Site-specific performance – acts of theatre and performative events at land-scape locations, in village streets, in urban situations. In houses, chapels, barns, disused factories, railway stations; on hillsides, in forest clearings, underwater. At the scale of civil engineering; as intimate as a guided walk.

Leading theatre artist and scholar Mike Pearson draws upon thirty years practical experience, proposing original approaches to the creation and study of performance outside the auditorium. In this book he suggests organizing principles, innovative strategies, methods and exercises for making theatre in a variety of contexts and locations, and through examples, case studies and projects develops distinctive theoretical insights into the relationship of site and performance, scenario and scenography. This book encourages practical initiatives in the conception, devising and staging of performances, while also recommending effective models for its critical appreciation.

Mike Pearson is Professor of Performance Studies at Aberystwyth University. He was an artistic director of Cardiff Laboratory Theatre (1973–80) and Brith Gof (1981–97). He continues to make performance with Pearson/Brookes (1997-present). He is co-author of *Theatre/Archaeology* and author of *In Comes I: Performance, Memory and Landscape.*

D0551622

Site-Specific Performance

Mike Pearson

First published 2010 by
PALGRAVE MACMILLAN

Palgrave Macmillan in the UK is an imprint of Macmillan Publishers Limited, registered in England, company number 785998, of Houndmills, Basingstoke, Hampshire RG21 6XS.

Palgrave Macmillan in the US is a division of St Martin's Press LLC, 175 Fifth Avenue, New York, NY 10010.

Palgrave Macmillan is the global academic imprint of the above companies and has companies and representatives throughout the world.

Palgrave® and Macmillan® are registered trademarks in the United States, the United Kingdom, Europe and other countries.

ISBN 978–0–230–57670–4   hardback
ISBN 978–0–230–57671–1   paperback

This book is printed on paper suitable for recycling and made from fully managed and sustained forest sources. Logging, pulping and manufacturing processes are expected to conform to the environmental regulations of the country of origin.

A catalogue record for this book is available from the British Library.

A catalog record for this book is available from the Library of Congress.

10   9   8   7   6   5   4   3
19   18   17   16   15   14   13   12   11

Printed in Great Britain by the MPG Books Group, Bodmin and King's Lynn

Contents

List of Images

Cover: Brith Gof, *PAX* (1991): preparations, Cardiff Bay. Photo: Brian Tarr

A chronology of site-specific performances created by the author with the Cardiff Laboratory Theatre, Brith Gof and Pearson/Brookes. This is followed by a chronology of solo performances and performances given by associated, Wales-based artists highlighted in the text.

Cardiff Laboratory Theatre
1979   *Special Event: Plasteg*, Mold, Wales (unoccupied country house)

Brith Gof
1981   *Branwen*, Harlech Castle, Wales (castle)
1983   *Ann Griffiths*, Wales (various chapels)
1984   *Rhydcymerau*, National Eisteddfod, Lampeter, Wales (disused cattle market)
1985   *Gwyl y Beibl* (*Bible Festival*), Llanrhaedr-ym-Mochnant, Wales (village streets); *Boris*, Welsh Folk Museum, Cardiff, Wales (barn)
1986   *Oherwydd y mae'r amser yn agos (For the Time is Nigh)*, St Davids Cathedral, Wales (cathedral nave)
1987   *Pandaemonium: The True Cost of Coal*, Morriston Tabernacle Chapel, Swansea, Wales (chapel)
1988   *Gododdin*, Rover car factory, Cardiff, Wales (disused factory)
1989   *Gododdin*, Polverigi, Italy (quarry); Hamburg, Germany (factory yard); Leeuwarden, Netherlands (ice hockey stadium); Glasgow, Scotland (disused tram depot)
1990   *EXX-1*, Chapter, Cardiff (studio theatre)
        Los Angeles, Rhymney, Wales (disused brewery)
        PAX, St David's Hall, Cardiff, Wales (concert hall stage)
        A Oes Heddwch? (broadcast video)
1991   *PAX*, Harland and Wolff, Glasgow, Scotland (disused shipyard); British Rail station, Aberystwyth, Wales (station platforms and concourse)
1992   *Gwynt, Glaw, Glo a Defaid (Wind, Rain, Coal and Sheep)*, Chapter, Cardiff, Wales (studio theatre)
        Patagonia, Taliesin Theatre, Swansea, Wales; Sherman Theatre, Cardiff, Wales (theatre auditoria)
        Haearn (Iron), British Coal works, Tredegar, Wales (disused factory)
        PAX TV: Y Fam, Y Ddeaear a'r Angel (The Mother, The Earth and the Angel) (broadcast video)
1993   *Arturius Rex 1: DOA*, Chapter, Cardiff, Wales (rear yard)
        Arturius Rex 2: Camlann, Cardiff, Wales (disused factory)

1994   *Arturius Rex 3: Cusanu Esgyrn*, National Eisteddfod, Neath, Wales (barn)
       Arturius Rex 4: Arturius Rex, Cardiff, Wales (industrial unit)
1995   *Estronwyr (Strangers)*, Barcelona, Spain (disused market)
       Tri Bywyd (Three Lives), Clwedog Plantation, Lampeter, Wales (forestry plantation)
       Y Pen Bas, Y Pen Dwfn (The Shallow End, The Deep End) (television programme)
1996   *Prydain: The Impossibility of Britishness*, Cardiff, Wales (disused factory)
2000   *Draw Draw yn ... (On Leaving)*, Lampeter, Wales (university assembly hall)

Pearson/Brookes

1997   *Dead Men's Shoes*, Welsh Industrial and Maritime Museum, Cardiff, Wales (museum gallery)
1998   *The First Five Miles ...*, Trefenter/Aberystwyth, Wales (landscape)
       The Man Who Ate His Boots ..., Aberystwyth, Wales (studio theatre)
2001   *Carrying Lyn*, Cardiff, Wales (multisite)
       Polis, Cardiff, Wales (multisite)
2002   *Metropolitan Motions*, Frankfurt, Germany (multisite)
       Raindogs, Chapter, Cardiff (studio theatre)
2004   *Who Are You Looking at?*, Chapter, Cardiff (studio theatre)
       There's Someone in the House, Phoenix Arts Centre, Exeter, England (studio theatre)
2006   *Strassen(w)ecken*, Frankfurt, Germany (studio theatre)
2008   *Something Happening/Something Happening Nearby*, Exeter University, England (studio theatre)

Solo

1991   *From Memory*, Welsh Folk Museum, St Fagans, Cardiff, Wales (cockpit)
1999   *Angels*, Aberystwyth, Wales (disused garage)
2000   *Bubbling Tom*, Hibaldstow, England (peripatetic)
       You Can't Tell by Looking (with William Yang), 'Mapping Wales' project, Wales (car journey; slide show)
2007   *Carrlands*, Ancholme valley, Lincolnshire (perambulatory audio work)
2008   *Winter*, Groeneveld Castle, Baarn, Netherlands (perambulatory audio work)

Other artists

1994   Eddie Ladd, *Unglücklicherweise*, St Dogmels, Wales (barn)
1996   Eddie Ladd/Cliff McLucas, *Once upon a Time in the West*, Welsh Folk Museum, St Fagans, Cardiff, Wales (museum field)
1997   Eddie Ladd, *St Matthew Passion*, Aberystwyth, Wales (unoccupied house)

1998   Eddie Ladd/Cliff McLucas, *Lla'th (Gwynfyd)*, Felinfach, Wales (unoccupied farm)

Simon Whitehead, *Tableland*, Lleyn Peninsula, Wales (perambulatory)

2000   Eddie Ladd, *Sawn-off Scarface*, Wales (various)

Eddie Ladd, *Scarface*, Wales (various)

Simon Whitehead, *Stalks*, Barcelona, Spain (perambulatory)

2001   John Rowley, *Sound Effects of Death and Disaster*, Sheffield, England (video)

John Rowley, *Lost Sounds of Wales*, Wales (broadcast video)

Simon Whitehead/Rachel Rosenthal, *Source to Sea*, Aberystwyth, Wales (perambulatory)

2002   Simon Whitehead, *2 mph*, Wales to London, England (perambulatory)

2003   Eddie Ladd, *Bonnie and Clyde*, Cardiff, Wales (disused factory)

Eddie Ladd, *Stafell A*, Aberystwyth, Wales (studio theatre)

2004   Paul Jeff, *Life in Perfect*, Peterstone Court, Wales (country hotel)

Eddie Ladd, *Stafell B*, Aberystwyth, Wales (studio theatre)

Marc Rees, *Shed*light*, Museum of Welsh Life, St Fagans, Cardiff, Wales (museum grounds)

John Rowley, *You Are my Favourite Chair*, St Pancras Hotel, London, England (video)

2005   Marc Rees, *The House Project*, Cardiff, Wales (unoccupied house)

John Rowley, *Dark Sounds for the City*, Cardiff, Wales (broadcast video)

2006   Eddie Ladd, *Stafell C*, Aberystwyth, Wales (studio theatre)

2007   Eddie Ladd, *Cof y Corff*, Wales (various)

2008   André Stitt *et al.*, *Trace: Displaced*, National Eisteddfod, Cardiff, Wales (Eisteddfod field)

Acknowledgements

This book has been long in gestation and results from personal experiences of professional performance making in Wales and elsewhere commencing in 1971; and from scholarly research over the past twelve years in the Department of Theatre, Film and Television Studies, Aberystwyth University.

There are then many people I need to thank. I owe an enormous debt to my many collaborators in Cardiff Laboratory Theatre (1973–80), particularly Professor Richard Gough and Sian Thomas, and in Brith Gof (1981–1997), especially Lis Hughes-Jones and John Hardy. Also thanks to the individual artists whose performances are considered here, several of whom I have had the pleasure of working with: Eddie Ladd, Richard Morgan, Marc Rees, John Rowley and Simon Whitehead.

Thanks to my academic colleagues Jill Greenhalgh, Dr Roger Owen and Dr Heike Roms; to Margaret Ames, Dr Andrew Filmer and Dr Carl Lavery who read early drafts; and to the students on BA Performance Studies and MA Practising Performance schemes in Aberystwyth who, in our small seaside town, continue to astonish with their practical embrace, interrogation and challenge of ideas included here. Also to Cathy Piquemal for her work on the index.

Thanks to photographers Jamie Andrews, Marilyn Arsem, Michelle Bogre, Ed Dimsdale, Tim Freeman, Hugo Glendinning, Paul Jeff, Rhodri Jones, Jens Koch, Dorian Llewelyn, Martin Roberts, Jesse Schwenk, Friedemann Simon, Brian Tarr and Pete Telfer for permission to include their images. Image 3.11 is courtesy of Trace Archive, Image 4.3 of Stan's Café, and Image 5.3 of Pixel Foundry Artists' Archive.

Work on the book has been framed by two important initiatives: the UK Arts and Humanities Research Council's 'Landscape and Environment' programme and the Brith Gof Archive Project, a collaboration with the National Library of Wales, Aberystwyth.

Within the AHRC programme my thanks are due to director Professor Stephen Daniels; to colleagues at Bristol University and the University of the West of England who participated in the 'Living in a Material World: Performativities of Emptiness' network, including principal investigators Dr Angela Piccini and Dr Jo Carruthers; and to Dr Iain Biggs. Thanks to the many academics from cognate disciplines encountered through the scheme, including geographers Dr J. D. Dewsbury, Dr Hayden Lorimer, Professor David Matless and Dr John Wylie. Thanks too to the advisory group of the 'Living Landscapes' conference of 18–21 June 2009 in Aberystwyth, especially co-organizer Dr Heike Roms.

Within the Brith Gof project, National Library archivist Mick Pearson has been wonderfully attentive, and former company members have contributed generously to public acts of collective recollection. Images 3.7, 4.4, 4.6, 4.9, 5.7 and 5.9 and the extensive quotations from unpublished works by Cliff McLucas are by permission of the Llyfyrgell Genedlaethol Cymru/National Library of Wales. I acknowledge too the generosity of the board of Ymddiriedolaeth Clifford McLucas and especially Margaret Ames, in allowing me to consult the personal deposit of Cliff's material, now housed in the Library.

Themes from this book have been rehearsed in many conferences and guest seminars and I am grateful to the organizers for the invitations to present.

Versions of sections of the text have already been published in the journals *About Performance*, 7 ('City' in Chapter 3; see Pearson 2007a), *Studies in Theatre and Performance*, 25, 3 ('Afterlife' in Chapter 6; see Pearson 2005b) and in the edited volume *Contemporary Archaeologies: Excavating Now* ('Inaccessibility' in Chapter 4; see Pearson 2009). I thank the editors Professor Gay McAuley, Professor Peter Thomson, Dr Angela Piccini and Dr Cornelius Holtorf for permission to include this material. I also thank Dr Iain Biggs, Dr Angela Piccini, Dr Jo Carruthers, Dr J. D. Dewsbury, Mike Brookes and Jennie Savage who have allowed me to use their texts verbatim.

My final debt is to the two artists, designers and theatre-makers with whom I have collaborated most closely over the past twenty years. Thanks to the late Cliff McLucas who worked with Brith Gof from the mid-1980s and who, prior to his untimely death in 2002, was the company's final artistic director. And thanks to Mike Brookes, my partner in our irregular performance company Pearson/Brookes. Their perceptions, often insufficiently credited, suffuse this book. They spring from *practice*, from expert, articulate practice, from – to upset current academic parlance – *research-led practice*.

The completion of this book is only made possible by a semester's research leave granted by my institution and a second one funded by the Arts and Humanities Research Council.

MIKE PEARSON

 Arts & Humanities
Research Council

The Practice of the Book

Structure

The Prologue outlines the background to, and basic intentions of, the book. It sketches the work of three companies from which the majority of its perceptions are drawn: Cardiff Laboratory Theatre, Brith Gof and Pearson/Brookes.

Chapter 1 introduces critical insights into articulations of site and of performance, as they are currently manifest in the field of theatre studies and beyond. To establish the terrain within which the particular standpoints of the book are situated, the conflicting and complementary definitions of a number of contemporary scholars are collated. They are included without extensive authorial comment in order to hold open an emergent field. Whilst formulations and manifestations of site-specific performance vary regionally, definitions are as yet barely contested. The chapter ends with a set of tentative distinctions between auditorium and site, as a point of departure for practical and analytical initiatives.

Chapter 2 suggests conceptual and theoretical approaches that help acknowledge and appreciate the particular nature of site-specific performance. It begins with a simple immersive model in which the reader is asked to imagine the variety of ways in which a site might be visited, both alone and in the company of others. It then draws upon other disciplines including human geography and architecture to describe better the experience of place and readings of its performative engagement.

Chapter 3 includes the description of ten works of site-specific performance created in different types of location and involving different modes of practice. Each part goes on to consider associated practices and other manifestations of performance in similar places elsewhere. The **Exercises** invite the reader to undertake research at a chosen location: to develop narrative strands from such enquiry; to engage in practical and physical exploration at such a place; and thereafter to develop ways of telling and ways of doing. The **Project** describes a specific site and series of performative activities undertaken there. The reader is invited to conceive a performance for the same location.

Chapter 4 includes the description of ten sets of geographical, architectural, social and cultural formulations, conditions and characteristics as they might inform and impact upon the conceptualization, creation and exposition of site-specific performance. The **Exercises** list a number of applied and previously tested explorations of site to inspire and stimulate practical initiatives by the reader. The **Project** describes a site and its current, highly restricted usage. The reader is invited to conceive imaginary performances at the same location that might further reveal or critique the particularities and complexities of the site and of its unique potentialities.

Chapter 5 describes and examines a cumulative series of conceptual and applied practices in making site-specific performance. The **Exercises** include recommendations towards the creation of effective dramaturgy. Two check-lists are included to demonstrate the intricacies of the multiple articulations of site and performance, and also to support practical applications. The **Project** describes a specific site and performance. The reader is invited to conceive performance for a similar site, in light of the operational conditions within such a ubiquitous location, as revealed in the example.

In Chapter 6 I espouse the educational potential of site-specific perform-ance and describe first-hand experiences of working with undergraduate and postgraduate students. I consider questions of documenting site-specific per-formance and proposals for archiving.

Application

Chapters 1 and 2 are largely theoretical and analytical. In them I consider the manifold relationships, both real and imagined, of site and performance. This leads to an appreciation of the particular nature of site-specific performance and to an expanded understanding of performative engagement through criti-cal optics drawn from a variety of disciplines.

Chapters 3, 4 and 5 involve the gradual evolution and elaboration of con-ceptual and applied practices for creating site-specific performance. *They are the core of the book.* Chapter 3 is largely descriptive of performances and their sites. Each part is discrete and can be accessed separately, though there is a trajectory to the examples, from empty field to website.

Chapter 4 is principally conceptual in aspect, addressing the application and operation of practices under specific conditions. In each part I consider a distinct set of circumstances, each of which can be accessed separately.

Chapter 5 tends towards practice, suggesting an integrated model for mak-ing performance and, reciprocally, frameworks for its analysis. Each part builds upon the previous section and they are best regarded in sequence.

In Chapters 3, 4 and 5 the **Exercises** may be undertaken at the desk – in the imagination – or in the field – at site. In the former, they may help explicate ways in which performative detail is generated. In the latter, they may guide creative activity leading to concrete outputs. The **Projects** are intended as test cases against which to assess the efficacy of concepts and practices previously introduced. The **Exercises** and **Projects** may be used independently or in con-cert, and without further reference to the text.

Chapter 6 examines the extension and impact of site-specific performance in other situations.

Bullet-points positioned irregularly throughout the text indicate significant questions. These moments of punctuation are intended to occasion further reflection on the nature and practicalities of site-specific performance. **Images** present further points of contemplation as much as illuminating passages in the texts. Readers are invited to picture themselves there and to imagine their range of responses as both performer and spectator.

In several places, unpublished documents from the archive of Brith Gof appear. These were composed for a variety of reasons and purposes including publicity, funding applications and extra-mural activities. In their various registers, they provide a series of snapshots of a professional theatre company at work. Of note are the extended texts by Cliff McLucas who died in 2002. Without the opportunity for him to respond, I have avoided ventriloquizing his intentions and critiquing his propositions. They are included verbatim and at length, without further comment.

Prologue

In which the scene is set, a personal history of practice is sketched and a particular context of performance making is delineated.

This is *a* book about site-specific performance. It is regional in aspect and does not pretend to completeness in its consideration of this elusive but enduring subject.

It is a book about *practice*: *concept*, *process* and *exposition*. About *strategy*, *method* and *technique*. About *orientations*, *organizing principles* and *rules of thumb*.

I avoid defining a *type*, be it site-determined, site-oriented, site-referenced, site-conscious, site-responsive, site-related. And the risk of being 'uncritically adopted as another genre category by mainstream art institutions and discourses' (Kwon, 2004, p. 1). According to Kwon, site-specific performance remains 'a problem idea, as a particular cipher of art and spatial politics' (ibid., p. 2). In this book I attempt to distinguish practices whose definition often begins with a negative, as performance using 'non-theatre locations' (Wilkie, 2002a, p. 149).

I prefer 'performance': to embrace the fullest range of practices originating in theatre and visual art, and to demonstrate affiliations with the academic field of performance studies.

I outline a series of creative *approaches* that attend equally to all terms under consideration – site, specificity and performance – and to their various articulations.

I do not propose an overarching model within which exemplars are positioned to illustrate or prove a thesis. Rather, I build upon a series of *exemplary practices*. The book is therefore partial and exclusionary, but I commend the benefits accruing from close inspection of specific experiences in a specific region.

I suggest that the conventions and techniques of the auditorium may be inappropriate or inadequate to the task of addressing 'site'. And that site-specific performance is other than a transposition and modification of stage practices. If the stage is essentially *synecdochic* – in which limited resources stand in for a complete picture, as when a table and chairs suggests a domestic scene – site is frequently a scene of plenitude, its inherent characteristics, manifold effects and unruly elements always liable to leak, spill and diffuse into performance: 'site-specific work has to deal with, embrace and cohabit with existing factors of scale, architecture, chance, accident, incident' (Persighetti, 2000, p. 12). In the auditorium, the audience is, we might assume, already orientated and paying

1

attention. What is operational, what under control, what an intended feature of intelligibility, what to be actively disattended, and what clearly apparent in a situation of excess – these then become key concerns at site. Although the stage is a site of imagination and site always inescapably itself, site may be transformed by the disruptive presence of performance seeking a relationship other than that of a ready-made scenic backdrop against which to place its figures.

This book tends towards theory of practice rather than adopting a position of critical spectatorship. It is descriptive, discursive and programmatic as much as analytical. It includes ideas, examples, evocations, speculations and exercises. It is citational, quoting at length, though much that is now part of the lingua franca of practice may pass unreferenced. In quoting documents from the 1980s and 1990s, it recalls the polemical trust of texts making often heated and exaggerated claims for regional practices outside the conventions of academic discourse.

My ambitions are pedagogical: I aim to encourage further initiatives in performance: there is then a tendency to overuse 'may' and 'might'.

I take up and extend positions expounded jointly with Michael Shanks in *Theatre/Archaeology* (2001) and in my *In Comes I: Performance, Memory and Landscape* (2006a). There is inevitably then an amount of reiteration and citation of personal work.

The book is informed by an experience of making performances in a particular set of artistic and cultural circumstances: in several companies – Cardiff Laboratory Theatre (1973–80), Brith Gof (1981–97) and Pearson/Brookes (1997–present) – and as a solo artist, primarily in Wales. There is then a tendency to overuse 'I', though this individual attempts to speak from within an experience of practice, as in both my previous volumes; after geographer Nigel Swift, 'I want to keep hold of a humanist ledge on the machinic cliff face. I hold to a sense of *personal authorship*' (Thrift, 2008, p. 13).

Cardiff Laboratory Theatre

In the 1970s Cardiff Laboratory Theatre created a number of *special events* under the direction of Richard Gough. The accent was upon *occasion* and *audience*: 'They are events for special times and places ... disused churches, deserted beaches, abandoned country houses ... They may celebrate particular dates ... draw attention to a specific building ... the life of a famous person' and take the form of a feast, a procession, a guided tour, a mystery outing in which 'each part of the journey is celebrated by music and action – the arrival at the theatre, the embarking, the trip, the disembarking' (Pearson, 1980, p. 32). The avowed intention was 'to relax the tension between performer and spectator', with new relationships only deemed feasible in other locations: 'In certain rooms, the spectators take up their own arrangement to see the action; in others they are seated ... In a Special Event everyone is a participant' (ibid.).

In this period there is no mention of site-specificity, though there is a clear appreciation of site and its potentials. Of the events:

> They are inspired by, and responsive to, non-theatrical environments. Each particular location conditions the work which takes place there. For instance, on a beach it is possible to use fire and natural sounds. The geography of a large building might suggest a guided tour ... occasionally we change the building, but in sympathy with it. (ibid.)

In 1979 the company mounted a special event at Plasteg, an unoccupied stately home near Mold in north Wales:

> A coach trip to a place made ready. The house was derelict, empty of furniture. But each room contained a strange inhabitant. In one there was a butler, who lived in a barrel, with his goat; in another, there was a man obsessed by birds. In a third, a woman in a feathered jacket was planting flowers in her garden. There was warm wine to drink and the sound of recorders drifted from closed rooms. It was a frightening experience, touring the crumbling house by the light of candles. Was it a mental asylum or just a museum for eccentrics? It was certainly a guided tour, reminiscent of those organised everyday in the great houses of Britain. Was this the night-time equivalent? Perhaps it was just a lament for a dying house. (ibid., p. 46)

These performances were usually created over periods of not more than a week, often conceived away from site, and semi-improvised in their public manifestation. In form, they were influenced not only by the celebratory works of Welfare State (see Coult and Kershaw, 1983) and IOU, but also by a series of residencies at Chapter Arts Centre in Cardiff in the mid-1970s in which companies including The People Show, the Pip Simmons Group and Waste of Time created peripatetic performances in the building, moving from room to room and staging scenes and sequences of differing atmospheres in each.

Brith Gof

On leaving Cardiff Laboratory Theatre, Lis Hughes Jones and I founded Brith Gof in Aberystwyth in 1981. In the initial period the emphasis shifted to 'events devised for special locations and occasions' (Pearson, 1985, p. 2). There was a sense of expediency about the choice of location, but also an increasing appreciation of cultural specificities and social congregation: 'we are working within a widely distributed population living in communities remote from the circuit of municipal theatres. Our performances often occur within the context of a local cultural, social, or even religious gathering. This may take place in a village school or in a barn' (ibid., p. 3).

The term 'site-specificity' has still yet to appear, but performance for special locations is cast as 'a celebration of the architecture within which a society works, plays and worships' (ibid.). Significantly:

> Such locations free from rules of decorum and prudence, allow us to use techniques unthinkable in a theatre. Theatre need not be signified as a distinct mode of expression. In *Rhydcymerau* two carpenters worked throughout the performance, their sawing and hammering counterpointing the pattern of poems and stories concerning rural decay, blurring the distinction between work and performance. (ibid., pp. 3–4)

Engagement with site had here a political and proselytizing aspect, challenging the 'withdrawal to the proscenium arch and the creation of stage illusion' (ibid., p. 3) and the hushed and darkened rows of the auditorium: in the development of a 'new, vibrant and distinctive theatre tradition in Wales' (ibid., p. 2).

From the outset the *fit* between location and performance was not always one of perfect congruence. The first Brith Gof performance, *Branwen* (1981), was staged with students from Aberystwyth in an inner bailey of Harlech Castle. From this spot the eponymous heroine, in a story from the collection of Welsh myths known as *The Mabinogi*, looks out towards Ireland. As the flocks of cackling jackdaws swooped in the gathering dusk and flaming torches, the audience was reminded of Branwen's lost brother Bran ('Crow'). But the enclosing walls of the castle were inescapably redolent of the occupation of Edward I.

Throughout the 1980s Brith Gof was resident in the Barn Centre in Aberystwyth, a range of historic buildings, originally an iron foundry and later converted by the university. Other occupants included artist Cliff McLucas who began to design elements of performance, such as the saw-horse used in *Rhydcymerau* (1984) (see p. 116). Subsequently, as a full-time member of the company, his training as an architect proved instrumental in helping instigate and elaborate new approaches to site, beginning with large-scale works such as *Gododdin* (1988–89) (see pp. 112–15), *PAX* (1990–91) (see pp. 69–70) and *Haearn* (1992) (see pp. 142–3). This led to operational definitions of 'site-specific performance', the term finally being applied to the work and the theorization that forms substantial parts of this volume.

> Site specific performances are conceived for, and conditioned by, the particulars of found spaces, (former) sites of work, play and worship. They make manifest, celebrate, confound or criticise location, history, function, architecture, microclimate. They are an interpenetration of the found and the fabricated. They are inseparable from their sites, the only contexts within which they are 'readable'. (Pearson and McLucas, no date, p. 2)

At this juncture, the company espoused site as a place of both artistic and cultural invention and innovation: 'a theatrical as well as a social enquiry'

(Wilkie, 2008, p. 95). 'The site of Brith Gof's performances might then be understood not just as a geographical location, but as a place in which cultural
identities and social relationships can be productively examined' (ibid., p. 93).
Later, in relation to *Prydain* (1996) (see pp. 73–4), Heike Roms observes that
'"being Welsh" must no longer be defined in reference to an originary pedagogical object (such as culture, language), but by the very performance of
"Welsh citizenship"' (Roms, 2004, p. 189).

Such was the scale of Brith Gof site-specific performances that it became
increasingly difficult for performers to monitor the immediate effect of their
activities and accordingly to react directly to audiences. In response therefore
I devised personal and autobiographical works of smaller scale, more intimate
and ultimately dialogic in nature, including *From Memory* (1991) staged at
the open-air Welsh Folk Museum and *Bubbling Tom* (2000) (see pp. 54–7) on
the streets of the village where I was raised.

Pearson/Brookes

The performances of Pearson/Brookes, an ongoing, irregular collaboration
with artist and scenographer Mike Brookes, reflect a shift away from architectural concerns with enclosure and modelling within bound spaces, to performance as place-making; and through the use of media, from taking audiences to
unusual sites to bringing unusual sites to them.

Companies such as Volcano Theatre (2009) and Earthfall (2009) continue
to make group performances at site in Wales, but in recent years a group
of solo artists has also emerged, through changes in funding regime, whose
advances in the field are considered here: Eddie Ladd, Marc Rees, John Rowley
and Simon Whitehead.

That such developments should occur in Wales is not entirely surprising.
With a relative paucity of indigenous dramatic traditions, with no mainstream
tradition setting what theatre should and ought to look like, with, until
recently, no National Theatre prescribing orthodoxy of theatrical convention,
performance has had options. Alternative practices have not been marginal-
ized, and since the early 1970s they have been substantially subsidized. With
only a limited range of auditoria, such practices have sought other sites.

Wales is a country of uneven demography, of scattered rural communities
and small towns in the north and west, and heavily populated post-industrial
conurbations in the south. Its languages are equally unevenly distributed,
though the renaissance in Welsh has been in urban areas. It has a recent history
of civil disobedience and a longer tradition of nonconformism, with an innate
suspicion of ostentation. It has the most highly subsidized television service in
the world. And it has a tradition of imagining itself, of reinventing itself, most
recently by statute in a new nationhood.

In Wales, there are places that resemble Pierre Nora's *lieux de memoire*:
'any significant entity, whether material or non-material in nature, which by

dint of human will or the work of time has become a symbolic element of the memorial heritage of any community' (Nora, 1992, p. xvii). Places such as Tryweryn where Liverpool Corporation constructed a reservoir, or Aberfan where a sliding coal tip engulfed the village school. At the time such events inspired protest movements and changed perceptions of industrialization. They continue to resonate as ever-present sites of claim and counter-claim. As sites of performance, they offer dense accretions of conflicting opinion. Whilst Nora's formulation is open to critique as being overly instrumental, it does help illuminate the role of the memorialization of place in a small, stateless nation: 'the goal was to exhume significant sites, to identify the most obvious and crucial centres of national memory' (ibid.).

And there are, too, particular Welsh expressions *of* placea, that help orientate both its practical engagement and critical apprehension: *y filltir sgwar* (see p. 110), *y fro* (see p. 111) and *cynefin* (see pp. 101–3).

All of which sets particular conditions for the location, presentation, form and content of site-specific performance.

1

Introduction

In which current understandings of site-specific performance and critical perceptions from within and beyond the field of theatre studies are detailed; and a set of distinctions between auditorium and site are proposed as a provisional point of departure.

Although the search for a practicable, encompassing definition of site-specific performance has long claimed scholarly attention, it remains slippery. In 1998 Patrice Pavis proposed:

> This term refers to a staging and performance conceived on the basis of a place in the real world (ergo, outside the established theatre). A large part of the work has to do with researching a place, often an unusual one that is imbued with history or permeated with atmosphere: an airplane hangar, unused factory, city neighbourhood, house or apartment. The insertion of a classical or modern text in this 'found space' throws new light on it, gives it an unsuspected power, and places the audience at an entirely different relationship to the text, the place and the purpose for being there. This new context provides a new situation or enunciation ... and gives the performance an unusual setting of great charm and power. (Pavis, 1998, pp. 337–8)

Pavis's observations relate specifically to practices originating in theatre: 'the play-as-event belongs to the space, and makes the space perform as much as it makes actors perform' (Wiles, 2003, p. 1). Shortly after, in the keynote volume *Site-Specific Art: Performance, Place and Documentation* (2000), Nick Kaye attends to a broader range of forms, stemming from both dramatic and visual art traditions. His characterization of site-specific art as 'articulate exchanges between the work of art and the places in which its meanings are defined' (Kaye, 2000, p. 1) sustains. He resists distinguishing common features within a putative genre, focusing upon process rather than object, and upon the relationship between 'an "object" or "event" and a position it occupies'; '... Indeed, a definition of site-specificity might begin quite simply by describing the basis of such an exchange' (ibid.).

Since the publication of *Site-Specific Art* related scholarship has burgeoned. Amongst many commentators, Miwon Kwon has extended Kaye's concern with visual art practices and Jen Harvie, Dee Heddon, Gay McAuley, Misha Myers, Heike Roms, Cathy Turner and Fiona Wilkie have all written substantively on performance. Most note a change in practice over the past ten years: from *fixity* to *mobility*; from *architectonic* to *peripatetic* manifestations; from *expositional* to *relational* modes; from 'the spectacular re-enactment to the quiet intervention, from remedial collaboration to dialogic, open-ended process' (Doherty, 2004, p. 11); and from general categorization – 'site-determined', 'site-referenced', 'site-conscious', 'site-responsive', 'context-specific' – to closer scrutiny of the specificity of each instance of performance. Daniel Libeskind's long lists of types of space – food space, interesting space, racist space, forgotten space, etc. – alerts us to both the folly and potential of classification as his students are asked to 'materialize, create, investigate, illuminate, construct, touch, redeem' spaces thus defined (Libeskind, 2001, pp. 65–8).

In her survey of site-specific performance in Britain, what she terms 'interventions into cultural spaces', Fiona Wilkie wrestles with *typology* whilst admitting that few instances are ever distinct and discrete. She identifies *site-sympathetic* (an existing performance text physicalized in a selected site); *site-generic* (performance generated for a series of like sites); and *site-specific* (performance specifically generated from/for one selected site (Wilkie, 2002a, p. 150).

But at base she appreciates the reciprocal *instrumentality* or *affordance* offered by the relationship: 'site-specific performance engages with site as symbol, site as story-teller, site as structure' (ibid., p. 158). 'Layers of the site are revealed through reference to: historical documentation; site usage (past and present); found text, objects, actions, sounds, etc.; anecdotal guidance; personal association; half-truths and lies; site morphology (physical and vocal explorations of site)' (ibid., p. 150). And she challenges notions of easy congruence between performance and site: 'that the "fit" may not be a comfortable merging with the resonances of the site but might be a reaction against them' (ibid., p. 149).

Wilkie canvasses companies and individuals. Brighton-based Red Earth describe their work as 'inspired by and designed to integrate with the physical and non-physical aspects of a specific location' (ibid., p. 149). Dartington artist and academic Sue Palmer comments: 'it's not just about a place, but the people who normally inhabit and use that place. For it wouldn't exist without them' (ibid., p. 145).

In subsequent research, Wilkie identifies two broad developments in practice: 'a shift in form (from *inhabiting* to *journeying*), and a shift in the nature of inquiry (from *this place* to broader questions of *site*)' (Wilkie, 2008, pp. 100–1). That is, from attention to the cultural resonances of one particular site, to an active rethinking of how 'site' is constituted – 'how art, and in our case performance creates a space of encounter'; 'Questions of *what* and *how* site "means" are teased apart' (ibid., p. 101). 'A shift in form can be noted from performance that *inhabits* a place to performance that *moves through* spaces'; 'from a concern with the political and cultural meanings of particular locations to a focus on broader questions of what *site* as a category might mean' (ibid., p. 90).

Rather than simply occupying an 'unusual setting', site-specific performance is adjudged to hold 'possibilities for responding to and interrogating a range of current spatial concerns, and for investigating the spatial dimension of contemporary identities' (ibid., p. 89), representing 'formal and aesthetic but also political choices' (ibid., p. 96). Not only does the use of non-theatre venues contribute to 'an enquiry into what theatre *is and might be*', it also incorporates 'a set of productive spatial metaphors, whereby practitioners use their focus on geographical space to explore a range of theatrical, conceptual, political and virtual spaces. Thus the potentially restrictive *specificity* of the work is expanded to allow for ambiguity and multiplicity' (ibid., p. 100).

Of the initiative in Scotland to create a devolved national institution, she opines that 'site-specificity offers a convenient marker of a set of ideas with which the National Theatre of Scotland wants to be associated: experiment, accessibility, the connection between art and everyday life, and a shift away from the primacy of the metropolitan theatre building' (ibid., pp. 87–8).

Jen Harvie indicates the potential of site-specific performance 'to explore spatial and material histories and to mediate the complex identities these histories remember and produce' (Harvie, 2005, p. 44):

> Site-specific performance can be especially powerful as a vehicle for remembering and forming a community for at least two reasons. First, its location can work as a potent mnemonic trigger, helping to evoke specific past times related to the place and time of performance and facilitating a negotiation between the meanings of those times. (ibid., p. 42)

Second, it is effective for 'remembering and constituting identities that are significantly determined by their materiality and spatiality, identities to do with, for example, class, occupation, and gender' (ibid.).

With regard to the Welsh context, Heike Roms retorts: 'it was frequently not the locations that invested the performances with a sense of identity, as Harvie proposes, but the performances that made these locations and histories associated with them representative of such an identity' (Roms, 2008, p. 115). For Roms, contemporary site-specific performance may involve a 'perceived potential to bring into correspondence the place of representation and the represented place in an attempt to create theatre work that expresses particular localized concerns' (ibid., p. 111), encouraging 'a different kind of audience-performer interaction' (ibid., p. 116).

Within an Australian context, Gay McAuley (2006, 2007) again outlines a schematic typology. Her first category of practice seeks in non-traditional sites 'those physical features and aesthetic qualities needed for a particular production', with the proviso that site 'may begin to tell its own story' (2007, p. 8). The second category entails engagement with a particular community. And the third category emerges from a particular place: 'it engages intensively with the history and politics of that place, and with the resonance of these in the present' (ibid., p. 9).

Whilst her preferred designation 'site-based' refers to performance 'in found spaces rather than in designated theatre buildings' (ibid., p. 7), in which site becomes the dominant signifier rather than simply being that which contains the performance, she is conscious of its capacity to enhance a 'deeper understanding of the spatialised nature of human culture' (ibid., p. 7), 'changing the way people perceive places' (2006, p. 151) – and to engage with social and political issues of ownership, power, identity, exclusion, memory. 'Work emerges from a particular place, it engages intensively with the history and politics of that place, and with the resonance of these in the present' (2007, p. 9), permitting 'the past to surge into the present' (2006, p. 150).

In regard to a history of colonialism, 'the placial turn' in theory and an appreciation of complexities of dwelling, occupancy and exclusion are significant in demonstrating the ethical responsibilities of site-specific practices, particularly those 'involved in activating and articulating the memories that circulate in relation to places of trauma' (ibid., pp. 171–2). 'Furthermore, locally based spectators experience an enhanced kind of creative agency in that their knowledge of the place and its history may well be deeper than that of the performance makers, and they will continue to frequent the place after the performers have left' (2007, p. 9).

Canadian scholar Kathleen Irwin also emphasizes the human dimension. For her, site-specific performance is 'extrapolated from the specificities of the site itself and, importantly, the communities that claim ownership of it' (Irwin, 2007, pp. 10–11). But it retains the capacity to unsettle and disturb: 'where physical traces of a building's past operate metaphorically to render absent present and function to introduce the spectator into other worlds and dimensions of our world that are *other*. The material traces evoke worlds that are intangible and unlocatable: worlds of memory, pleasure, sensation, imagination, affect and insight' (ibid., p. 37).

Drawing upon her practical experiences as a member of Exeter-based company Wrights and Sites, Cathy Turner concurs with the creative potency of an uneasy fit. For her: 'each occupation, or traversal, or transgression of space offers a reinterpretation of it, even a rewriting' (Turner, 2004, p. 373). In addition, 'the "ghost" is transgressive, defamiliarising, and incoherent' (ibid., p. 374), creating a fruitful disjuncture. She characterizes site-specific performance as a 'range of lens'. Its critical appreciation, apprehension and account requires:

- ■ A rhetoric that situates us not as within but as elements of the space of site-specific performance.
- ■ A vocabulary which provides better metaphors for the co-creative aspects of inter-subjectivity.
- ■ A greater emphasis on phenomenological experience.
- ■ A greater emphasis on social interaction, including play. (ibid., p. 379)

In addressing the provisionality and contingency of ephemeral practices based upon other than architectonic principles, she appeals to psychoanalysis:

> By referring to this body of work, one need not return to notions of either site or self as fixed or finite entities. One need not imply an unproblematic notion of a located self, or a resolution of the tension between conceptual and 'real' sites. One need not make an absolute distinction between material and human objects. (ibid.)

She favours the inclusivity of Winnicott's 'potential space' (ibid.) within which all elements, human and material, are envisaged as co-creative.

In both her critical and artistic work Dee Heddon has concentrated upon the local and personal: 'performances that fold or unfold autobiography and place, particularly outside places, I have conceptualised them as being autotopographic' (Heddon, 2008, p. 90). She suggests '"autotopography" renders the self of the place, and the place of the self, transparent' (ibid., p. 15). Her writing juxtaposes 'the factual with the fictional, event with imagination, history with story, narrative with fragment, past with present' (ibid., p. 9), in order to 'write place'. In their latest joint project 'The Art of Walking: An Embodied Practice', Heddon and Turner set out to challenge walking in landscape as 'male, solitary and self reliant', 'rhapsodic and epiphatic' (Wylie, 2005, p. 235).

Architect Jane Rendell characterizes her 'site-writing' as a form of site-specific/critical spatial practice:

> To achieve its objective the research brings spatial understandings from a number of disciplines to spatialize the concepts/processes/subjects of writing through an exploration of the relationship between the material/cultural/political qualities of the site, the associated sites remembered/dreamed/imagined by the writer, and the spaces of writing itself. (Rendell, 2009; see also 2010, forthcoming)

Miwon Kwon's sustained examination of practices with roots in the visual arts are broadly illuminating, particularly as she elaborates ways in which 'our understanding of site has shifted from a fixed, physical location to somewhere or something constituted through social, economic, cultural and political processes' (Kwon, quoted in Doherty, 2004, p. 10) – and from phenomenologically orientated practices to 'an "intertextually" coordinated, multiply-located, discursive field of operation' (Doherty, 2004, p. 30). Site-specific practices:

> initially took site as an actual location, a tangible reality 'its identity composed of a unique combination of physical elements: length, depth, height, texture, and shape of walls and rooms; scale and proportion of plazas, buildings, or parks; existing conditions of lighting, ventilation, traffic patterns; distinctive topographical features, and so forth. (Kwon, 2004, p. 11)

They were:

> initially based in a phenomenological or experiential understanding of site, defined primarily as an agglomeration of the actual attributes of a particular location (the size, scale, texture, and dimension of walls, ceilings, rooms; existing lighting conditions, topographical features, traffic patterns, seasonal characteristics of climate, etc.), with architecture serving as a foil for the artwork in many instances. (ibid., p. 3)

Current perceptions of site have moved 'from a physical location – grounded, fixed, actual – to a discursive vector – ungrounded, fluid, virtual' (ibid., pp. 29–30), effectively relocating meaning from the art object to the contingencies of context. Kwon adds: 'it can be literal, like a street corner, or virtual, like a theoretical concept' (ibid., p. 3).

Kwon identifies three paradigms for practice: phenomenological, social/institutional and discursive. But she stresses that this is not a progressive chronological ordering: 'rather they are competing definitions, overlapping with one another and operating simultaneously in various cultural practices today (or even within a single artist's single project)' (ibid., p. 30). All involve 'an inextricable, indivisible relationship between the work and its site' (ibid., p. 12), the work addressing 'the site itself as another *medium*, as an "other language"' (ibid., p. 75). Whilst site-specific art might constitute a form of institutional critique and more intense engagement with the everyday world, it has the capacity to articulate and cultivate local particularities, accentuating difference in the face of globalizing tendencies. However, it may also work in opposition to the constraints of context so that the work cannot be read as an affirmation of 'questionable ideologies and political power' (ibid.).

Contemporary societal deterritorialization and the fluidity of a migratory model of experience introduce 'possibilities for the production of multiple identities, allegiances, and meanings, based not on normative conformities but on the non-rational convergences forged by chance encounters and circumstances' (ibid., p. 165), producing 'symptoms not codes', or 'spaces of affect' understood in contrast to 'effecting space' (Hauptmann, 2006, p. 11). Nevertheless we may maintain 'a secret adherence to the actuality of places': 'Despite the proliferation of discursive sites and fictional selves, however, the phantom of a site as an actual place remains, and our psychic, habitual attachment to places regularly returns as it continues to inform our sense of identity' (Kwon, 2004, p. 165).

It is not a matter of choosing sides, between models of nomadism and sedentariness, 'between space and place, between digital interfaces and the handshake': 'This means addressing the uneven conditions of adjacencies and distances *between* one thing, one person, one place, one thought, one fragment *next* to another, rather than invoking equivalences via one thing *after* another' (ibid., p. 166).

There are here echoes of Nicholas Bourriaud's conception of *relational aesthetics*. Within relational practices the nature of the encounter is fundamental, aiming at the 'formal construction of space–time entities that may be able to elude alienation, the division of labour, the commodification of space and the reification of life' (Bourriaud, 2004, p. 48), encouraging 'moments of sociability' (Bourriaud, 1998, p. 33). 'The political value of the relational aesthetic lies in two very simple observations: social reality is the product of negotiation and democracy is a montage of forms' (ibid.). So site may be produced *through* and *in* interaction, momentarily. Relations make spaces rather than occurring within them: 'place as formed out of the specificity of interacting social relations in a particular location; place as meeting place' (Massey, 1994, p. 168).

Misha Myers's performances (see p. 27) in Plymouth 'activate and invite modes of participation' (Myers, 2009, pp. 107ff.). Her shared and remote walks, within which the knowledgeable participant or *percipient* can alter and determine outcomes, encourage conviviality and companionability, particularly with disadvantaged communities. Those present are asked to recall other times and places that become projected upon and are part of the cityscape traversed in performance.

In appreciating the shift from attitudes regarding site as vacant space awaiting performance, the appearance of new kinds of informational site in changing technological circumstances, and the role of human agency in place-making in a transitory moment of absorption of actors and things and an intensification of affect, the perceptions of cognate disciplines such as geography and anthropology, are instructive for both the critical apprehension of and creative initiatives in performance.

In human geography, the *new mobilities paradigm* aims 'at going beyond the imagery of "terrains" as spatially geographical containers for social processes' (Sheller and Urry, 2006, p. 209). It is a reflection upon the effects of deterritorialization and nomadism – the increasing flow and travel of people, information and image – whilst acknowledging that in movement not everyone is free in the same way. Connections of social life, it is proposed, are 'organised through certain nodes':

> Mobilities thus entail distinct social spaces that orchestrate new forms of social life around such nodes, for example, stations, hotels, motorways, resorts, airports, leisure complexes, cosmopolitan cities, beaches, galleries, and roadside parks.
>
> Or connections might be enacted through less privileged spaces, on the street corners, subway stations, buses, public plazas and back alleys where the less privileged might use pay-phones, beepers, or more recently short-text messaging to organize illicit exchanges, meetings, political demonstrations or 'underground' social gatherings. (ibid., p. 213)

> Places are thus not so much fixed as implicated within complex networks by which hosts, guests, buildings, objects, and machinery are contingently brought together to produce certain performances in certain places at certain times. Places are about relationships, about the placing of peoples, materials, images and the systems of difference that they perform.

> At the same time as places are dynamic, they are also about proximities, about the bodily copresence of people who happen to be in that place at that time, doing activities together. (ibid., p. 214)

There are then new kinds of site, more or less stable, within and through which performance might be enacted – and new kinds of (performative) relationship within and through which site might (temporally) materialize.

Also in geography, Nigel Thrift's *non-representational theory* is towards '*the geography of what happens*' (Thrift, 2008, p. 2). It concerns movement: 'movement captures a certain attitude to life as potential' (ibid., p. 5). In sum, it attends to the 'onflow' of everyday life. It concentrates on practices 'understood as material bodies of work or styles that have gained enough stability over time, through, for example, the establishment of corporeal routines and specialized devices to reproduce themselves' (ibid., p. 8); as well as upon 'the vast spillage of *things*'; 'Things answer back' (ibid., p. 9). It is experimental. It stresses affect and sensation. And it returns to consideration of space.

In addressing the consequences of technological advance, Thrift sees no reason to reduce everyday experience and understanding of spatial complexity to 'a problematic of "scale"': 'Actors continually change size. A multiplicity of "scales" is always present in interactions' (ibid., p. 17). There is a proliferation of the 'actor's spaces that can be recognised and worked with', redefining 'what counts as an actor' (ibid.).

Although demanding in its range of references, Thrift's work concerns *performance*. It is about dealing with the everyday as it comes at us, as sophisticated social improvisation in a thinned out world, 'whereby a given locale is linked indifferently to every (or any) other place in global space' (Casey, 2001, p. 406) and where we no longer know quite how to go on but are always 'on the go', where regulated or habitual practices may prove ineffective.

Significant concepts related to 'performance' in the work of geographers such as John Wylie and Hayden Lorimer are creative practice, mode of representation, embodied enquiry and analytical trope and *affect* ('an intensity, a field perhaps of awe, irritation or serenity which exceeds, enters into, and ranges over the sensations and emotions of a subject who sees' (Wylie, 2005, p. 236); 'the augmentation or diminution of a body's capacity to act, to engage, and to connect, such that autoaffection is linked to the self-feeling of being alive – that is aliveness or vitality' (Clough, 2007, p. 2)). They undertake performative activities and they write of the sensual and physical experience in situations where materialities, motilities and corporealities are of equal account.

In 2002 Wylie conducted a solo walk along a 200-mile stretch of the South West Coast Path (Wylie, 2005). His account 'aims to describe some of the differential configurations of self and landscape emergent within the performative *milieu* of coastal walking' (p. 236). Hayden Lorimer, in his research on 'sites of special interest', focuses on:

> notable or overlooked landscape features (e.g. paths, gates, stiles, dykes and walls, flagstone steps, sheep pens, cattle grids, shooting butts, bus shelters, bothies,

scarecrows, gang-huts). Such folk geographies of things-in-places would focus on narratives, tales, memories and material remains of the not-so-distant past. (Lorimer, 2009)

Both have noted a resurgence in popular topographical writing in Britain pursuant upon the success and pervasive influence of W. G. Sebald, whose *Rings of Saturn* (1999) traces a long-distance walk in Norfolk. In *Waterlog* (1999) Roger Deakin swims across England. In *The Wild Place*s (2007) Robert Mcfarlane visits inaccessible locations. In *Connemara: Listening to the Wind* (2007) Tim Robinson continues his detailed mapping of one region in western Ireland. Each has performative aspects: movement, dwelling. Each is a personal account of experience and of place.

Both have acknowledged the work of American anthropologist Kathleen Stewart, particularly her attempts at 'narrativizing a local cultural real' (Stewart, 1996, p. 3) in coal-mining communities in West Virginia. Stewart invites the reader to imagine a deprived community through its own understandings of place and the memories they enshrine:

It tells its story through interruptions, amassed densities of description, evocation of voices and the conditions of their possibility, and lyrical, ruminative aporias that give pause.

It fashions itself as a tendon between interpretation and evocation, mimicking the tension in culture between the disciplinary and the imaginary. (ibid., p. 7)

Her work is 'a dwelling in and on a cultural poetics contingent on a place and a time and in-filled with palpable desire' (ibid., p. 4).

This resonates with the linked ideas that anthropologist Tim Ingold outlines in *The Perception of the Environment* (2000), which have been widely taken up in associated fields:

A place owes its character to the experiences it affords to those who spend time there – to the sights, sounds and indeed smells that constitute its specific ambience. And these, in turn, depend on the kinds of activities in which its inhabitants engage. It is from this relational context of people's engagement with the world, in the business of dwelling, that each place draws its unique significance. (ibid., p. 192)

For Ingold, landscape is also *taskscape*: a work-in-progress, perpetually under construction. It is a matrix of movement, with distinct places as nodes bound together by the itineraries of inhabitants (ibid., p. 219). It is differentiated, but it better resembles a network of related places, some revealed through our habitual actions, some through familiarity and affinity and some through particular moments and events stored in communal memory. Moving between places, *wayfinding*, more closely resembles story-telling than map-using, as one situates one's position within the context of journeys previously made: 'every place holds within it memories of previous arrivals and departures, as well as expectations of how one may reach it, or reach other places from it' (ibid., p. 227). Perceiving landscape is thus 'to carry out an act of remembrance' (ibid., p. 189); 'places do not have locations but histories' (ibid., p. 219).

There is no privilege of origin: a place owes its character not only to the experiences it affords as sights, sounds, etc. but also to what is done there as looking, listening, moving. Both 'being' and environment are mutually emergent, continuously brought into existence together. And here performance might represent a place of work or special moment within landscape (see Pearson, 2006a, pp. 152–62).

Site then is also a function of the social: '*Topophilia* is the affective bond between people and place or setting' (Tuan, 1974, p. 4):

> a notion of place where specificity (local uniqueness, a sense of place) derives not from some mythical internal roots nor from history of relative isolation – not to be disrupted by isolation – but from the absolute particularity of the mixture of influences found together there. (Massey, 1999, p. 18)

And here site-specific performance may not only highlight such investment, such heterogeneity, it may also become a lasting part of the story of that place: 'potentially constitutive of aspects of the world' (Myers, 2009, p. 34).

Provisional distinctions

Given an expanded notion of site – 'reimagining place as a situation, a set of circumstances, geographical location, historical narrative, group of people or social agenda' (Doherty, 2004, p. 9) – and an extended range of practices, can anything then be said, in general, to define site-specific performance?

Whilst 'that undertaken in non-theatrical spaces' is now barely adequate, the auditorium might yet provide a *control*, an abstracted set of conditions, against which to extrapolate the particularities of site work, all that might absorb and impact upon practice (whilst acknowledging that the auditorium is itself a site, equally susceptible to conceptual readdress):

▪ The auditorium is cloistered.	▪ At site, bounds and perimeters may be extant or installed.
▪ In the auditorium environmental conditions are stable.	▪ At site, environmental conditions may change and need to be accepted or actively countered.
	▪ Site is only dark or quiet if chosen for such qualities or rendered so.
▪ The auditorium is dark and quiet.	

In the auditorium performance is scheduled.

In the auditorium performance is located in one place.

In the auditorium the arrangement of the audience is fixed.

In the auditorium, the audience is cast as audience: purposefully assembled, expectant, disposed, potentially appreciative.

In the auditorium the audience may have been before.

In the auditorium the scene is singular.

In the auditorium events occur in the middle distance.

In the auditorium effects are confined and controlled.

In the auditorium the machinery of production pre-exists performance.

In the auditorium artifice is disguised.

In the auditorium established techniques are more or less sufficient to the task of production.

In the auditorium one thing of singular importance is happening.

The auditorium is designed to facilitate repetition.

In the auditorium previous occupations are erased.

In the auditorium this sort of thing has happened before.

At site, there may be a transitory discontinuity in the social fabric.

At site, performance may be distributed as moments of rhetoric intensity.

At site, there may be multiple dispositions: organized; fluid; negotiated in performance ...

At site, the audience may be incidental – those present in the same place at the same time – and obdurate.

At site there are no regular theatregoers. If they have been before, it is in another guise.

At site, the prospect is complex unless otherwise framed.

At site, events occur at varying and changing distances.

At site, effects may intrude and compete for attention.

At site, it may be installed or modified from that otherwise existing, or rendered surplus to requirements.

At site, performance is in plain view unless masked.

At site, techniques may be invented or appropriated.

At site, many things may be happening: performance may need to establish and proclaim its own presence.

At site, there may be no recourse, no second chance.

At site, they are evident and operative, though not necessarily alluded to.

At site, it is always as if for the first time.

2

In which conceptual and theoretical approaches are proposed and examined in order to acknowledge and appreciate the particular nature of site-specific performance. An immersive model is introduced. Reference is made to the insights of other disciplines, including human geography and architecture to describe better the experience of place and the nature of performative occupancy.

Visitation: going and doing

Imagine Esgair Fraith ('Speckled Ridge'), a farmstead first occupied during the enclosure of common land near Lampeter, west Wales, in the early nineteenth century. Often mistakenly described as a hamlet, its buildings, walls and paths appear too numerous for an upland agricultural concern. From the outset, they were more than this. The first occupier was a weaver, an out-worker in the regional woollen industry. The buildings were always partly industrial, with manufacturing and cloth-storage sheds near the house, dams in the river and the remains of a horse-whim, perhaps to assist fulling. By the late 1880s the family was much reduced: eventually only one daughter lived there, with her own illegitimate daughter, masquerading as her aunt. The next occupants, the Davies, took Esgair Fraith solely as a farming enterprise around 1890. A dated stone of 1904 from the garden marks their energetic tenure. Mrs Davies died in 1926 and the old man lived alone until 1941 when the farm was finally abandoned. The roof was missing by 1949. Local memory has Mr Davies engaged in smithing, tinkering and cobbling, and incredibly in one of the collapsed outbuildings there are traces of his work: fragments of baths and pans, pieces of leather and nails. Esgair Fraith is now in ruins. Its story is that of just two families, of two sets of biographies.

For almost fifty years Esgair Fraith lay deep in the Clwedog Forest, planted by the Forestry Commission between 1956 and 1959 in two adjoining parishes in the long-term post-Second World War strategy to ensure essential resources. It is composed mainly of non-indigenous sitka spruce, with some pine. But the farmstead was never quite hidden. The deciduous trees, beech and sycamore, that matured in the garden and surrounding hedges always marked its location in the coniferous canopy. Gradually a thick blanket of moss and lichen coated its fabric in the resulting microclimate. And it took on symbolic significance: through the state-organized processes of land requisition and afforestation, it became one of those places in Wales, along with reservoirs and military ranges and open-cast mines, where land disappeared, was 'disappeared', and with it too, by implication, language. In this, land itself is not regarded as separate from the lived experience. Each episode of loss inspired poetic reflection and political response, campaigns of civil disobedience, the formation of organizations of resistance: each a veritable *lieux de memoire* (Nora, 1996, pp. 1–20). This was always a complex matter, involving issues of homeland and native soil, of place, culture, idiom and identity intimately entwined. The late Welsh scholar Bedwyr Lewis Jones suggests that 'land and language are two strands that tie the Welsh-speaker to his *cynefin* or locale'. 'There are other links', he adds, 'such as remembrance of things past' (Lewis Jones, 1985, p. 122).

In what follows it might help to bear Esgair Fraith in mind. But picture too a street corner or a library or a telephone kiosk or a beach or a swimming pool or ...

If site-specific performance involves an *activity*, an *audience* and a *place*, then creative opportunities reside in the multiple creative articulations of *us*, *them* and *there*. In the model that follows, each postulate poses particular questions, both offering and demanding different forms and modes of engagement. In acts of visitation and meeting, it begins with me, the same me as 'me-performing' in *Theatre/Archaeology* (Pearson and Shanks, 2001, pp. 15ff.) or the 'I' of *In Comes I* (Pearson, 2006a): a self-reflective practitioner.

I go there and you and they do not

To outline stances, attitudes and presuppositions:

- Who am I and what am I doing?
- What are the conditions of my access?
- Am I there by invitation or am I intruding or trespassing?
- Am I there for the first time or is this a place of familiarity?
- Is it in the public or private domain?
- Is what I might see or do either prescribed or proscribed?
- What are the circumstances of my presence?
- Am I a stranger or an inhabitant?
- Do I pass unnoticed or do I stick out?
- Are my actions clandestine or do I draw attention to myself?
- In what guise do I visit?

As *tourist*: wandering with varying degrees of attention and disinterest, or watching the aurora borealis from the specially darkened cabin of an aircraft north of Shetland.

As *walker*: sauntering – *sans terre* – 'equally at home everywhere' (Emerson and Thoreau, no date, pp. 71–2), 'validated by its effects on the body – from sweat to heart rate to muscle stretching' (Thrift, 2008, p. 68). Looking, and being looked at, following 'the thicks and thins of an urban "text" they write without being able to read it' (Certeau, 1988, p. 93). 'The moving about that the city multiplies and concentrates makes the city itself an immense social experience of "lacking a place" – an experience that is, to be sure, broken up into countless tiny deportations (displacements and walks)' (ibid., p. 103).

As *wayfarer*: moving from one familiar place to another. 'The wayfarer is continually on the move. More strictly, he is his movement' (Ingold, 2007, p. 75).

As *flâneur*: 'at home in the ebb and flow, the bustle, the fleeting and the infinite' (Baudelaire, 1972, p. 399) yet with the freedom to loiter, to witness and interpret passing scenes and incidents, diverse activities, unpredictable juxtapositions, fleeting occurrences, multifarious sights and sounds. Moving through the flux of the city in awe of dazzling consumer spectacles: gazing, grazing, consuming. As scenes of the modern city channel my gaze and limit my objects of pleasure, my circulation becomes disciplined.

As *derivist*: 'in a dérive, one or more persons, during a certain period, drop their usual motives for movement and action, their relations, their work and leisure activities, and let themselves be drawn by the attractions of the terrain and the encounters they find there' (Debord, quoted in Andreotti and Costa, 1996, p. 22). The *dérive* ('drifting') as 'a technique of transient passage through varied ambiances' (ibid.), distinct from the stroll. Michele Bernstein notes that the taxi journey might constitute our most immediate experience of disorientation and discovery (quoted in ibid., p. 47).

As close relative *psycho-geographer*: 'the element of chance is less determinant than one might think: from the dérive point of view cities have a psycho-geographical relief, with constant currents, fixed points and vortexes which strongly discourage entry into or exit from certain zones' (ibid., p. 22). A complete insubordination to habitual influences without subordination to randomness. It is orientated neither by attraction to a particular era nor to an architectural style nor by the exoticism that arises from exploring a neighbourhood for the first time. But Debord suggests that it is not aimless, for we seem drawn to certain locales, differentiated, complex and unnerving, that offer a density of experience, with significant effect upon the emotions and behaviour of individuals: this he calls *psycho-geography*. His modes of enquiry in search of such places include slipping by night into houses undergoing demolition, hitch-hiking non-stop, wandering in subterranean catacombs.

As *nomad*: shifting across the smooth space of the urban desert using points and locations to define paths rather than places to be. The enemy of the nomad is the authority that wants to take the space and enclose it and to create fixed and well directed paths for movement. And the nomad, cut free of roots, bonds and fixed identities, is the enemy of the authority, resisting its discipline (see Deleuze and Guattari, 1988, 380ff.).

As *rambler*: rethinking the city as a series of flows or movements in pursuit of pleasure, moving between sites of leisure, consumption, exchange and display. Rambling as 'a mode of movement which celebrates the public spaces, streets and excitement of urban life from a male perspective' (Rendell, 1998, p. 75):

> Urban design organises bodies socially and spatially, in terms of positioning, displaying and obscuring. Architecture controls and limits physical movement and sight-lines; it can stage and frame those who inhabit its spaces, by creating contrasting scales, screening and lighting ... Such devices are culturally determined, they prioritise certain activities and persons, and obscure others according to class, race and gender. Urban space is a medium in which functional visual requirements and imagery are constituted and represented as part of a patriarchal and capitalist ideology. The places of leisure in the nineteenth century city represent and control the status of men and women as spectators and as objects of sight in public arenas. (ibid., p. 84)

As *field-worker*: in pursuit of objects of study:

- What are my objectives? Have I gone prepared? How is my visit planned in advance? Am I on a quest? Do I have an itinerary? Am I purposefully lost in space, trying to get my bearings? Do I have tasks to fulfil?
- How do I orientate myself? Do I need a map to get around or am I drawn to, and moving between, old haunts on familiar routes in an 'archi-textural meshwork' (Ingold, 2007, p. 80)? Am I met and shown around, my attention drawn to this or that which I might otherwise not have noticed?
- Am I directed by the exhortations, admonitions and signposts of others? Am I pursuing quarry, following the tracks of animals or the flight-paths of birds?
- Do I seek out the traces, archaeological traces, of other (former) visitors and occupants? As I move around do I leave marks: 'to walk is to leave footprints' (Roms, quoted in Whitehead, 2006, p. 4)
- Am I simply enthralled by the place? Or is it difficult to know where it ends and I begin?
- Is my journey a private, performative undertaking occasioned by the nature of the place: pilgrimage, 'walkabout'?

Australian Aboriginal landscapes are marked by ancestral acts, sedimented with human significances. To travel across such landscapes is to remember them into being. The pathways are song-lines, long narrative excursions that remember places in song, singing the world into being again.

> For journeys through these places, with the narrative song cycles that articulate their numinosity for the initiated, constitute performative re-makings, re-earthings,

> re-memberings of imaginary happenings here now, fusing place, body and spirit at the intersection of secular and sacred time. To walk the story is to revisit and rehearse the itineraries of a tradition that maps the complex interrelatedness of cultural spaces and identities, pasts and possible futures. (Williams, 1998, p. vii)

These are, contra Nora's assertion of disappearance, environments of memory: 'settings in which memory is a real part of everyday experience' (Nora, 1992, p. 1): *milieux de memoire.*

■ How am I affected? What do I feel? What do I perceive? What do I experience?
■ How far is this informed by predispositions and previous experiences?
■ To what do I attend? Natural landscape and built environment; sky as well as land; night as well as day? In foul weather as well as fair?
■ And upon my return, how do I reconstitute 'there' here?

By configuring the physical materials I bring back. In his project *Rupture and Residue* (2004) Simon Whitehead took six sea-washed ash sticks to Queensland and returned with six sticks to place on his home beach (Whitehead, 2006, pp. 76–7).

By showing the recorded evidence, drawings, diaries, video tapes, audio recordings, of what I did there. As *exhibition* or *installation*, as manipulated and enhanced sounds – as in *Arctic*, Max Eastley's recordings of bearded seal, kittwake, little auk, etc., as well as Aeolian flutes and harps made during northern voyages (Eastley, 2007).

By relating what I did there, at another time, in another place, as *story-telling*, some equivalent of the explorer's account, the traveller's tale. As Walter Benjamin noted, 'when someone goes on a trip he has something to tell about' (Benjamin, 1992, p. 84).

In his reflection on reindeer herding in Scotland, geographer Hayden Lorimer notes: 'landscapes told as a distribution of stories and dramatic episodes, or as repertoires of lived practice, can be creatively recut, embroidered, and still sustain original narratological integrity' (Lorimer, 2006, p. 515). Perhaps this is a work of *autotopography*, a performance that folds or unfolds autobiography and place: 'a creative act of interpretation and invention, all of which depend on where you are standing, when and for what purpose' (Heddon, 2008, p. 91).

By combining documentary footage from there with all that may be created here to stand in for the experience in *multimedia* performances: in Brith Gof's *Patagonia* (1993) (see pp. 164–5), accounts of personal journeys to Welsh emigrant communities in Argentina were fused with the story of the shooting of Llwyd ap Iwan there in 1909 by US outlaws Butch Cassidy and the Sundance Kid (Pearson, 1996).

We go there and they do not

We may be of the same ilk, fellow artists, our conversation addressing emergent matters from similar standpoints. But our expertise may be in different disciplinary areas. On a fieldtrip – doing *fieldwork* on a geological *excursion* for instance, trekking from one exposure to another – either of us might expound particular knowledge, pointing out this or that. Our discussions might mutually illuminate and extend extant positions: between performance and archaeology, between performance and geography. In 'Performing a Visit' (Pearson and Shanks, 1997) archaeologist Michael Shanks and I reflect upon Esgair Fraith from different perspectives. On the 'Littoral' workshop, during the 'Living in a Material World: Performativities of Emptiness' network project (see pp. 133–4), archaeologists, geographers and artists gathered:

> On Sunday January 26th four of us made a transect using a single line of string. We did this at a point approximately two-thirds of the way along the 'littoral' between Severn Beach and New Pill Gout heading towards Avonmouth. The line sat at approximately ninety degrees to the foreshore and ran from the curb of the A403 to well below the high water mark. In the process it crossed under the railway and over the footpath which runs parallel to the A403 at this point. (The littoral is taken here as the long strip of land from Severn Beach to Avonmouth marked by the road inland and the low tide mark out in the estuary). This transect was begun shortly after the turn of high tide (10.14 a.m.) and was completed at about 1.30 p.m. Each participant selected (or asked to have given them) a task. My task, given by Penny at my request following discussion of my sampling habits following our first preliminary exploration of themes during and after the walk on Saturday, was to sample every five strides, using the toe of my left boot as a marker and reporting what was next to the object that first took my attention while trying to pay attention to the full sensory range of my experience, including any memories that appeared. (Biggs, 2008, p. 1)

Every ten paces I paused and attempted to list all the *horizontals* I could see, bottom to top: to demonstrate the manifold instances of human intervention: pipelines, railway tracks, security fences, bridgework. And to appreciate Jean-Luc Nancy's supposition that 'all landscape painting paints a horizon' (Nancy, 2005, p. 60).

You go there, I and they do not

From a different disciplinary standpoint, you may still employ approaches analogous to those of performance and performance writing. In geographer John Wylie's account of a single day's walking on a coastal path, he describes 'sensations of anxiety and immensity, haptic enfolding and attenuation, encounters with others and with the elements, and moments of visual exhilaration and epiphany' (Wylie, 2005, p. 234). He suggests that walking involves specific corporealities and sensibilities: moments, movements, events. He is in the landscape but also up against it: 'to be dogged, put-upon, petulant, breathless' (ibid., p. 240).

They go there, you and I do not

In anticipation of their visit, what is to be done? First, nothing: we leave it as it is, facilitating access, saying little, allowing the remains to 'speak' for themselves, letting visitors address them in their own ways. For at Esgair Fraith the tumbled walls are equivocal, serving as a backdrop or scenography for any narrative or fantasy that might be projected onto them, any knowledges and aspirations that might be brought to them, any interpretation that might be read 'onto' and 'into' them. Yi-Fu Tuan suggests that a visitor's experience of the same place may invoke reactions and associations entirely differently from that of the inhabitants: it is possible to be in a place without realizing its significance for the groups of people who have historically inhabited it, though 'the visitor's judgment is often valid. His main contribution is the fresh perspective' (Tuan, 1974, p. 65). For some, the response will be aesthetic and personal: the romance of the ruin. For others the very ruination is evocative of the cultural trauma that it seems to represent, with the deciduous growth representing a kind of dogged resistance. A pile of old stones to walk your dog over then, or the defeated hopes of a nation? The visitor decides. Whichever, the senses are engulfed by the smells of decay, the textures of moss and dead leaves, the image of collapsed walls, fallen lintels, the gloom of forest shade. Here, the very processes of the 'archaeological' are apparent: mouldering, rotting, disintegrating, decomposing, putrefying, falling to pieces ... Apparent too is that sense of the passage of time, of entropy, and of our own mortality perhaps, that the manicured sites of 'heritage culture' often seem keen to disguise. Here, one realizes, 'it was then, it is now and all points in between'. And the visitor is aware that each surviving doorway was once entered, each window was once looked through. At Esgair Fraith, on this bleak hillside, where it will inevitably rain during a visit, people have struggled, survived and lived a life.

Or they are orientated and directed by our sketch maps and instructions. What they may need is some sense of *scale*, a *key* to the symbols and some idea of which way is up, though what gets onto the map will always be partial. In that these order movement around the site, suggesting routes for walking and pausing, for instance, they could also recommend or demand corporeal involvement *with* the site. They might come to resemble choreographic scores or diagrams with the visitor as participant/performer. Such choreography could be *of* the site, following existing paths, crossing thresholds, entering rooms. Equally, it could delineate unusual trajectories of movement traversing the remains: straight lines, circles, arcs. Revealing unexpected viewpoints, demanding altered physical stances and body attitudes. All of which serve to unsettle the visitor, inviting him or her to look afresh at detail and at vista. And we might suggest not only where to look, but also how to look: in close-up, in long shot, with wide-angle, as people have always done at Esgair Fraith. And they may be encouraged to touch and smell and listen as much as look: 'changing the way people perceive places' (McAuley, 2006, p. 151).

Or they take our guidebooks, texts that supplement the phenomenological experience of being present. These we could term *deep maps*, or *incorporations*: juxtapositions and interpenetrations of the historical and the contemporary, the political and the poetic, the factual and the fictional, the discursive and the sensual – that include plan, axonometric section, photograph and artist's impression adjacent to, and overlapping, poem, topographic details, local folklore. The conflation of oral testimony, anthology, memoir, biography, natural history and everything they might ever want to ask. Texts adequate to the task of elaborating the complexity of narratives that have accumulated and that are in contest here. These are proactive documents: their parts do not necessarily coalesce. They leave space for the imagination of the reader. The interpretive instinct of the visitor is not denied, and meaning is not monopolized. *In Comes I: Performance, Memory and Landscape* (Pearson, 2006a) is structured as a number of *excursions* in my home region: guiding the reader, be they in an armchair or in the field, through a sequence of locales, pausing at each for personal and critical reflection on themes related to, or evoked by, that place: mixing themes biographical, familial, topographical, archaeological. A *chorographic* approach to the visitation of individuated places.

In specially designed guidebooks integrating text and image, Exeter-based performance company Wrights and Sites offers 'the stimulus for a series of actions, or performances, to be created and carried out by readers who become walkers in the city's spaces' (Turner, 2004, p. 385). Some 'walks' offer specific routes, others imaginative games or provocations: 'loiter without intent'. In *An Exeter Mis-Guide* (Hodge *et al.*, 2003) the city is revealed through oblique engagements, with proposals such as 'Borrow a dog from a friend. Let it take you for a walk'. Their recent project *A Mis-Guide to Anywhere* is transferable to any city. 'Go exploring with children – let them choose a special way of travelling: As if the city were underwater ... or a mountain' (Wrights and Sites, 2006). In what Turner terms *mythogeography*, the personal, fictional and mythical are placed on an equal footing with factual, municipal history: 'the whole city becomes a field of transitional objects, part created, part discovered' (Turner, 2004, p. 386): the city becomes a 'potential' space, a place of enquiry and invention.

Or they encounter what *we* have altered there, the traces we have purposefully made or left behind, both *additive* and *reductive*:

A line drawn with charcoal on paper, one with chalk on a blackboard, is additive, since the material from the chalk forms an extra layer that is superimposed on the substrate. Lines that are scratched, scored or etched into a surface are reductive, since they are formed by the removal of material from the surface itself. (Ingold, 2007, p. 43)

The practices of land art may be instructive for further performative activities, often themselves inviting participation. At Robert Smithson's *Spiral Jetty*, 'you can look at it, look from it, look with it, be in it, be part of it, connect it up with yourself and the surroundings in a number of different ways' (Wylie, 2007, p. 142). Mark Pimlott's *La Scala*, situated on the piazza in front of Aberystwyth Arts Centre, is a large concrete staircase: 'one can climb the stair to be closer to the sky and higher above the world. I want people to feel as though they are suspended in the air, leaving the world, as monumental as the architecture and landscape around them' (Pimlott, 2006, p. 271). The structure prefigures activities of climbing, sitting, sunbathing, talking, looking out to sea. At Drenthe in the Netherlands, PeerGrouP's *Strokasteel* (2005) is a temporary auditorium in a rural setting constructed from 11,000 straw bales (Schuring, 2008, pp. 38–43).

Or they are led towards and move between what we have left there for them, such as the clockwork audio sources of recorded information on local natural history currently attached to trees in certain plantations by the Forestry Commission in Wales. Or the twenty radio transmitters in Graeme Miller's work *Linked* (2003; Miller, 2009) broadcasting recorded testimonies of those who once lived and worked on a three-mile route where a motorway now runs through 400 demolished homes in London, conspiring 'an odd sense that the activity of the walker is somehow triggering these recollections' (Wilkie, 2008, p. 100). Or on the numerous and proliferating platforms of exposition within urban contexts: the multiple hoardings and screens of the contemporary city, in the street, on public transport. Monitors on Cardiff buses now show BBC World News intercut with views of the passing street from multiple cameras.

Or our relationship is mediated in the emergent genre of audio-walks, increasingly familiar in museum trails and artistic practices; or conjoined in Paul Auster's memorial tour of the site of the World Trade Center (Auster, 2005). My own project *Carrlands* (2007b) (see pp. 80–3) is composed of three sixty-minute compositions for locations in an agricultural river valley in north Lincolnshire with recommended walks.

You and I and they go there together

We accompany them. Of course they may already be there: this is their place and they may know far more of it than we do. Or we may be equally unfamiliar: in 1997 I led a guided tour at a disused steelworks near Bochum in Germany, that neither I nor they had visited before. Going equipped, but only one step ahead of the game.

We may have arranged to transport them there, the journey becoming part of the performance: a brass band on the coach. Or the journey, the performance itself: Forced Entertainment's *Nights in this City* (1995) took the form of a coach trip in Sheffield.

> The text we created – pointing out buildings, street corners, car-parks, patches of wasteground – was always overlaid with other texts – with the whispered or

even shouted texts of other passengers ('That's where I used to work ...' 'That's the place where ...') and the silent text of actions created by those living and working in the city as the bus moved through it. (Etchells, 1999, p. 81)

Once there, performance, both expositionary and dialogic, is conceivable at any number of scales.

In *The Best Place* – 'an encounter with inhabitants, places, stories and images' (Feenstra, 2007, p. 231) – Dutch artist Waapke Feenstra invites suggestions for the 'best' local place. In *Former Farmland* (2008) she walks the land with individual farmers, augering the soil, looking at its composition, reflecting upon land-use as 'site of memory for an agrarian community'. Misha Myers's 'conversive wayfinding' projects (Myers, 2009) are enacted through the contingent effort of conversation, shared walks encouraging companionability. She warns however that 'there are conditions, which the artist may create space for, but cannot predetermine, such as weather, transformations of the landscape, walkers' corporeal rhythms, capacities, desires and mood' (ibid., p. 104). 'The artist asks the instigating question, listens, sets a context for action, creates an aesthetic milieu in which an event is mutually created. The exchanges depend on the talents of the speakers to respond to the insights, fallibilities and allure of each other' (Heim, 2006, p. 203). In Myers's work 'they' are refugees, bringing memories of another place.

It might be a solo narrative akin to a guided tour in which the interpreter is foregrounded and interpretation becomes a performative practice. This can exhibit a high order of intertextuality, of dialogue between texts. It can include truth and fiction, lying and appropriation: the fragmentary, the digressive, the ambiguous – anecdotes, analects, autobiography. The description of people, places and pathologies, poetry, forensic data, quotations, lies, memories, jokes ... Here there are no hierarchies of information and no correct procedures. Indeed, it must vacillate between the intimately familiar and the infinitely strange, if the visitor's attention is to be held. The teller is inevitably at the centre of events. Here in the grain of the voice, and in all the rhetorical techniques of the performer's art, is where the story comes to life: in physical re-enactments, impersonation, improvised asides ... Thus language is potentially brought back to places that were silenced as a rearticulation. Performance occasions reinterpenetration.

Or it might be a large-scale scenographic work in which what we say here, do there, need not be solely *about* or *of* the place. In 1994 Cliff McLucas hauled three tons of scaffolding up to Esgair Fraith to create *Tri Bywyd* (*Three Lives*) (see Kaye, 2000, pp. 125–37), a site-specific performance about three deaths, about the domestic in the landscape.

No one goes

There are places that under normal circumstances remain out of bounds: places difficult to access, such as Antarctica, though Chris Cree Brown's composition *Under Erebus* (Brown, 2000) demonstrates the primacy there of sound over sight, the ear ever attuned to the cracking of ice.

Other places are where entry is inadvisable, such as war zones, though Peter Cusack's audio recordings (Cusack, 2009) made in the area of exclusion around the Chernobyl reactor in his *Sounds from Dangerous Places* series teem with the animal and bird life that flourishes there, free from human disturbance.

And there are new kinds of places into which our entry is prohibited, such as the detention centres at Guantanamo Bay and Abu Ghraib, though this should not prevent us simulating their effects elsewhere.

There is no here and there

There are places betwixt and between, such as border regions and security areas where actions and motives are under extreme scrutiny, where we submit ourselves to the will of others. Guillermo Gomez-Pena's early work takes place on both sides of the US–Mexican border and the cross-cultural, hybrid work this might generate.

And some places seem neither here nor there, or nowhere in particular, unpatinated, untouched by history: 'today all of our circulation, information and communication spaces could be considered non-places' (Augé, 2000, p. 10). 'A non-space comes into existence, even negatively, when human beings don't recognise themselves in it, or cease to recognise themselves in it, or have not yet recognised themselves in it' (ibid., p. 9).

There are new kinds of place – digital platforms – established through advances in information technology: performance as broadcast, as webcast, as GPS/satnav configuration. We can visit the expeditionary huts in Antarctica without damaging them. We can join a round-the-world yachtswoman every-day as she sails the South Atlantic. We may even be able to visit places once unimagined, in domains such as Second Life.

There is no us and them

And our mutual and/or respective presence and/or absence is enabled and problematized by social networking websites and mobile telephony. As *avatars* we become multiple, as do they. Who is who may be difficult to discern: 'flash mobs' gather unannounced and the dancers at 'silent discos', each listening to their own soundtrack on an MP3 player, invade a railway station concourse.

Or we do other

We direct our energies to direct action and *implementation*.

Everything at Esgair Fraith has recently changed. The cash-crop timber has been harvested, and the finds of this felling are spectacular: across this hill-side a dozen similar derelict farms have emerged. We never expected them to return. Their absence allowed us to romanticize their very disappearance, to revel in their loss. Now they challenge us, particularly those of us who have benefited economically and artistically from them, to readdress them.

What might this mean in practice? For the owner, Forest Enterprise, these places are increasingly regarded as a leisure resource: it is eager to provide public access. Since they are to be revisited, we might base the framework of a research project around the notion of the *visit* and its close relative the *guided tour*. Further, Forest Enterprise is legally obligated to plant more deciduous trees. Questions emerge about the policies and politics of such replanting, and of future land use. And here *we* might intervene. Could we design interpretive trails across the landscape, in which the farms and their mature hedges and gardens become significant locales, places to visit, with newly planted avenues linking them? Unfortunately, such is the degree of ruination that the Health and Safety Executive will never allow it. And as one forester retorted, 'it is a perfect place to grow spruce'.

Phenomenology: experiencing

Imagine a winter landscape.

Your senses working overtime: you shiver and squint, stamp and blow. Only then perhaps do you look, listen, touch. You flog through the snow. Your feet and fingers freeze. To your left, a flock of scavenging rooks takes flight. You are aware of *surface*, *climate* and *ambiance*.

Your sensual engagement is *phenomenological*. The emphasis is on bodily contact, corporeality, embodiment: 'body and environment fold into and co-construct each other through a series of practices and relations' (Wylie, 2007, p. 144). This is as much a *weatherworld* as landscape, and it conspires to bring about *affects*.

Gradually you begin to make *perceptual judgements* about distance and direction, near or far, this way or that way: to make distinctions between left/right, top/bottom, within reach/beyond reach, within sight/beyond sight, here-and-there polarities – difficult enough in this whiteness. And all informed by past experiences of how similar and how dissimilar this is to places you have known.

The environment might oblige you to respond in certain ways, prefiguring performance, spread-eagled on thin ice: performance as a practice of involvement. During a Cape Farewell project expedition to Spitzbergen, dancer Siobhan Davies notes:

> The best movement is to walk or to run. Dance here is then reduced to the familiarity, the straightforwardness, the elegance of the walk and the run. Our walking turned into slipping on ice or pushing our heels down into snow to help us keep upright while going steeply down hill. Every kind of putting one foot in front of the other had its use. (Buckland *et al.*, 2006, p. 86)

You may take up its challenges in practices that intensify sensual experiences: rock climbing, skydiving, snorkelling …

Such experiences you might assist others to encounter. Of his *Locator* workshops (1995–2005) Simon Whitehead writes: 'my role as guide is to encourage people to get lost' (Whitehead, 2006, p. 38). Or you might tell others about elsewhere. Or help them to imagine. My own *Winter* (2008) was conceived and written for the Groeneveld Forum, a symposium primarily for agriculturalists to consider the potential of the arts to inform environmental policy. The thirty-minute audio work, combining spoken word and musical composition by John Hardy, was made available ready loaded on MP3 players to accompany an optional lunchtime walk in the grounds of Groeneveld Castle near Baarn in the Netherlands, a late eighteenth-century arrangement of lakes, paths and plantings referred to locally as an 'English landscape'. The equipment was provided, with a lunch bag, to delegates who were advised that they could walk alone or in groups. In the event they were also provided with umbrellas, as it poured with rain.

My quandary was how to create a work for a location I had visited only once and with little further opportunity to research its history, either in archives or through interviews. The solution: to invite the audience to imagine this place in a different guise, to picture it in deepest winter. The text makes reference to the familiar paintings of Hendrick Avercamp and Pieter Bruegel. It recalls the bad winters of 1780, 1947 and 1963. And it asks them to remember: their memories became part of a personal *reverie*, a projection onto the autumn landscape. It concludes:

> And if, and when, the snow comes no more ...
> What will you remember of childhood delights, of work in the fields?
> The feel of snow: its textures ... dusty, watery ... caked into woollen gloves ...
> The look of ice: glazing windows in leafy patterns, falling as spikes from the roof ...
> Frozen toes in rubber boots ...
> What we called 'hot aches' as the blood seeped back painfully ...
> Your skin ... in new tones ... red and blue and purple ... chapped knees ...
>
> And if I asked you to remember the place of your childhood in winter ...
> And if I asked you to write a postcard, describing it in five words ...
> What would you write?
>
> And if I asked you, to recall adventures, and incidents, and accidents, in the snow ...
> And if I asked you to write one sentence to describe one such experience ...
> What would you write?
> And if, and when, the snow comes no more ...
> How will you describe the awesome power of the snowstorm and the sublime and terrible beauty of a world turned black-and-white?
>
> When you begin with the words 'I remember ...'
> What will you tell them?
> And when *you* say to them 'Imagine this', what will they imagine?

Several delegates listened twice. Most took the players home and listened again, frequently at night and in bed. Many returned from the walk with stories and anecdotes of their childhoods. Individuals revealed detailed experiences of landscape, affirmed in the immediate response of others present, that might otherwise not have emerged within the conventional protocols of conference proceedings.

Chorography: differentiating

> To be a place, every somewhere must lie on one or several paths of movement to and from places elsewhere. Life is lived, I reasoned, along paths, not just in places, and paths are lines of a sort. (Ingold, 2007, p. 2)

Picture the place where, if asked, you would say you come from, have attachments with.

The nature of *chorography* is to distinguish and espouse the unique character of individual *places*. At particular scales of apprehension, it identifies and differentiates sites of significance as, potentially at least, places to visit within a given *region*. Chorography attends to the local: it concerns specificities, particularities and peculiarities. In demonstrating preference, it ignores or chooses not to acknowledge other places that fall outside its sphere of interest. It displays partiality. Its outcomes, its representations of a region, are partial.

For Edward Casey a choric region is a 'locatory matrix for things' (Casey, 1998, p. 34). Seventeenth-century English chorographies collected and arranged natural, historical and antiquarian information topographically in a region, place by place, village by village, without necessarily relating it to larger spatial frames or to the broader concerns of disciplinary enquiry, largely because disciplines, anthropology for instance, did not yet exist or were in nascent form. In their inclusion of details of antiquities and flora and fauna, however, they presage the development of both archaeology *and* natural history.

In the form of a gazetteer, they involve the systematic description of a region's natural and man-made attributes, its emplaced *things*. Its scenic features. Its inhabitants, their histories, laws, traditions and customs. Ancient sites and relics. Property rights, and the etymology of names. They incorporate elements of historical narrative and biography, with pictorial maps and architectural sketches. They often seek to legitimize claims to title and land. And whilst they discriminate – 'Regard this rather than that', 'Visit this rather than that' – they draw together diverse phenomena into a heterogeneous collection that not only seeks to evoke the special qualities of a region, but may even come to define, to stand in for, that region as viewed from somewhere else. This is not necessarily however how the inhabitants would choose to represent themselves.

With region as the optic, chorography offers conceptual and analytical approaches to site-specific performance, regarded here as one of Casey's distinct *things*: a feature of topography, a function of landscape, a component of local history, related as much to immediate conditions of geology or traditions of agricultural land-use as to ostensibly similar practices elsewhere. In that it professes itself attached to a particular locale, such performance is better viewed in relation to other cultural practices and to geophysical conditions there, rather than being considered the local enactment and expression of common traits within a putative genre: 'site-specific performance'. It arises from and is articulated in direct relation to sets of historical, social, cultural and environmental circumstance, and in juxtaposition with all else that constitutes the grain of the region. It need not be considered as the manifestation of transferable techniques and technologies in search of a suitable location. Specific in form, content and function in a specific place, it finds itself adjacent to, drawn into juxtaposition with, owing allegiance to, other *things* – mutually illuminating things, awkwardly dissimilar things – across the terrain and through time within a choric region. It becomes a local feature of, and an active contribution to, the distinctiveness of a region. It may indeed be the most interesting *thing* that has ever happened at this site. And given our particular *sphere of interest*, our disciplinary partiality, we could conceive a chorography that favours moments of performative exposition. Casey's other things may include all manner of celebratory, ludic and performative activities: modes of traditional practice – folk drama and calendar custom – and manifestations of contemporary devised theatre are thus copresent in a regional chorography (see Pearson, 2006a).

But in addressing the very particularities of its engagement with a location, any chorographic account of site-specific performance as a thing will necessitate detailed description, paying equal attention to that which is of the site and that which is brought to the site, the inextricable binding of place and artwork, to demonstrate its uniqueness.

This might resemble what Michael Shanks and I called a *deep map* (Pearson and Shanks, 2001, pp. 64–6): an attempt to record and represent the substance, grain and patina of a particular place, through juxtapositions and interweavings of the historical and the contemporary, the political and the poetic, the factual and the fictional, the academic and the aesthetic … depth not as profundity but as topographic and cultural density. In this it is perhaps akin to anthropologist Clifford Geertz's *thick description*: the detailed and contextual description of cultural phenomena, to discern the complexities behind the action, and from which the observer is not removed (Geertz, 1973). It may further reference his *blurred genre*: as Shanks and I appropriated it, 'a mixture of narration and scientific practices, an integrated, interdisciplinary, intertextual and creative approach to recording, writing and illustrating the material past' (Pearson and Shanks, 2001, p. 131).

It also requires explication of the scope of the region and the character of the locatory matrix itself: the sphere of interest. This may be a physical landscape entailing consideration of geomorphology, climate, traditions of land use, dialect, architectural traditions. Or it may be a domain circumscribed by personal predilection or biography or memory. Or a creative construct: a work of invention and imagination.

Art: modelling

In identifying a series of potential relationships between visual artist and landscape, Kastner and Wallis's typology of land art (1998) might provide a useful analogue for that between performance and site. They suggest the following:

Integration: the manipulation of the material landscape in its own right, the artist adding, removing or displacing materials – marking, cutting, rearranging – to create sculpture, drawing out the relationships between existing character- istics of site and evidence of human intervention. This is often monumental in scale, as in Robert Smithson's large-scale construction *Spiral Jetty* (1970).

Interruption: the intersection of environment and human activity by employ- ing non-indigenous, man-made materials to draw attention to, frame or harness natural elements, often in a transgressive material as in Christo's major works such as the wrapping in fabric of the Reichstag in Berlin.

Involvement: the artist in a one-to-one relationship with the land, using his or her body in forms of ritual practice, of transitory and ephemeral action or subtly rearranging elements, as in Richard Long's *A Line Made by Walking* (1967).

Implementation: the artist demonstrating environmental awareness, with the environment as ecosystem and depository of socio-political realities and not as a blank canvas or an endlessly exploitable resource, involving clean- ing, planting, remedial work, as in Joseph Beuys's planting of 7,000 oak trees (1982–87). Or Anthony Gormley cutting blocks of snow to represent one kilo- gram of carbon dioxide, 'roughly the volume occupied by a coffin' (Buckland *et al.*, 2006, p. 31).

Or *imagining* the land not as physical matter but as metaphor or signifier, as concept or historical narrative: planting, statuary and architectural fol- lies becoming part of an iconography symbolizing culture, civilization and morality.

Such scenarios presuppose *ad*-venture, the realm of the Latin prepositional *accusative – in, inter, trans* – of motion towards and into: of mobility, of entry and encounter, of the pursuit of choreographic strategies, of interlocutory occupations, of the documentation of traverse and sojourn. But what might be the nature of performance prefixed with *clam*, 'unknown to'; *ob*, 'in front of'; *juxta*, 'close to'; *penes*, 'in the power of'? And what of the ablative, 'the instrument, manner or place of the action described by the verb': *ex*, 'from'; *cum*, 'with'; *coram*, 'in presence of'; *simul*, 'together with'?

Richard Long's work is immediately performative as he moves materials, marks the land and supplies us with maps and diagrams upon which are traced his walk across a landscape or a list of observations he made on a particular walk. His walking may be measured in time or distance and in the form of line, circle, rectangle. Whilst Long is extremely sensitive to nature, his work is artificial, pursued on trajectories and for durations at odds with the lie of the land and diurnal rhythms. But as we look at the oft-reproduced photograph of *A Line Made by Walking*, where is the performance? Out there or here in the gallery? And where is the audience? Was anyone present at the time, the photograph being but an incidental record of the event? Or were we always the intended audience?

How is landscape addressed performatively by those who dwell there? What of the *insiders*, the figures of Barrell's 'dark side' (Barrell, 1980)? 'To apply the term *landscape* to their surroundings seems inappropriate to those who occupy and work in a place as insiders' (Cosgrove, 1984, p. 19). With enviable etymological facility, Jean-Luc Nancy elides *pays, paysan, paysage* (Nancy, 2005, pp. 51ff.). Country, peasant, landscape. Location, occupation, representation. *Pays* he characterizes as a corner, delimited by some natural or cultural feature, the corner from which one comes. One can only be from one corner. It is, he suggests, something based on belonging: a matter of *holding* (I hold it, it holds me, it holds together) and *pertinence* (it corresponds, it responds, it makes sense at the very least as a resonance). Taken out of one's *pays* one feels estranged, unsettled, uncanny. One no longer knows one's way around – no more familiar landmarks, and no more familiar customs. A countryman is someone whose occupation is the country, and the land. He occupies it and takes care of it, and he is occupied with it. That is, he takes it in hand and is taken up by it. He works *on, at, in the land*. This embrace is mutual. And pagan: in painting, landsmen can appear as but elements of landscape: it is itself the entire presence, absenting all other presence that would possess any authority or any capacity for sense. No more civic life.

But if there is no need, desire or facility to bring landscape into visual representation are there activities that make manifest, explicitly state, confirm, Nancy's embrace of this holding? There are performance practices and events within the purview of folklore that form special *occasions* and *opportunities* to animate and reflect upon landscape as 'nature, culture and imagination within a spatial manifold', such as the Haxey Hood (see pp. 47–50).

Architecture I: occupying

Picture an unoccupied building: a disused factory.

In the mid-1990s Cliff McLucas and I made a series of programmatic statements in public presentations and unpublished Brith Gof company documents on mutual understandings of nature of site-specific performance. These informed subsequent workshop practice:

> Site-specific performances are those conceived for, mounted within and conditioned by the particulars of *found* spaces: existing social situations or locations,

both used and disused; places of work, play and worship – cattle-market, chapel, factory, cathedral, railway station, museum. (Pearson, 2007c)

You can either use the word 'found' or 'chosen'. We choose these places. (McLucas and Pearson, 1996, p. 215)

They rely, for their conception and their interpretation, upon the complex coexistence, superimposition and interpenetration of a number of architectures and narratives, historical and contemporary, of two basic orders: that which is *of* the site, its fixtures and fittings, and that which is brought *to* the site, the performance and its scenography: of that which *pre-exists* the work and that which is *of* the work; of the *found* – the site – and the *fabricated* – the performance of the past and of the present. They are inseparable from their sites, the only contexts within which they are intelligible.

Performance recontextualises such sites: it is the latest occupation of a location at which other occupations – their architectures, material traces and histories – are still apparent and cognitively active. Conversely, site relocates the dramatic material and suggests the environment, equipment and working processes that might mediate and illuminate it. Site is not just an interesting, and disinterested, backdrop. (Pearson, 2007c)

The real power of site-specific work is that it somehow activates, or engages with, the narratives of the site in some kind of way. That might be with its formal architecture, or it might be with the character of the building. It might be to do with the history of that building. (McLucas, quoted in Morgan, 1995, p. 47)

They acknowledge and utilise the particular nature of these places in their form and content. 'Specificity' to site, here, is to be discovered in an encounter with that which lies beyond the obvious elements of the piece, through intrusion of the 'found', *in looking*, into the incompletions of the 'fabricated'. (Kaye, 1996b, p. 66)

Site may be directly suggestive of subject matter, theme, dramatic structure; it will always be apparent as context, framing, sub-text. (Pearson, in Pearson and McLucas, no date, p. 7)

Performance, in turn then, may reveal, make manifest, celebrate, confront or criticise site or location, and the architecture, history, function, location, microclimate may be apparent as subject matter, framing, subtext. (Pearson, 2007c)

Following the creation of the scenography for *PAX* (1991) in which a section of a Gothic cathedral was built from scaffolding and through which the site was always apparent, McLucas began to characterize site-specific performance as the coexistence and overlay of two basic sets of architectures, those of the extant building or what he later called the *host*, that which is *at* site ... and those of the constructed scenography or the *ghost*, that which is temporarily brought *to* site. The site itself became an active component in the creation of performative meaning, rather than a neutral space of exposition – 'it's the "host" which does have personality, history, character, narrative written into it' (McLucas, quoted in Morgan, 1995, p. 47).

> To construct another architecture within the existing architecture, imposing another arrangement, floor-plan, map or orientation which confounds everyday hierarchies of place and patterns of movements.
> Significantly these two might have quite different origins and they might ignore other's presence; they are co-existent but not necessarily congruent. The performance remains transparent. (Pearson, 2007c)

'Within those two the performers are then almost guided into what they should do, because there are ways to move in all that stuff' (McLucas, quoted in McLucas and Pearson, 1996, p. 221). There may however be a mismatch between host and ghost, their relationship 'deeply, deeply fractured' (McLucas, quoted in Morgan, 1995, p. 51). Site may facilitate the creation of a kind of purposeful paradox – tension not congruence – through the employment of orders of material seemingly unusual, inappropriate or perverse at this site: an opera in a shipyard, an early Welsh epic poem in a disused car factory.

As a trained architect McLucas proceeded from the premise that 'within the normal everyday world that everybody walks around, these are vital terms – distance, space, volume, direction, orientation' (ibid., p. 47). But he began to apply the term 'architecture' to structural components both physical and dramaturgical:

> *Haearn*'s seven orders or 'architectures' of materials commingle with the host's component orders to create a complex architectural/structural poetics. His poetics is rich in metaphor, opportunity and language, and can generate theatrical detail, action and narrative. (McLucas, quoted in Pearson and McLucas, no date, p. 12)

Drawing upon Bernard Tschumi (see pp. 38–40) he observed:

> Techniques of congruence (hand in glove relationship between event and site), confrontation (transgression of site by event) and ignorance (unreconciled and unactivated or 'blind' non-relationship between event and site) are all available ... It might even be that each of these three occurs at different points in the work. (McLucas, quoted in McLucas and Pearson, 1995, p. 2)

> It is not possible to view one and not the other: the spectator develops an interpretation of what she sees and understands of the *two*. Interpenetrating narratives jostle to create meanings. The multiple meanings and readings of performance and site intermingle, amending and compromising one another. Such sites begin to resemble a kind of *saturated space* or *scene-of-crime*, where, to use forensic jargon, 'everything is potentially important'. (Pearson, 2007c)

In *Haearn*, the shifts and slippages between forms and media would open the viewer, *in looking*, to a relationship *to be made* with site. (Kaye, 1996b, p. 66)

Despite his architectural inclinations, McLucas quickly shifted to a tripartite model:

> Site-specific work takes things a stage beyond the simple staging of a theatre work in an odd location and seeks a whole new form of work in theatrical terms. That new form of work is composed of three integral and active elements: 1 the performance; 2 the place; 3 the public. And it is the deep engagement of these three elements that constitute site specific works. (McLucas, 1993, p. 5)

Within this matrix, he further describes the three *agents*:

> The performance is an active agent and embodies all of the performers' and musicians' efforts, all scripts, sets, music and action. This is the most controlled by the prior conceptual work of the 'authors' and is the totality of what is normally, in theatre, referred to as the 'piece' or the 'work'. However, in site specific work, this 'performance' must be conceived in order to engage with its other two partners to create a new, developed notion of 'the work'.
> The place (emphatically not site, space or building) is an active agent – either formally (in architectural or spatial terms) or socially and culturally (in political, ownership or historical terms).
> The public is an active agent and theatre doesn't exist until it/they is/are engaged. As such, they may define, in very large part what is happening – what the piece is; they may leave with different versions of the event, having chosen what is significant and why, from a field of activity and information. (Note: this does not mean that Brith Gof's material is 'open-ended'.) (ibid., p. 6)

> Such works bring together a gathering of interpenetrating, but discrete, discourses jostling to create meaning. They take on the characteristics of a hybrid. As a hybrid the work's parts will never fully coalesce – and it will contain irreconcilable 'differences' within its field of material. (McLucas, quoted in Pearson and McLucas, no date, p. 14)

In *Tri Bywyd* (1995), conceived at the ruined farmhouse of Esgair Fraith, McLucas now identifies the active components as 'the host, the ghost and the witness' (McLucas, quoted in Kaye, 2000, p. 128). He notes the need for 'a number of foreign pollutants' to avoid 'the trap of romanticisation and nostalgia' (McLucas, 1998, pp. 13–14). 'Host might always be haunted by other ghosts – not of the theatrician's making, and Ghost might also come with an inbuilt Host – a ready made event architecture of its own' (McLucas, quoted in Kaye, 2000, p. 129); 'the transparency of architectures means that all the images are compromised' (ibid., p. 135). He concludes: 'they are constellations of effects, attitudes, ownerships, built materials, histories, firmly held beliefs and so on. They constitute a temporary but unique ecology' (ibid., p. 129). In the era of analogue technology, performance involved the construction of a big, noisy machine.

Architecture II: programming

Picture a new building: the Welsh Assembly Government building in Cardiff, designed by Richard Rogers.

> There is no architecture without event, without program, without violence. (Tschumi, 1994, p. xx)

Whilst teaching at the Architectural Association in London in the 1970s, Bernard Tschumi began to critique prevailing characterizations of architecture as the history of style, or as the articulation of surfaces. He devised creative models for understanding, animating and taking responsibility for the relationship between action and space: the entangled nature of object, human subject and event. They inform critical approaches to the analysis of site-specific performance. They also provide inspiration and orientation for initiatives in practice.

For Tschumi, architecture is not necessarily prescriptive. It doesn't simply tell us what to do, how to behave. Whilst we may give names to rooms in the profound hope that that is what will happen there, we know that murders are committed in bathrooms. Events can have an independent existence, rarely are they purely the consequence of their surroundings. He suggests that spaces are qualified by actions just as actions are qualified by spaces. Architecture and events constantly transgress each other's rules. Bodies not only move in, but also generate spaces, produced by and through their movements. He describes the intrusion of individuals into a controlled, pure, architectural space as an act of violence. They violate the balance of precisely ordered geometry, their bodies rushing against established rules, carving new and unexpected spaces, through fluid and erratic motions. Movements of dance, sport and war are for him the intrusion of events into architectural spaces, against the assumed order. Acts that reveal potential.

The relationship between action and space is not always symmetrical. Simply, one may dominate the other. And most alternate between independence and interdependence. Tschumi identifies three categories:

- *Reciprocity*, when events and spaces are totally interdependent and fully condition each other's existence.
- *Indifference*, when spaces and events are functionally independent of, or neutralize, one another.
- *Conflict*. (ibid., pp. xxi–xxii)

All three can be manifest in sequence or parallel, from time to time, in a given location. And the 'arrow of power' may alter: space can come into conflict with event, event with space. It's not a question of knowing which came first – movement or space – or which moulds the other, for ultimately a deep bond is involved: architecture ceases to be a backdrop for actions.

In sum, in order to examine and represent this complexity, Tschumi devises hypothetical *programmes* (ibid., pp. 7–12): sequences of events ('moments of passion, acts of love and the instant of death'; ibid., p. xxi) and movements ('the inevitable intrusion of bodies into the controlled order of architecture'; ibid., p. xxi). He projects them onto autonomous spatial architectures, frame after frame, room after room, episode after episode, as a form of motivation and suggestive of 'secret maps and impossible fictions'. He then proposes transformational devices that can apply equally and independently to spaces, events and movements: devices that can permit the extreme formal manipulation of the sequence, such as repetition, superposition, distortion, 'dissolve' and insertion. Devices in which the content of contiguous frames can be mixed, superimposed, faded in or cut up, suggesting endless relational possibilities of action, event, people and place: between an architecture and its habitation. His aim is to create disjunction between form and anticipated use. And he has a fascination with the dramatic. His explorations frequently involve violence and crime. For him, events have their own momentum and are rarely the consequence of their surroundings: 'the definition of architecture may lie at the intersection of logic and pain, rationality and anguish, concept and pleasure' (ibid., p. xxviii).

In *The Manhattan Transcripts* (1994) he outlines a series of theoretical projects that simultaneously direct and witness activities and incidents as 'intrusions into the architectural stage set' (ibid., p. 7). He adopts the discrete *frame* as a structuring and representational device, juxtaposing maps, plans, axonometric projections, news photographs, line drawing, choreographic diagrams, and photographs of people and places in sequences of frozen moments in order to examine better, express and document our discontinuous experience of the city. Through sequences of jump cuts, he supposes that the viewer will maintain memory of the previous frame in the creation of imaginary narratives. He claims to introduce the order of experience and the order of time – moments, intervals, sequences – into exploration of the limits of architectural knowledge. 'Programmatic violence ought to be there to question past humanist programmes that cover only the functional requirements necessary for survival and production, and to favour those activities generally considered negative and unproductive' (ibid., p. xxviii).

Tschumi's *programmes* are conceptual and provocative. They envisage and propose action. At the same time, as 'architectural inquest', they document what are also past occurrences. And they are of profound significance in the apprehension of site-specific performance. The layering, juxtaposition and superimposition of images he conceives in his *theoretical projects* resemble the performance scenario. They provide ways of understanding potential relationships between place and action. But performance itself might best manifest the multiple articulations of event and space that he conceives, the transformational techniques he craves. What performance offers to Tschumi is time. It gives dynamic to the frame and duration to the event. It can conspire to bring about simultaneity – difficult to represent on the page – and it draws attention to all that the frame disattends: sound, odour, climate, social milieu, historical depth and all that is adjacent. The detail behind the architectural facade and all that makes a place distinctive. And this it can achieve as much through artistic indifference and conflict as reciprocity: through the oblique, the disquieting, the truly disturbing. Overheard, caught out of the corner of the eye.

Performance might then be in conflict with or indifferent to site as well as reciprocal – and vice versa – though only through *studied indifference* would it demonstrate its specificity. 'Good architecture must be conceived, erected and burned in vain. The greatest architecture of all is the fireworkers': it perfectly shows the gratuitous consumption of pleasure (Tschumi, 1995, p. 19).

Mobility: sauntering and loitering

Picture a deserted street.

> Many key urban experiences are the result of juxtapositions which are, in some sense, dysfunctional, which jar and scrape and rend. (Thrift, 2008, p. 209)

If site-specific performance of the 1980s and 1990s was concerned with taking audiences to locations to which access was under usual circumstances restricted, more recent practices have or rendered familiar places unfamiliar, or taken unfamiliar locations to the audience. Since 2001 Mike Brookes and I have created two separate bodies of work that mark a shift from the architectonic approaches of Brith Gof and the occupation of bounded spaces within which scenic devices can be organized and contained: 'banishing nearness as the measure of all things'; 'I want to substitute *distribution* for nearness or ambience' (ibid., p. 17).

First, a series of multisite works: attempts at performance that exists in a number of places simultaneously, at dispersed locations in the urban environment, and for several audiences. These include *Carrying Lyn* (2001; see Pearson and Jeff 2001; Pearson 2006a) and *Polis* (2001; Pearson 2007a) in Cardiff, *Metropolitan Motions* (2002) in Frankfurt, Germany, and *There's Someone in the House* (2004) in Exeter. Such works involve the registration, return, assemblage and subsequent projection of video material recorded in the public domain by both performers and audiences. In *Carrying Lyn*, bicycle couriers transported tapes shot by the performers themselves to an audience waiting in a studio theatre (Jeff, 2009) (see pp. 96–8). In *Metropolitan Motions* couriers returned with footage made by various sections of the audience, itself travelling through the city (see pp. 70–1). In *Polis* the audience was given sole responsibility for identifying and recording performers. In *There's Someone in the House*, staged in and around the Phoenix Arts Centre in Exeter, a standing audience gathered in a studio theatre around a long, gridded table along which were placed texts and blank videotapes. Over a period of thirty minutes, I moved down the table reading the texts, about dogs mainly, in strictly timed sequences. In cycles of five minutes, Paul Jeff took a tape, placed it in a camera and departed to a locale in the same building where he created a two-minute scene with John Rowley and Steve Robins reminiscent of footage from Abu Ghraib prison. In these sequences the essential relationship was between protagonist and camera as much as oppressor and victim. Two men sit drinking beer whilst a naked third lies in a lift doorway, the door closing and shutting on him. Jeff then returned, placed the tape on the table and took another, departing to meet the performers again at a different location in the building. And so on. Mike Brookes projected the returning tapes on a large screen in a rapid cycling of material. The effect here is of events happening 'just now, just over there'. But were one to want to intervene where would that be?

In a second set of studio performances conceived in collaboration with Welsh playwright Ed Thomas, *Raindogs* (2002) (see pp. 153–4) and *Who Are You Looking at?* (2004) performance was constituted as a purposeful arrangement of mediated fragments – video, photographic, audio – created elsewhere, at some other time. The performers were prerecorded at locations or from new viewpoints inaccessible to a theatre audience.

In both, the city becomes the location of performance. Performance serves to present recognizable places in unfamiliar ways, from unexpected perspectives. And to reveal unfamiliar locales: rarely visited but just adjacent to the flow of everyday life. But the prospect is a partial one. In this, performance resembles Bruno Latour's *oligopticon*, 'seeing a little, very well, but just a little' (Read, 2006, p. 62). 'Oligoptica are just those sites since they do exactly the opposite of panoptica: they see much *too little* to feed the megalomania of the inspector or the paranoia of the inspected, but what they see, they *see it well*'. 'From oligoptica, sturdy but extremely narrow views of the connected whole are made possible – as long as connections hold' (Latour, 2005, p. 181).

Performance is generated and apprehended in several places, from which performers and spectators may be excluded or absent. As an *itinerant* practice, it momentarily occupies nondescript or indistinct sites, or places overlooked through familiarity. It draws attention to all that might not be immediately apparent: details of fabric, moments from history. It does so as much through fiction as fact, and through theoretical asides as much as drama. In *Carrying Lyn* the ten-minute sections of twin projection, juxtaposing the returned video with footage of the same locations at midday, were interspersed with five-minute audio recordings of short theoretical and critical textual reflections on the contemporary city to allow time for rewind, referencing and quoting Marc Augé on spatial forms of anthropological place (Augé, 1995, pp. 56–7) – path, crossroads, monumental centre, and the activities they might engender: itinerary, meeting, gathering. And Michel de Certeau on the rhetorics of walking, tactical delinquency, and 'the relationships and intersections of these exoduses that intertwine and create an urban fabric, and placed under the sign of what ought to be, ultimately, the place but is only a name: the City' (Certeau, 1988, p. 103). And Walter Benjamin on *flânerie* – 'The space winks at the *flâneur*: "What do you think may have gone on here?"' (Benjamin, 1999, p. 418). And Deleuze and Guattari on the *nomad*. And Jane Rendell on gender and the urban experience. And Guy Debord on the *dérive*.

The auditorium now rendered *porous*, with information flowing in and out and through it, rather than a place that ensures a singularity of looking and listening: 'through a ceaseless transport of information' (Latour, 2005, p. 182).

The performance exists in a multitude of places, some of which may even be out of sight, in a work potentially as large as the city. It refuses to coalesce, make itself available for total scrutiny. There is no one place from which one can see it all. It is never one thing. It is a *field* rather than an *object*. And it is already archaeological in aspect. To understand its scale, let alone its narrative, the individual spectator pieces together video sequences, photographs, maps, texts, overhead conversations and interrogations in acts of interpretation. A *reconstitution* of the past from its surviving fragments ...

Archaeology: marking

Picture a boarded up shop.

> Time in its passing casts off particles of itself in the form of images, documents, relics, junk. Nobody can seize time once it is gone, so we must make do with such husks, the ones that have not yet succeeded in disintegrating. (Sante, 1992, p. ix)

In reflecting upon the specific relationship between place and performance, we might usefully borrow other disciplinary optics. We might realign such performance as an active agency within adjacent fields of endeavour: geography, architecture, urban planning. In practical and theoretical convergence between performance and archaeology the closest collaboration may yet result from a shared concern with the notion of the 'contemporary past'.

How is this 'contemporary past' manifest? First, we engage in small acts of *curation*, in creating a present that is itself multitemporal. Juxtaposing today's milk bottle with flowers bought last week with a photograph taken twenty years ago with a family heirloom.

Second, at the most intimate of scales we inscribe the urban fabric, with varying degrees of permanence. Both private and public domain are marked by our presence and by our passing. From 'Kilroy was here' to modern graffiti, we deliberately 'tag' the environment: proclaiming identities and affiliations, demarcating territory. But inadvertently, quietly, continuously in the touch of flesh on metal and stone, we also leave signature *traces*: the prints of our bodies. In certain places, our marks accumulate, the signs of our regular and habitual contact: patterns of grubby handprints around doorhandles, greasy smears on the street outside the fish-and-chip shop. In others, our bodies abrade and erode. We wear things out with our hands, our feet, our backs, our bottoms, our lips: the step is worn shallow, the handrail rubbed naked of paint, the wall is scored by generations of resting bicycle handlebars. In the very passage of pedestrians, in places of multitudinous swarming, the pavement is ground down. Elsewhere, there are the marks. Of singular actions: scuffs, scratches, cuts and stains. Of traumatic events: accidents of fire and explosion, incidents of anarchy and unrest. Of transitory occurrences: dropped groceries, vomited kebab. Sometimes they are no more than the faintest swish and sometimes awful to behold: scenes of crime, 'arcs of blood, quantities of semen'. And on the street corner, dogs sniffed urgently, cocked their legs, left a jumble of spoors in the wet concrete. The unintentional, the random, the intimate unplanned touch of history's passing ... that attest to our presence and also, of course, to our absence ...

Through our passage, movements, moments, actions, encounters, we constantly mark our material surroundings. These are the authentic traces of the performance of everyday life: the result of routine, tradition, habit, accident, event, social ritual, of long-term evolution and unconnected short-term ruptures and singularities, of nearness, of dwelling. Our physical contact constitutes an ongoing archaeological record, and microchronology. Even the most mundane set of circumstances has a depth or density: the character of the place. But recognizing this depends upon looking at them in oblique ways, observing texture and detail. What is banal at one scale of viewing may be minutely detailed in close-up, complex stratigraphies of decoration and structural alteration lurking in the domestic and the ordinary.

These marks we make, these traces we leave, are ineffably archaeological: 'an archaeology of us', of contemporary material culture, of the recent, of the immediate. This is the realm of what has been termed, in an oxymoronic way, 'the archaeology of the contemporary past', an 'archaeology of us' (Buchli and Lucas, 2001, p. 5). That addresses 'those aspects of experience that are non-discursive, inarticulate and otherwise unconstituted practices (either through suppression or otherwise ... tensions, contradictions, exclusions, pains, etc.)' (ibid., p. 14). Restoring an absent present, that we risk ignoring and losing. As a field of enquiry, it involves a renewed sensitivity to the fabric of the present and attention to those details distinct and differentiated that signal our presence, but that we consciously disattend or casually ignore or commit to collective amnesia. Or what French archaeologist Laurent Olivier has termed a 'relationship of proximity maintained regarding places, objects, ways of life or practices that are still ours and still nourish our collective identity' (Olivier, 2001, p. 175).

If the unturned calendars in the sandwich bar were anything to go by, 44 and 46 James Street, Cardiff were abandoned in August 1989. After breaking in, we found traces of those who lived and worked there. Wear patterns around doorways and stains on skirting boards attested to their presence, and also to their absence. They indicated how the habitual actions and chance moments have shaped the place. But we should beware. The life-story of these shops did not cease simply because they were removed from the histories of the people who once worked there. They began to decompose, to fall apart, significantly and confusingly for us, of their own volition. Visibly changing as we visited them, drawing our attention to the way that nothing in the material world is ever fixed, always tending towards entropy. Slates became dislodged, paint peeled, a veneer of dust settled, pigeon droppings accumulated. Michael Shanks has called this, in that we do not perceive it, the secret life of things. Places and objects are constantly in motion, changing in ways that condition how we observe and make use of them.

Archaeology is, I suggest, a process of cultural production – a form of active apprehension, a particular sensibility to material traces – that takes the remains of the past and makes something out of them in the present. A contemporary creative work.

There is here an implicit repoliticization of a discipline that has its nascence in foundational processes of nation-state building, as a form of active apprehension, as a particular sensibility to traces. As it poses the question, who made these marks?, it addresses social and ethical issues, engaging with questions of identity, community, class and gender. In an examination of the relationship between material culture and human behaviour, it inevitably concerns aspects of activity and experience that are non-discursive, resulting from practices of labour, trade and social life. It might reveal inarticulate, unregarded or disregarded practices. Anonymous, silent, silenced, suppressed, forgotten, ignored, such as patterns of social smoking or profligate street urination or covert sexual activity. It might challenge familiar categorizations, such as assigned usage and the spatially constructed order, through the identification of delinquent events and practices: shortcuts, transgressions and acts of trespass that privilege the route over the inventory. The lateral skids of skate-boarders. Places where the bye-laws of the city are clearly broken: by gum chewers and public drinkers and drug users. It might presence absence, indicating the traces of those departed or who live a life of a different timetable, such as night workers and club-goers. It might indicate small acts of vernacular defiance in the personalization of domicile and business.

Performance is an interpretive and representational practice, a medium that can juxtapose, superimpose and elide different orders of material. Both are social practices: together they might fuse critical and technical experiment, making creative use of the fragments of the past, in an attitude critical and suspicious of orthodoxy, of any final accounts of things. An enacted romanticism.

Performance might demonstrate the partiality of our understanding of the occupancy of the city, revealing that which escapes usual discourses of urban theory and planning. It might be redemptive and therapeutic, but equally troubling and disruptive. With the accent on detail, on that which we barely notice, the archaeologist might enquire of inhabitants and workers what marks their activities and occupations produce and about how such traces reveal difference and distinctiveness – about the genesis and history of existing marks within the locale and how they serve as a mnemonic for the events that caused them, leading to a fuller appreciation, through the stories and experiences of others, of the microchronologies and polyphonic geographies that make up the urban present, to the city as a temporal as well as a spatial phenomenon. In these traces, *can* we discern the movements, moments and encounters involved in their making: maps of practices and behaviours? If our very walking is archaeological then these are surely the true spoors of archetypal figures of the modern city. But to track them we may need a taxonomy, a field guide of marks ordered and identified according to type, location, density and time-scale. Can we discern the movements involved in their making?

In the attic in James Street a man's suit quietly rotted beside three Coca-Cola cans and a tray of cutlery spilled across the floor in an unwitnessed moment. But can we ever be sure that human agency was involved in what appears now as an event? Was the chair knocked over and the cutlery scattered in an emotional outburst, or as an accident during evacuation, or later as the result of perching birds? Accidental arrangements of objects, particularly when framed in the viewfinder of the camera, suggested narratives for an eye adjusted by the forensic 'turn': pen, four cups, knife; shoe, bird's nest, wooden cash till, betting slips, jacket; single knife; single toothbrush. Tools and utensils bore chips and abrasions that attest to their usage, to events they had witnessed, things that had happened to them, signs of ageing, time and use: the carving knife ground thin on the doorstep, a favourite mug cracked and handle-less ... We removed them, intending to integrate them into performances elsewhere. But out of context they became so much detritus, already left as surplus to requirements by their former owners. We threw them away. Artist Emma Lawton intended to hack into the shops. To cut, hammer and slice their fabric. And then to order and reorder the fragments of brick and mortar: by size and colour elsewhere. But they were demolished quickly, without our knowing, to make way for a car park for the Cardiff Bay Development Agency. But I can still stand on the street and tell the story of our forced entry.

In works of site performance that evince the transitory and the mundane, we might demonstrate for the popular imagination how we ourselves and our immediate environment are part of the historical process, how constituents of material culture exist within overlapping frames and trajectories of time, drawing attention to how we are continuously generating the archaeological record. Whilst little is at risk here, everything of value might be at stake: communality, generational communication, sense of place. As modes of cultural production, archaeology and performance might take up the fragments of the past and make something out of them in the present, in an attitude critical and suspicious of orthodoxy, of any final accounts of things.

Such works might resemble small acts of resistance to the excesses of mediated, global culture, drawing attention to the local and particular, identifying and energizing regionalized identities, without monopolizing interpretation. In a renewed sensitivity to ephemerality, to an everyday rendered unfamiliar, an enacted archaeology might provide insights into the personal and the emotive, at scales that as yet escape the scrutiny of CCTV surveillance. Addressing tensions, contradictions and exclusions. Evincing the grain of a place, its history, and its changing nature. It might celebrate the fact that we do and can still mark – insubordinate to the imperatives of public cleansing, architectural sanitization, social decorum – in acts that are colloquial, vernacular, detailed, social. And that in this, we are not alone. Perhaps this concern with the dirty and the discarded is a symptom of late modernism, a nostalgia for a public domain in dynamic dialogue with its inhabitants, counter to the current genrefication and gentrification of the urban landscape, the deterritorialization of social life and retreat into the unmarked domain of cyberspace. A restoration of the absent present ...

But if performance is to be an active agency of contemporary archaeology, it might be as much a *reading onto* as a *reading from*. It might *avoid* pointing to this or that, whilst nevertheless making them evident through its very presence.

3

Site: Places

In which ten locations, their attendant performances and the linkages between them are described in detail, with the additional consideration of associated practices and other manifestations of performance in similar places elsewhere.

Field: Haxey, Lincolnshire

Image 3.1 *The 'Sway'*, Haxey Hood, North Lincolnshire, 1975 (Michelle Bogre)

A field. A group of men, some in costume, some in working clothes, most in boots, pushing ...

It's 3.30 p.m. on 6 January in the village of Haxey, in that area of reclaimed fenland known as the Isle of Axholme, in north Lincolnshire, and these men are involved in different ways in the Haxey Hood, a *succession* of *passages* and *nodes* of activity of varying durations, rhythms and intensities, and opportunities for public participation, culminating in the playing of an enduring, wide-ranging game (see Newall, 1980; Cooper, 1993; Parratt, 2000; Pearson, 2006a). It's already been a long day and, although the planned *schedule* may have slipped, they've followed the *itinerary*, faithfully as ever. Breakfast in the Loco. Daubing the face of the Fool in the Carpenter's Arms in Westwoodside, and singing the songs – *John Barleycorn, A Farmer's Boy, Cannons*. Singing again in the King's Arms, with official photographs at the old market cross outside. The long walk up Main Street where until recently the Fool would thwack children with his weighted sock-on-a-stick. Singing in The Loco. Singing in the Duke William. Pursuing the Fool and hoisting him onto the mounting stone outside the church, where he welcomes the gathered crowd as a fire of damp straw is lit beneath him. Walking up to the field en masse. Throwing the sack hoods for youths to struggle over. An accented and punctuated continuum interspersed with periods of drinking and socializing. Now the expectation is palpable. They become excited, massing, pushing forward, attention focused as a dignitary chants and throws the *hood*, a metre-long leather cylinder, into the air. There is a surge and crush of bodies as a large tightly bound scrummage forms. Their *task* and purpose is to get the hood into one of the public houses on Axholme, where it will remain for the coming year. It will take several hours of conflicting toing and froing, purposefully and in earnest, in field and street.

The Haxey Hood takes place in a particular place on a particular date through the concerted offices and efforts of a particular group of people. It resides within, and is inseparable from, a set of topographical, cultural and social conditions. It is essentially site-specific. Elsewhere and on a different day it might resemble public disorder. Elsewhere the functionaries – the Lord and Chief in their red coats and feathered top hats, the Fool in ribboned tunic, the Boggins in red shirts – might appear incongruous or ridiculous. But here it persists through communal approbation as a marker of distinctiveness. There is a local appreciation of the unique practices that define and set it apart, and tolerance at least of transgression within prescribed limits, of the demonstration of passion and exaggerated endeavour under restraint.

There is a shared appreciation of, and adherence to, traditions of practice, of how and where things should go on. The event passes through differentiated locales where specific activities occur. The Boggins elbow room to sing in the bars. The Fool stands on his stone, gains height and employs changes of voice and formalities of language. The Lord locates the spot at which to plant his staff and commence the game by aligning it on a particular distant hedge. The performative and ludic overlay, displace, confound, supplant and suspend the everyday, within a given landscape for a limited period of time. Site and performance are caught in an embrace, intimately entangled. Performance draws attention to the details of location, valorizing them, pulling them out of the everyday into relief, acknowledging them, staking claim to them in passing, as places to be, to do, to watch. And the land, in its specificities of slope and texture, occasions certain kinds of physical and emotional engagement and response.

The Haxey Hood constitutes a form of strategic and tactical engagement with the land, of working on, at it and in it. It is an act of communal delinquency and trespass, challenging laws of tenure and ownership, reappropriating the land under the wholly illusionary sanction of *no law*. The sway itself is ambivalent to matters of law and order and it is wilful, occasionally destroying hedges and walls. Its accompanying crowd tramples crops indiscriminately. But this is no free-for-all. As the Fool announces in his introductory address, in the setting of the *rules*: 'now this is a sway hood, not a running hood and I remind you that it must be swayed at all times'. At the very core of the action is its *mantra* chanted in each pub after the singing of the songs, chanted by hundreds of people along with the Fool, called out by the guest thrower:

> House against house
> Town and against town
> If a man meets a man
> Knock him down
> But don't hurt him.

Such rules in the form of shared understandings mark off the activity, protecting the tentative and restraining the over-enthusiastic.

The sway is a *fluid* entity, oozing across the landscape. Within its body, social conventions of the everyday are confounded. Men hug men in the creation of an ad hoc communality, of evanescent effort. Yet again and again, it collapses. At each fall voices cry 'Man down'. It pauses and strangers drag strangers out of the pile, up from the mud before re-engaging and moving on, in dynamic flow. In the description and critical apprehension of this organism, it may be as useful to concentrate upon *proxemics* and *haptics*: upon interpersonal distances and the touch of self and others and how they vary moment-to-moment as upon overt performative gestures, though there are recurrent moments of rhetorical heightening – in speeches of welcome and incitement in admonitions from the Lord.

In the sway, there is nothing *scapic* or *scopic*, nothing scenic or visual about land. It's underfoot and then not. Suddenly it's in your ears and under your nails and up your nose. And what you see is another man's greasy hair and what you smell is beery breath and diesel fuel, and what you feel is sweat-soaked shirts, and what you hear is oath and exhortation. The swaymen know landscape through feel rather than perspective. Any contours are felt not measured. Landscape as *somatic space* as much as visual construct. And they know it at the most intimate of scales: as surface and slope and angle and facade, as foothold, as slight advantage, as the best place to attempt or achieve this or that, as the locations where danger lurks. All are trying to get purchase from the land. Their effort is mediated by topography, body and land inextricably linked. If their experience here is *phenomenological*, their engagement is *ergonomic*: body-to-body and body-to-environment. Movement is both enhanced and compromised as they attempt to apply strength against all odds in the sway, struggling to maintain an effective posture, their reach restricted. There is no separation of self from scene. This is not simply a matter of performance appropriating landscape as a scenic backdrop against which to place its figures. And it need not be regarded through the analytical lens of landscape painting and its close relative the proscenium stage. We might rather attend to the convergence of figure and ground, to surrender and *immersion*, and the degree – 'the concussiveness and largesse' (Scarry, 1999, p. 37) – of the contact, in a shift from *optic* to *haptic* understanding of site-specificity.

The swaymen make the land, giving this apparently featureless terrain significance through action. They mark it, with varying degrees of permanence: a collapsed wall here, a filthy pub carpet there. And it marks them, with bruises and sprains. They play within a historical dimension. The Haxey Hood purports to enact a foundational myth, a thirteenth-century story in which a local lady lost her riding hood which was retrieved by peasants, ancestral Boggins, working in the field. Beyond this, they do things, many of them, as their fathers did, ever vigilant of the correct ways to go on. The strategies reflect accumulated knowledge, past made present. It is *reiterative*: 'If only Haxey can get it onto the road!'. The winning barely matters. This is an expenditure of energy in an expression of common purpose – push for your village, for your pub – and cross-generational links, though allegiances may change over the course of the day.

Spectators can choose to see things in close-up, from far away, approaching, passing, from the top of a wall. Occasionally, desirous of attention, it extends itself towards them. But once the sway commences there are always too many bystanders for a clear view, the landscape too flat to privilege any one perspective. Often all one sees is steam rising and the tracks it leaves in the mud. As night falls, it becomes a tsunami in the neon-lit streets, its approach announced only by the arrival of those fleeing to avoid it. It is fluid too in its composition as there is a constant flux of those entering, stepping out to rest and watch, re-entering. And there is always a chance that you may be swept up, inadvertently subsumed or impelled to lend weight. If you abide by the rules, there is no impediment to your participation.

Eventually, the hood emerges from deep in the sway, from the experienced hands that have held it upright. The publican waves it at her door and all cheer. The King's Arms fills.

Landscape 1: Mynydd Bach, Ceredigion

A hillside. Two men, one in costume, one not, walking ...

It's 23 August 1998 and we are struggling across Mynydd Bach, near the village of Trefenter, south of Aberystwyth: following footpaths, sheep trails, farm tracks and wind-farm access roads from Llyn Eiddwen to Pwllclai. The wind is strong, the clouds low, the rain intermittent. I am dressed as an early nineteenth-century gentleman, but also wearing a radio microphone, battery unit, earpiece and receiver, and carrying a halogen lamp. Mike Brookes is lugging a backpack radio transmitter. We are not alone. On the summit is a BBC engineer in a relay truck. In the Radio Ceredigion studio in Aberystwyth are

Image 3.2   Pearson/Brookes, *The First Five Miles* …, Trefenter, West Wales, 1998
(Brian Tarr)

two other colleagues. And scattered across the landscape are groups of people, some huddling together, others sitting in their cars, uncertain of where to look in the encroaching darkness, but all doing something now unusual: listening communally to the radio. We are all engaged in, and with, *The First Five Miles/ Rhyfel y Sais Bach*, a performance work for broadcast and live performer (Pearson and Shanks, 2001, pp. 143–6). Mike and I aim to cover the five miles in one hour. Our route winds along a straight line: the expression of 'reason, certainty, authority, a sense of direction' (Ingold, 2007, p. 167). It mirrors the aspiration for a new order that our story will relate. Although we have reconnoitred the route, we have not rehearsed under these conditions.

The *concept* is simple. At 9 p.m. our local radio begins transmitting a previously recorded bilingual drama/documentary. It concerns the abortive attempts of an English gentleman from south Lincolnshire, Augustus Brackenbury, to enclose 850 acres of peat bog and common near Trefenter in the 1820s, and the concerted efforts of local people, in defence of their traditional land rights, to prevent him, which involves nocturnal meetings, riotous assembly in disguise, destruction of property, parading effigies and rough music. Simultaneously we begin walking. Our journey will last the duration of the programme. From time to time, my voice, as Brackenbury, is mixed 'live' into the programme. The signal travels from me to Mike to the BBC vehicle to a satellite and thence to Aberystwyth, perhaps through Goonhilly Down in Cornwall, perhaps via an automatic tracking station in Norway. I deliver the text on cue without being able to hear its effect within the sonic matrix. But its inevitably fractured quality, given the context of its registration, combined with the ambient sounds of the hillside, surely contrasts dramatically with the studio-produced material: a voice from elsewhere, from the past. The performance makes no attempt to re-enact historical events, favouring rather a sophisticated application of contemporary media that never disguises anachronism. I am a costumed figure engaged in a technical task as much as a character. But, like Brackenbury, my application to the job is unswerving. The performance resides within and emerges from the expertise and cooperation of a number of operatives in dispersed locations. Any individual failure will result in systemic failure.

- What then are the parameters of the work?
- Where is its site, for it extends beyond the horizon?
- Where is it being generated, in one place or many places?

The programme is in stereo, with the Welsh texts panned towards the left channel and the English towards the right. Through this, and by attributing the two languages to actors' voices of different gender and timbre, we attempt a form of bilingualism that is other than direct translation, through the juxtaposition of complementary texts. In English, I speak the legal depositions of Brackenbury, full of invective yet comic in the inflated sense of self-worth, and in the accounts of nightly, and highly performative, visitation, often including men dressed as women. The only way to hear me is on the radio. In addressing questions of *scale*, we conspire, in effect, an enormous amplifier, making performance as large as landscape with limited means. Multiple options appear for the audience. They may choose to sit at home or to be out on the mountain with a transistor radio, or positioned anywhere in between. *How and where is it being received, in one place or many places?*

Just minutes before we begin, the system breaks down. The police helicopter cannot fly. It was to have tracked my walk with a circular pool of light, illuminating me but always moving on, never turning landscape into a pictorial backdrop for performance, never appropriating or laying claim to it, never revealing it fully, never pretending that this story of appropriation is *of* the place. A travelling point rather than a perspective: the landscape as a place to be provisional on rather than set against, with viewpoints neither recommended nor favoured. As Brackenbury stalks his estate, we are all literally in the dark.

But we persist in our task, somewhat vainly perhaps. We pass ruined farms, deserted during changes of agricultural practice, abandoned when the land was cropped to exhaustion by poor husbandry. We walk beneath the wind turbines, contentious not only within environmental debates but also in their allocation, and the uneven distribution of ground rents amongst landowners. We remember the houses of incomers who bring different cultural expectations and innovations too: Trefenter, Venture-town. The theme of *The First Five Miles* is specific. It refers to no other issues directly, in this landscape of contest. But its very presence may throw them into relief, drawing attention to all else that might be in play here, to regional anxieties. Just as Brackenbury came here with bullish intentions, so performance might arrive as an *intrusion*, self-sufficient and lacking local approval. In this, it is potentially divisive. It may then choose to tread carefully, to disclose its true allegiances in the turn of a phrase. Can I deliver Brackenbury's last words, concerning the treacherous and deceitful nature of the local populace with enough irony to show where I stand? In the end, perhaps the hubris of our endeavour perfectly matches Brackenbury's excessive ambition, ultimate failure and withdrawal.

Several weeks later, we stage *The Man Who Ate His Boots* in a studio theatre in Aberystwyth to replicate some of the effects of *distanciation* in *The First Five Miles*. I stand with sixty audience members. An overhead spot lamp provides a little light at the centre. Around us at the four cardinal points of the compass are small projection screens showing images shot at regular intervals across Mynydd Bach. I am wearing a dark suit and a radio microphone. The audience wears simultaneous-translation headphones, familiar equipment in a bilingual country. I am able to speak directly and intimately into their ears. At the same time, the soundtrack of *The First Five Miles*, a ramshackled music for violin, guitar and drums, plays at high volume in the room, experienced corporeally by the audience, their headphones acting as mutes or earplugs. As I roam the room telling the stories of Brackenbury and explorer John Franklin and two others from Lincolnshire, occasionally in the light, often indistinct in the darkened topography of the crowd, there is a *dislocation* of aural from visual effect. As I appear to address others over there, gesturing for them, I continue to whisper in your ear.

In September 2000 I accompany Chinese–Australian artist William Yang to Mynydd Bach (Pearson, 2001). As part of the Centre for Performance Research 'Mapping Wales' project I am invited to collaborate with William in creating an alternative cartography of Wales. Challenged to drive from Cardiff in the south to Holyhead in the north in a single weekend and to create a map of our impressions and encounters, I decide to stay off the beaten track and to take him to ten places away from coasts and castles and coalfield heritage sites. Unmarked places slow to reveal themselves. Places that resist immediate scrutiny, where it is difficult to discern from the scenery either the events that occurred there or their cultural and political significance: reservoirs, plantations, spoil heaps. At each location, I ask William to take a photograph before describing its history to him. What does he do? He too resists the vista, his emerging strategy two-fold. First, he records detail: the grain of slate, berries on a tree, foam on wave tops. Second, he photographs words – house names, gravestones, road signs – in acknowledgement I suspect of the importance that others have ascribed to this place and not that, to this thing and not that. Later he makes a slide show of our journey in that deceptively simple format for which he is renowned. The commentary, in his gentle seductive voice, is a mixture of memory and invention, for as Walter Benjamin notes of experience: 'what the storyteller knows from hearsay is added to his own' (Benjamin, 1992, p. 107).

At Mynydd Bach, it takes two hours for Mike and I to slither and squelch the five miles. Long after the broadcast has finished, we are still walking. *Five Miles Further* in which one female performer walks in the city, one male in the country, each accompanied by a helicopter and linked in radio broadcast, is yet to be realized.

Village: Hibaldstow, Lincolnshire

Image 3.3   Mike Pearson, *Bubbling Tom*, Hibaldstow, Lincolnshire, 2000 (Hugo Glendinning)

A village street corner. Several people standing, one man sitting …

It's 26 April 2000 and I'm perched awkwardly on the step of my late grandfather's fish-and-chip shop in Hibaldstow in north Lincolnshire, relating how from this spot in the mid-1950s we would watch and wave at the infrequent passing traffic. With me is a group of family, friends, local inhabitants and visitors. Over the next two hours we visit ten such locations in the village, places where significant and memorable things happened to me: sites of earliest and formative experiences. Autobiographical landmarks: school, churchyard, stream, and others less notable. *Bubbling Tom* is a guided tour of my 'square mile' (see p. 110), of the landscape I knew at the age of seven, a leisurely stroll pausing to remember events and people in a rolling sequence of performed texts and orchestrated movements (see Pearson, 2000; 2006a, pp. 21–9; Wilkie, 2001; 2002b; Heddon, 2002; 2008, pp. 96–102). Occasionally it draws itself into moments of expositional formality, as I stand apart to relate this or to show that. Otherwise it just rambles. En route, I point out this that still survives: my great-grandmother's grave; that which has altered, the school gate now bricked over; and that which has disappeared, the corrugated-iron church hall. I recall friends long dead and I reveal the odd family secret. I touch and point, mimic and gesticulate. I pose and imitate and impersonate. I speak in dialect. I even include the odd quotation from Gaston Bachelard, Georges Perec and Raymond Williams – 'theory-lite' perhaps. I animate a familiar landscape, frequently to comic effect: climbing the school wall. I evoke this place fifty years ago: performance as a lens or *filter*, residing exactly over the current everyday.

I've composed and learned a long text. I've walked the route previously, quietly mouthing the words. I've been noticed doing it. In the event, I can, at times, barely get a word in. I am constantly interrupted: by others with additions to, and corrections and contradictions of my story. For there are always those who remember us, remember for us, better than we do ourselves. And as soon as I stop talking others begin, with other memories of these same places at other times, for this was the landscape of their childhoods too, many of them. These differentiated places act as 'containers' (of memories, stories and legends), as 'aggregations of metaphorical and physical layers' (Wilkie, 2001, p. 2), as *palimpsest*, named and marked by the actions of ancestors. Topographical and architectural features function as prompts, as *mnemonic*, and *Bubbling Tom* quickly becomes *dialogic*. I enter an unfamiliar realm of performance – of planned sections, but also improvised exchanges and casual asides; of close encounters. What holds it together is the constant reference back to place and our mutual acquaintance with it, with where we are now, or once were: 'place inscribed in bodies, accents, local habits and the microphysical environments' (Heddon, 2008, p. 99). This involves much pointing to, and pointing out. I shift register as subtly as I can, as I declaim and reflect. 'Just as Pearson responded, in the moment, to his spectators' contributions, so did the physical architecture of the guided walk enable the spectators to leave behind the formal script that typically guides "spectatorship"' (ibid., p. 168). They are charged with 'replotting and reshaping it' (ibid., p. 101). And as anyone might intervene and contribute – as inhabitant engages visitor, doubtless opening with the words 'So, where are you from?' – it avoids becoming exclusionary, though there are passages so specific that only two or three present will fully appreciate them. Private entering the public domain, local knowledge ... Inevitably there are things best left unsaid that will offend or damage.

My aim is to devise ways of telling that are both intimate and opinionated, that mix autobiographical material and useful information about vernacular attributes, characters, occurrences with the pleasure of telling. And that can include personal and familial, factual and fictional: description and evocation, testimony and confession, history and fantasy, in equal measure. My inspiration and model is the tumbling flow of *gossip*, in its juxtapositions and elisions of this, that and the other, in the sudden jumps it effects in person, place and time. My *mode* of performance employs a repertoire of gestures to indicate, demonstrate, locate and shape the details of a writing that was not separate from a telling, often informal, at the edge of performance itself. In composing this *solo narrative* I first revisited places I once knew at a different scale, in search of physical marks and traces I left there. I used the rediscovered landscape as a reminder of happenings and feelings and personal reveries. Relocating myself in a place once close. Re-embodying half-remembered actions. I sought evidence of me in these places – photographs. Studying the details of stance and posture, eventually adopting the same positions in performance, at a different scale, drawing attention to all that has changed, in me and in it. Seeing me then, others now. I recorded the memories of those who remember me and my actions up to the age of seven, particularly non-family members, relating to particular events such as Coronation Day 1953. I considered the constitution of my own body, physiognomy, morphology, demeanour, that combination of heredity, habit and conditioning that were engendered in this landscape – how I clasp my hands like my father. I thought too about physical scars, for the body bears the marks of its history and the skin is a map of accident and injury. I gathered objects, my father's knife, a toy gun, each bearing the patinas of age and usage. I looked at maps, seeing the landscape from above, reminded of the dawning appreciation of symbol – red road, green wood, blue river – scale and direction. And I attempted to recall all those surrogate inciting incidents, those thresholds, those entrances and exits with which we measure the passing of our lives. I worked with fragments, with material traces, in order to create something, a meaning, a narrative, a story, that stands for the past in the present. This address to memory in a contemporary project embraces critical romanticism and nostalgia, as a regenerative force. Place and memory are animated through the momentary presence of performance, though the effect may be lasting.

These are the questions that *Bubbling Tom* poses:

■   How can site-specific performance play a role in an active engagement with place, helping make sense of the multiplicity of meanings that resonate from landscapes and memories?

■   What mechanisms for enacting the intimate connection between personal biographies, social identities and the biography of place can it provide?

> ▪ Can it work at a variety of scales of rhetoric, within different scales of landscape?
> ▪ Can it return as a simple 'telling', akin to anecdote and tall tale?
> ▪ Can a conversational form engender a provisional and contingent communality across generations within a particular location?

Such performance works *with* memory, raking over enduring ones, stirring half-suppressed ones. It can demonstrate multitemporal densities of experience within a given location. It acknowledges that the local is always heterogeneous, that there is no essential reading here. It might indicate for the popular imagination how we ourselves, and our immediate environment, are part of a historical process. How constituents of material culture exist within overlapping trajectories of time ('it was then, it is now and all points in between'). And ways in which we are generating the archaeological record continuously. It draws attention to the constituents of the present. It reveals memory, living memory, to be one of the principal objects of retrieval and examines the complex curation of memory itself. 'So what is remembered, and how it is remembered is always subject to the concerns of the present' (Wilkie, 2002b, p. 8).

Dee Heddon suggest that those present as contributors possess *agency* 'with a right to write and rewrite their location and, as such, to rewrite the script of *Bubbling Tom* and the place of Hibaldstow (Heddon, 2008, pp. 167–8), the performance helps 'wrest "nostalgia" from its reactionary position' (ibid., p. 98). They become 'equal participants in the performance event and in the performance of place, charged with replotting and reshaping it' (ibid., p. 101).

Early in 2002 Heddon literally followed in my footsteps in Hibaldstow (Heddon, 2002). In a form of active apprehension and creative interpretation of site-specific practices, she retraced my route with relatives, interviewing them and using surviving performance documentation as orientation. Eventually she positioned herself as I had done. In a resulting series of photographs, we transmogrify. Her written account is a complex fusion and interpenetration of my text, the recollections of others of both *Bubbling Tom* and their memories of these places it engendered, and her own childhood. Of times and places elsewhere. A clamour of voices.

Bubbling Tom is a spring in Hibaldstow, its exact source a constant source of local disagreement. My performance ends in semi-darkness, as a group of elderly citizens speculates on its location. Calling out, laughing …

House: Marine Terrace, Aberystwyth

A house. A group of people sitting …

It's May 1997 and we are crushed together in the front, ground-floor room of an empty four-storey house on the seafront in Aberystwyth, some

Image 3.4 Embracing an audience member: Marc Rees, *The House Project*, Cardiff, 2005 (Rhodri Davies)

on chairs, others on cushions. On a pile of video monitors, we witness scenes from the 'Stations of the Cross', played out in rooms to which we are denied access throughout the house, by a group of students directed by Eddie Ladd. Strategically placed cameras allow us to look through doorways, along corridors and into interiors. All the scenes are precisely framed and timed, all technical installation concealed. A visual edit that switches viewpoints, allows one station to be set up as another is being performed. Performers and technicians move through the house in a complex choreography that keeps them out of shot in the interim, often crawling below the level of a camera, hiding momentarily in niches. What appears as the reverential portrayal of the religious theme is achieved only through feverish activity. In our room a recording of Bach's *St Matthew Passion* provides the continuous soundtrack, establishing the emotional tenor of the work. Occasionally acoustic sounds are evident elsewhere in the house, most poignantly as we hear running water and struggle as Christ is drowned in a bath that must surely be directly above our heads.

In March 1998 Ladd developed the use of closed-circuit television in *Lla'th* (*Gwynfyd*), a solo performance created in and around an empty farm south of Aberystwyth in collaboration with Cliff McLucas. 'The geography of her movements is determined by the strange imposition of one system – the Stations of the Cross – onto another, the real geography of Penlanwnws' (McLucas, 1998, p. 18). '1. The shed: Jesus is condemned to death. 7. The kitchen: Jesus falls for a second time' (ibid., p. 17). Ladd was observed by nine security cameras in farmhouse and yard, and viewed remotely on monitors by an audience seated on straw bales in the barn. As she travelled from room to room, so she moved from screen to screen, often seen from different angles on several monitors at once. But the religious theme was superimposed upon and infused with two other narratives: the flight of astronaut Yuri Gagarin and the killing of a farmer by his bull during Ladd's childhood. Maps, photographs and audio descriptions of these events appeared in the mix of image and soundtrack that again included the *St Matthew Passion* as its foundation. This combination of a 'large' narrative space flight and a small – local – tragedy is a recurrent signature in Ladd's exploration of the complexities of contemporary rural experience. The use of sophisticated technology in such settings became a hallmark of Brith Gof's *Prosiect X*.

Although the employment of media enhances performative opportunities within the constraints of dwelling spaces, live performance remains feasible. In the late 1970s Lis Hughes Jones presented a story-telling performance for family groups in Welsh farmhouse kitchens, accompanied by the exotic sounds of Irish bagpipes and the eccentric manoeuvres of the musician. The *visitation* of strangers, but present only by *invitation*, and good mannered in their awareness of, and address to, the various generations present.

In April 2005 Marc Rees staged *The House Project*, 'a labyrinthine walk-in novel' in 5 Llandaff Road, Cardiff, based on *7 Rooms, a Prologue, a Bridge and an Afterward* by Montreal-based author Michael Topping, itself a document of a previous project (Rees and Tyson, 2004; Topping, 2004). Each room corresponded to a chapter in the book, with words inscribed, pinned and gouged on walls, ceilings and floors. In each space, an individual artist created actions and scenes in response to his or her allocated text. The small audience was at liberty to roam through the three-storey house, pausing to read, drawn to animated rooms as noise attracted their attention. Retracing their steps, losing track of time, reinforcing 'the notion of visiting and re-visiting, of snapshot, collage and palimpsest' (Adams, 2004, p. 5). Without narrative sequence as structure, the timed orchestration of dissimilar activities in which the sounds of one room might accompany another was paramount. A spider-woman in the master bedroom dances to the sound of a pounding keyboard in the basement. The atmosphere induced was of claustrophobia, of entry into a private, hermetic world: the *intrusion* of strangers.

Sometimes access is denied or inadvisable or inappropriate. In telling the story of the murder of Lynette White on 14 February 1988, an appalling crime that led to a serious miscarriage of justice, we never sought entry to 7 James Street in Cardiff dockland. But on 2 October 1998 Mike Brookes and I sat in his red Series 3 BMW one hundred yards from the scene of the crime, fifty yards from Butetown police station. We had arranged to meet a small audience on a site close to the now-demolished Casablanca Club. At the appointed time, we drove up. I was wearing a radio microphone. As I began to relate the sequence of events, pointing out places, naming names, locating the narrative on this landscape, the audience clustered around the car, my voice only audible on its radio. Very quickly then: family memories, defendants' testimonies, media articles, eyewitness accounts, police interviews, pathologists' reports, scene-of-crime reconstructions, my own DNA test ... In an account that attempted to make sense of an event in which many were implicated through geographical proximity – our company office was directly opposite, hence the blood test – and through an unease that awkward matters were being settled too quickly, in the thrust of civic development. Hit-and-run performance, in a place where feelings still run high and time has not healed. Then off and away to a pounding 'dub' soundtrack: performance *adjacent* to but never *at* the actual scene. In *Bonnie and Clyde* (2003) Eddie Ladd extended this makeshift broadcast technology: 'the audience drives in, parks up, and watches the action, which references the careers of the Depression era outlaws played against a soundtrack broadcast live through their car radios'.

In 1994 Cliff McLucas reconstructed 7 James Street deep in the Clywedog plantation in west Wales. At Esgair Fraith, he created *Tri Bywyd (Three Lives)*, a site-specific performance about three deaths, a performance about the domestic in the landscape (see p. 161; see Kaye, 2000, pp. 124–37). Rather than re-enacting the place and its history, he built two new architectures at, and indeed through, the site, and through each other, with three tons of scaffolding. Each structure consisted of a cube divided into twenty-four separate 'rooms' eight feet square. Formality in the forest: wood and steel; straight against curved; neon strips and large hanging light bulbs. 'Ghostly' in their presence. Each frame represented a specific building: 7 James Street; Llethemeuadd where Sarah Jacob 'the fasting girl of Llandysul' starved to death. All furniture – beds, chairs, tables – was constructed from scaffolding. In these three coexisting architectures were located three separate stories. Taking 1860 as the datum, one story was of period but not site – Sarah Jacob. A second of site but not period – a reflection on contemporary rural suicide. And a third of neither site nor period – Lynette White. In performance, the narratives unfolded simultaneously, one always seen through or in juxtaposition to the others, whilst never quite acknowledging each other's existence. 'The transparency of architectures means that all the images are compromised' (McLucas, quoted in Kaye, 2000, p. 135). On several misty nights audiences were brought to Esgair Fraith by coach, to sit in a grandstand in the trees. Performance as the *pretext* and vehicle for visitation of this isolated location. Places from elsewhere brought here: James Street *relocated*. But in order to avoid 'the trap of romanticism and nostalgia' McLucas needed 'a number of foreign pollutants' (McLucas, 1998, p. 14). The horror of the domestic – the banal combination of DIY and dead bodies in the crimes of Fred and Rosemary West – shadowed the concept.

Tri Bywyd was the singular manifestation of what McLucas referred to as *architectureeventspace*, a hybrid of architecture and event: 'a set of attitudes that would bring together built and conceptual architectures, and implode use and enclosure' (ibid., pp. 13–14). His ambition was to generate 'complex interrelationships between the formal, the thematic and the cultural and mobilize them to resonate within a particular social or historically specific context (ibid., p. 16). Such hybrids he regarded as 'constellations of effects, attitudes, ownerships, built materials, histories, firmly held beliefs and so on. They constitute a temporary but unique *ecology*' (McLucas, quoted in Kaye, 2000, p. 129). However, in the haemorrhaging of location, event and audience into each other, 'each will always generate More or Less than is required by the other – leading to conditions of surplus or starvation' (ibid., p. 128).

The domestic room provides a point of reference and frame in Eddie Ladd's latest series of projects, informed by Roman Polanski's film *Repulsion* (see Ladd, 2009). In *Stafell A* (2003) she improvised physically in a row of three interconnecting fabricated wooden rooms. In the live version of *Stafell B* (2004) she danced in the same structure and text was available on headsets. It includes mixed extracts from Catherine Deneuve's performance with accounts of the bombing of the Tryweryn reservoir construction site and the activities of M15 in Aberystwyth University. The web-based version overlays documentary material with 'live' webcam imagery. In performances of *Stafell C* (2006) video of the choreography is mixed with specially generated footage, the audience negotiating between live and mediated image.

Chapel: Morriston Tabernacle, Swansea

Image 3.5 Brith Gof/Lis Hughes Jones, *Ann Griffiths*, West Wales, 1983 (Mike Pearson)

A chapel. A group of people sitting ...

It is 24 March 1987 in Morriston Tabernacle chapel, the 'cathedral of Welsh non-conformism'. From the high pulpit at centre front, a minister announces the first hymn. He can see all before him and all can see him. Behind him on the sweeping balcony are three choirs, the nurses in uniform, as some will depart shortly for night duty, the ex-miners in matching blazers. The audience, cast in the role of congregation, stands and sings in harmony without prompting. As in the standard order of service, the minister then begins his opening address. But there is unrest in the pews and gradually figures, barely noted before, begin to reveal themselves. They are dressed anachronistically, after the fashion of the early twentieth century: working class men in Sunday suits, women in best shawls, a female Salvation Army officer. So commences *Pandaemonium: The True Cost of Coal*, Brith Gof's imaging of the aftermath of the Senghenydd mining disaster of 1913 in which 436 men were killed in a catastrophic gas explosion and gallery collapse. The dramatic conceit is that the explosion has occurred and that a service is taking place whilst the men, most probably now dead, are trapped underground. In the heightened tensions of this situation emotions run raw, accusations fly, conventions of propriety break. Distraught women express their anxieties and bitterness, and union leaders argue with mine owners. Accusation, denial, claim, rebuttal ...

There follows a series of re-enactments and allegorical scenes. Struggling to understand the accident. Demonstrating how rescue might be effected. Expressing communal hope and support.

Pandaemonium utilizes the formal spatial and architectural conditions of the chapel to disperse its constituents. The only scenographic installation is a single plank runway supported on the backs of pews from front to back upon which the ghostly figure of a miner, burnt and mangled, will ultimately appear, lit from behind by the only theatrical lighting. All activity happens amongst the audience in the rows of wooden seating, in the aisles where the intrusion of a 'reporter' from *The Times* is roughly dealt with, and in and around the pulpit. At its base is the *seiat fawr*, the 'big seat', a semicircular bench for the deacons, equipped in Morriston with a moveable top to create a temporary stage for concerts. It is here that the performance culminates in a long, semi-improvised confrontation between a proto-union leader and black-suited owner on procedures for mine safety. As the cause of the explosion is revealed – an electric spark in a faulty signalling system – members of the men's choir nod spontaneously in affirmation. At the end, three female performers appear in their own street clothes and unfurl an original banner of one of the women's support groups that played a crucial role in sustaining the miners' strike of 1984.

Morriston Tabernacle is a functioning chapel. In *Pandaemonium* the fabric of the building is untouched, its ascribed function undisturbed. Respect for operative sensitivities and sensibilities recommend prudence in conception and restraint in operation. However, extant practices suggest a dramaturgical structure, as performance adopts the practices of the chapel. The audience is, in large part, conversant with how to conduct themselves in here. For many, it is their place of worship. They sing when encouraged to do so, aware of the constraints the site might impose upon performance, and of the historical issues in play and their resonance as thinly veiled metaphor. Here performance is compatible with site in form, content and style, although the fit is not exact. The songs of Heather Jones resemble 'the blues' as much as Welsh hymnody, her voice amplified against the surging Hammond organ. Performers shout, run and blaspheme, conspiring 'a personal and communal hell which transcends the time and place' (Pearson, 1988, pp. 6–7).

Pandaemonium was the last in a series of works by Brith Gof for religious contexts in Wales. For *Gwyl y Beibl* (1985), an outdoor event commissioned to celebrate the four-hundredth anniversary of the translation of the Bible into Welsh, Cliff McLucas designed forty, five-metre-high banners each bearing image and text above head height, for the books of the Old Testament (Pearson, 1988, pp. 8–9). These were hung from buildings, including the church tower, and on scaffolding frames in gardens and fields throughout the village of Llanrhaedr-ym-Mochnant. At the climax of the processional performance – that repeatedly paused for Biblical readings delivered, for example, from the balcony of the public house – Polish company Theatre of the Eighth Day appeared from side streets in clouds of orange smoke. On a range of ladders rigged from railings around the village green, they hoisted antithetical banners bearing images of raw meat. To the discordant sounds of electric violin, they tore bibles and ripped them with their teeth on the roof of the bus shelter, dumping mannequins from wheelbarrows into flames below. As climbing figures were targeted with carbon dioxide fire extinguishers, causing them to fall and climb again, a large black plastic sheet bearing words from the Book of Revelation was drawn over the whole spectacle – a scene at once appropriate to the theme of the event but disturbing of the gentler overall aesthetic and to the mood of the celebrants.

Oherwydd y mae'r amser yn agos/For the Time Is Nigh (1986), again commissioned to celebrate the translation of the Bible, was created in the cathedral of St David (Pearson, 1988, p. 7). Given its ambiguous role in liturgy, the choice of Revelation was at once proper and contentious. At the core of the production was an improvised sermon on the theme of the 'New Babylon' preached from the pulpit by a well-known minister, actor and ballad singer. Descended from several generations of nonconformist clergy, he emulated the techniques of his forebears, his voice beginning to sing in *hwyl*, becoming wordless, talking in tongues, his emotional and visionary abandon an affront to Anglican rectitude.

In this fragile and pristine building, visibility was a key concern. The large audience was seated in the nave and was addressed by placing the Four Horsemen of the Apocalypse on stilts. As these looming, cavorting figures entered there was a sense of irreverence, countered by the appearance of an equally elevated

St Michael. Since the performance was presented only twice, once in English, once in Welsh, the costumes were made of folded and pleated paper, impressive but insubstantial, sufficient to the task but redolent of the ephemeral presence of performance. In front of the chancel screen a small dais raised the figures further. Against the screen they joined the frieze of sculptured saints, their activity framed, visual irrelevance disattended. Across the screen arch was a paper hanging, bearing a series of seals, removed as extracts from the text were enacted. On top stood two narrators, their voices amplified. The accompanying musical score for solo soprano, small orchestra and cathedral organ was atonal and distinctly non-celebratory, echoing the large photographs of the contemporary apocalypse eventually hung from the screen in an essentially two-dimensional combination of elements.

Ann Griffiths (1983–86) was created for small and often elderly congregations, in rural chapels in Wales and in Patagonia (Pearson, 1985, p. 20). The solo performance by Lis Hughes Jones combined the letters and lyrics of the charismatic young hymnist, tracing her increasing devotion and the rapture of her conversion at the turn of the eighteenth century. Presented in small vestries or delivered from pulpits, the physicality of the white-dressed figure was restrained, the overt expression of passion confined to the singing voice. Whilst remaining respectful of its documentary sources, the work was unsettling. The songs were set to the archaic tunes and folk melodies Ann Griffiths herself would have known, rather than those of mid-Victorian composers through which her words are now known. Each location necessitated adjustments in tone and dynamic to take advantage of, and to compensate for, features of architecture, decor, furniture and acoustic. How best to communicate when visible only above the waist?

Religious buildings come freighted with history, with established routines of observance, with atmospheres of piety. Performance here might constitute a trivial pursuit. In the early work of Brith Gof we saw an opportunity to annex the techniques of oratory and song of nonconformism, to locate performance within its architectures, and to use the pervasive nature of religious knowledge in identifying subject matter.

In September 2008 Aberystwyth MA student Rhiannon Morgan took up these dormant notions in a solo performance in Bethesda chapel, Aberystwyth. Starting with an account of her own earliest experiences of being in chapel, of its customs and characters, that offered an opportunity of shared acknowledgement in her audience, she then expanded the range of her narrative to encompass her square mile and the idiosyncrasies of her personal and family history.

Close to the end of his life, Cliff McLucas proposed filling a chapel with water, in a further reflection upon the drowning of Capel Celyn during the building of the reservoir at Tryweryn. He approached it as a work of civil engineering. In risking structural damage and collapse, he highlighted the fate of so many deserted chapels in Wales, and the passing of religious adherence itself.

Barn: National History Museum, St Fagans, Cardiff

Image 3.6 Brith Gof, *Boris*, Hendre Wen, Welsh Folk Museum, Cardiff, 1985 (Mike Pearson)

A barn. A group of people sitting, and a horse ...

It's November 1985 and an audience huddles in Hendre Wen, a reconstructed barn in what was then the Welsh Folk Museum. It is a simple rectangular building with stone walls topped by timber planking. Above animal stalls there is an open-fronted hayloft. The two large wooden doors opposing each other once facilitated winnowing. One end is dressed with furniture and ornaments as a rural kitchen, after the manner of museum practice here. At the other, a few items suggest cruder living conditions, table, chair and stove. The audience of sixty is seated on tiers of straw bales down the long walls, facing inwards and leaving a narrow performing space on the central axis. Some events they will see in extreme close-up, performers addressing them directly, face-to-face. Others they will watch like a tennis match, as the dramatic focus swings between the two settings. It is cold, but they have come prepared. The occasion bears resonances of the *noson lawen*, a once-common form of rural gathering for songs, stories and skits.

From the stalls, a horse calmly watches the proceedings. A door opens and a figure enters, with a sheepdog on a length of rope. So begins Brith Gof's *Boris*, prepared by John Berger from his short story (1983) and subsequent drama in French, and translated into Welsh. It tells of an ill-fated shepherd who falls in love with the wife of the local driving instructor and whose inevitable abandonment leads to suicide, in that clash of rural and urban expectations and behaviours, familiar from Berger's sustained writing on communities in the French Pyrenees. Boris's story is told through three voices. Two local inhabitants talk not only *to* him but also *about* him, in asides and confidences. In a crucial moment demonstrating his state of distraction, Boris opens the door and a flock of sheep enters. In rehearsal they were extremely animated and disruptive, bounding around the space. In performance, they slowly amble in and out, disinterestedly.

Hendre Wen presented problems and opportunities for performance in equal measure. As a museum exhibit, its fabric had to remain unmarked. All attempts to heat it through a small upper window failed. Yet as a robust place of work it could accommodate animals and their associated mess, the hay that Boris would bring down a ladder from the loft, the oily chainsaw he would test, the leaves that would fall on his dying body in the open doorway.

Conceived in the late 1940s by Welsh curator Iorwerth Peate and based on the model of Danish open-air museums, the National History Museum includes a range of buildings from around Wales, dismantled and relocated to the parkland of St Fagan's Castle: cottages and farmhouses, water mill, chapel. With the initial aim of rescuing rural structures at risk, the site now includes a row of terraced houses, a miners' institute, a village store, a post-war 'pre-fab'. Essentially performative in nature, in the recreation and evocation of place and period, St Fagan's has long provided an environment for the staging of dramatic activities. In the 1990s it employed its own theatre company to animate buildings such as the Victorian school, with role-playing actors and visiting school classes in costume, engaged in modes of 'live interpretation'. Enactments of traditions such as the *mari lwyd* – a house-visiting custom involving visitation by a performer covered in a white sheet and bearing a horse's skull, and an improvised singing contest with the inhabitants (Owen, 1987, pp. 49–58) – still mark its calendar, as do regular visits from re-enactors such as the Sealed Knot that in 1998 staged the battle of St Fagan's.

The museum's many architectures have also afforded opportunities for site-specific work. In 1991, I presented the first two sections of the trilogy *From Memory*: the first, a monologue on my childhood and the death of my father, in the circular containment of the cockpit; and the second, an account of the shooting of Llwyd ap Iwan in Patagonia in 1909, in the yard of the tannery. In 1996 Eddie Ladd and Cliff McLucas created *Once Upon a Time in the West* in a small paddock. Again in Ladd's work, two disparate themes were combined – that of the film *Shane* (1953) starring Alan Ladd, and of accusations levelled in 1994 against her aunt for mismanagement of farmland, resulting in a landslip. 'Both narratives deal with justice and revenge and the show reformulates Hollywood iconography for a west Wales setting' (Ladd, 2009). Ladd's solo performance was enacted at prepared locations across the field, often far from the audience which was seated in a temporary grandstand. Her activities were videoed live and the imagery relayed to a bank of monitors. The audience thus watched some scenes at a distance, some in close-up, some off screen and, with the camera crew clearly at its work, some *being registered*.

In *Shed*light* (2004) Marc Rees constructed a replica of a shed for storing dynamite in the Swansea Valley that was the site of his first sexual encounter. The original is a brick structure with a heavy concrete roof. The interior and exterior of the replica was covered with specially designed wallpaper that 'emulates the ivy that covered the original shed but is also embedded with subtle male erotica that echoes the rites of passage experienced within the building's history' (Rees, 2009). Hundreds of tiny penises were woven into the pattern. The work takes up museum conventions of, and expertise in, reconstruction and display, and quietly subverts them, drawing attention to a mundane and neglected building outside the operational order at St Fagan's, and to the importance of lived experience.

Lotte Svinhufvud-Lockett's family home in Finland has become a national museum. Her PhD project tracks its transition from domicile to institution (Svinhufvud-Lockett, 2008). 'Kotkaniemi' is a wooden *dacha*, built in the late nineteenth century. Purchased in 1908 by her great-grandfather P. E. Svinhufvud, the third president of independent Finland, it was the space of her childhood. She was brought up with the possessions of the president and the handicrafts of his wife – embroidery, painted plates – as everyday familiars. Each summer her mother would open the house to guests, informally showing them the family heirlooms. In the 1990s the building was transferred to state ownership and converted into a museum, with her mother as official guide. Initially the family continued to occupy part of the house. They now live in the converted byre. In a series of performances for her PhD, Svinhufvud-Lockett examined the mechanisms and repercussions, personal, familial, regional, of this change in status: the reordering of the layout, with new restrictions on access; the change in the nature of objects to iconic national treasures; the addition and removal of artefacts in the redressing of rooms; the erasure of orders of marking caused by recent periods of habitation. Infused with memories of geographies of childhood ...

In a preliminary work, she photographed the four walls of the dining room at Kotkaniemi. These she then projected onto the exterior surfaces of a cube of tracing paper constructed in a studio in Aberystwyth. Inside, audiences were invited by a recorded soundtrack to regard objects they could see but not touch, in a form of virtual guided tour. A second performance was conceived and performed on site in Kotkaniemi. Using her mother's script and dressed in her guide's uniform, Svinhufvud-Lockett led the audience around the house, gradually subverting the official interpretation with anecdotes of her own memories of these places and objects, and of the understandings of family lore. Indicating the best places to hide Easter eggs, the nails where the polar bear skin once hung. Without pause or shift in register, she then entered her parents' living accommodation, pointing out and commenting upon details of the everyday – the scuffs and marks of habitual actions, the traces of dwelling – through the formal discourse of visitor interpretation. The tour culminated in her former bedroom. In a third version, she presented the original text, orientated by the geography of the same tour, in another building – the mansion of Nanteos near Aberystwyth. Here the effect was both comic and eerily disconcerting for the audience. Clearly the portrait of P. E. Svinhufvud was not hanging in the place described. Yet the stove in the kitchen was indeed a stove, if not quite the Finnish original. This transfer questioned the generic nature of historical reading and offered knowing approaches to awaken the interest of the weary tourist.

In a final performance, the entire floor plan of Kotkaniemi was outlined in white tape, at an oblique angle, in a large studio in Aberystwyth, in emulation of Lars von Trier's film *Dogville* (2003). A few objects on pedestals and several silent performers – P. E. Svinhufvud knitting, his wife devouring crayfish as she famously did from her own self-decorated tableware, and Svinhufvud-Lockett's husband in a bath – wryly referenced both museological display and 'live interpretation'. For the audience, the guided tour now constituted a work of imagination, as one site was evoked in another through performance.

Institutions frequently offer secure and resourced sites for performance, though conditions of occupancy may be prescribed by prohibition and parameters of conduct. In the management of, and forms of address to, audiences, their procedures may both inform and be open to critique by performative exposition.

Public building: Aberystwyth railway station

A station platform. A group of people standing, and a train.

Image 3.7   Brith Gof, *PAX*, Aberystwyth railway station, 1991 (Cliff McLucas)

It's 16 October 1991 and an audience gathers on a platform of Aberystwyth railway station. As the 19.57 departure for Shrewsbury pulls out, horn sounding by arrangement, the performers of Cyrff Yswyth, a local dance company with several disabled members, are revealed across the tracks on the platform opposite. Over the next fifteen minutes, their choreographic routines avoid the large trolleys from which 'ground-workers' vigorously spread soil and spray water and envelop them in smoke – workers who will then drag felled trees through the audience, shepherding them into the glass-roofed station concourse where all will eventually congregate: where a small orchestra, vocalists and narrators perch on the roof of a newspaper kiosk and four performers are suspended on pulley systems from the ironwork rafters.

PAX, the second of Brith Gof's large-scale works, involved a descent of angels: fragile when examined and persecuted by the workers, vengeful in their retribution and eventual ascent. Announced as 'a reflection on the state of the planet in ten movements', its dramaturgy attended two questions: could angels survive in current environmental conditions? Would we know them if we saw them? It was originally conceived for the incongruous setting of the St David's Centre concert hall, Cardiff, where the aisle of a Gothic cathedral was built to scale in scaffolding, jutting obliquely from the stage into the auditorium, the suspended performers hanging in the arches and swinging out over the heads of the audience. It would take twenty-nine men seventeen hours to construct: scenography at the scale of civil engineering and with the skeletal structure occupying the building for a limited period of time, giving rise to the notion of *host* and *ghost*. As a result of venue programming and hire costs, it was only achieved close to the performance premiere.

This pressured constituents such as music and physical performance, restricting opportunities for experimenting with instrumentation, compositional formats and specialist techniques on site. It led to two initiatives. First, the creation and public presentation of preliminary études at other sites: to examine aesthetic and technical aspects of the larger works. *Los Angeles* (1990) was created in a disused brewery building in Rhymney, the highest space locally available, with just two angels and two ground-workers but without the eventual musical soundtrack. This was being tested simultaneously in concert elsewhere, from Westminster Abbey to the Powerhouse Club in London. In the brewery, angels descended into a tank of freezing water – a scene replicated in Cardiff but not Aberystwyth – and landed on a circle of sawdust lit by detuned television sets. Second, the installation of a functioning rehearsal 'rig' in another empty space, a tall shed in Cardiff docks. Here, under scrutiny, performers could research and rehearse sequences that would function when viewed at an angle, or directly from below. Fundamental problems quickly emerged. Performers were initially reticent about giving their full weight to the harness, tending to grip the rope for safety's sake and to resist extending the body fully in space. Challenged to work three-dimensionally, it took a considerable time to orientate the body: to distinguish 'up' from 'down'; to engage the *body envelope* equally in all directions; to devise and remember actions in relation to a *line*, the rope – rather than a surface, the floor.

In Cardiff the flying used the counter-weight system traditionally employed to hoist theatre scenery. Hanging from the thinnest of wires, the performers had to be tied off, in the instant of touching the ground, to avoid pullers having to support their full body weight. In Aberystwyth the system reverted to ropes and yacht pulleys. The performers were free to move at ground level whilst still attached, though with no brakes or shunts on the ropes to slow the descent, other than the skills of the pullers.

Set within the public domain at a site in constant commercial use, *PAX* in Aberystwyth was restricted in both available space and schedule for completion. Its scenography was of necessity simple and mobile. Rehearsal involved as much walking and talking through the scenario as concerted physical activity. Whilst responding to the layout of the station, the performance did call upon a set of pre-existing, formal *building blocks*, including libretto and music, and established attitudes and demeanours of the angels and workers, to be modified in new circumstances. The performance had to be concluded, the platform cleaned, before the arrival of the next train from Shrewsbury.

PAX was resolutely expositional in its scale and modes of address. Later works in railway stations have been less assertive. *Metropolitan Motions* was created in August 2002 in Frankfurt, Germany with thirty university students. After gathering at the studio of the municipal theatre, one audience of forty remained in the auditorium. Four others of ten individuals immediately left by tram, subway, taxi and on foot, for separate, dispersed locations in the city, including the main railway station. They were then guided back through the city by performer-guides speaking semi-improvised texts about the urban experience, about architecture, history, citizenship – mixing theoretical insights with anecdotes and local understandings. At several points on these journeys each individual group met a performer – on a river bridge, on top of a sky-scraper, in a city square – repeatedly registering and returning video record-ings of their encounters to the audience in the theatre by cycle courier. As a redheaded performer descends from an arriving train, she is met by a group of strangers, her audience. She seems in distress, asks for directions in broken German and disappears into the crowd. They will meet her next in a launder-ette as her story advances.

As videos were replayed, those who had stayed could observe how the nar-ratives of the four individual performers related in any one moment across the city, how they were part of the same story, how they were in search of each other. But all the journeys were moving towards the theatre and the work culminated with all the performers on-stage and all the audiences in the auditorium.

For audiences in the street: the challenge of negotiating presence, intruding into the social scene, building narrative coherence from fragmentary meetings. For performers: of existing in the urban flux, making themselves apparent without drawing attention. For the guides: of creating a non-stop commentary whilst attending to the imponderables of the moment and the need to meet pre-cise schedules. In the theatre: the task of forensically scrutinizing for linkages in the multiple videos shown on a row of monitors, as on-stage other performers physically and verbally sample and reiterate aspects of the taped imagery.

In August 2004 Lotte Svinhufvud and I completed a research exercise in the central railway station in Helsinki that shifted our attention from the visual to the aural. Our objective was to locate and identify 'relic' sounds that would have existed at the opening of the station in the 1920s and that still survive, though relocated within the audio spectrum: the opening of a certain door, the crash of crockery, urine splashing into a flute-shaped urinal. Ten such sounds each inspired a short poetic text that, with documentary photographs of loca-tions in the station, were posted on a website. In the same project, archaeolo-gist Victor Buchli sifted through the station's rubbish bins, examining a single day of detritus, building stories from what had been discarded. And Angela Piccini showed her fourteen-minute videowork/live, spoken-word perform-ance *Guttersnipe* (Piccini, 2009, pp. 183–99). Shot with a camera strapped to a child's pram, this is a continuous tracking shot of a kerb and gutter in Bristol over which is laid a creative commentary that relates the history of the dis-trict from its vernacular detail, occasionally referring to objects observed and passed.

On 10–12 October 2006, Bristol Temple Meads station was the setting for the first workshop of the research network 'Living in a Material World: Performativities of Emptiness'. For three days scholars and artists roamed the station, particularly at night when its nature changes fundamentally: taking photographs, making films of its silent desertion. On a Saturday afternoon Heike Roms and I completed a listening exercise that we called 'One pair of good ears, one pair of bad'. As a starting point we took an early plan of the area showing the outlines of the stockyards that existed prior to the construction of the Victorian station. Using the wall of one of these corrals to orientate our work, we identified ten equidistant points on a transect across the station. Walking along the line, we paused for precisely one minute at each location – in the buffet, on various platforms, in an underpass – listening to and noting its sounds, making no distinction between human, animal and mechanical – and taking a single photograph with a camera purchased from a station shop. On site, our endeavours were barely perceptible, our actions like those of tourists or trainspotters, recording us in this place and features of the locality. Later Roms created a webpage, with our widely divergent texts and the photographs taken superimposed on the early plan. The exercise was conceived quickly, for a site with which we were unfamiliar. It might suggest a transferable methodology. It certainly highlighted the efficacy of station information and its accessibility for various kinds of disability. For me, all announcements were garbled.

Disused building: Ferry Road, Cardiff

Image 3.8   Brith Gof, *Arturius Rex*, industrial unit, Cardiff, 1994 (Jens Koch)

A derelict warehouse. A group of people, some in jackets with fluorescent shoulder patches, standing.

Doors open, a van drives in and performers pile out of the back. Someone announces:

> Welcome. Those of you who have chosen to be spectators, please feel free to move at all times. And remember – the place you are watching from is never the best place to watch from. For those of you who have chosen to participate with us, it will be risky, but it won't be dangerous. Well it could be, if you want.

So begins Brith Gof's *Prydain: The Impossibility of Britishness* (1996) (see Roms, 2004, pp. 186–9): part building site, part performance, part rock concert and part 'rave', a phenomenon already past its zenith at that time, that *subsumed* audiences into its aural and visual environment and that frequently involved the illegal occupation of empty industrial buildings. A hybrid of action, soundtrack, architecture and audience: for five physical performers; ten technicians; two music groups, the 'extreme metal' band of German–Slovene composer Robert Merdzo and the 'drum and base' mixes of Welsh band Reuvival; forty individuals, identified by the coloured yoke on their work clothes, who nightly volunteer to participate; and a standing audience. The central conceit is that all technical and scenographic resources arrive on the backs of lorries: small generators, battery amplifiers, industrial and mobile lighting, props, building fabric, rostra, plastic sheets. Stage managers, directors, performers and participants utilize this repertoire of equipment to construct, stage and activate events and their attendant effects practically as they happen. Only four installations pre-exist the performance: two large scaffolding frames seemingly flung randomly across the space like toppled ziggurats; and the technology to produce wind and rain. Performance as a *kit* of parts, materials and movements: to be assembled anew each night.

'What do you know about Britain? It's an island. It rains. It's violent. Shakespeare,' the publicity demanded caustically. Two hundred years previously in a Europe in turmoil, poets, politicians and preachers had imagined other definitions of, and futures for, 'nation' – visionaries such as William Blake and Iolo Morgannwg who had dared to imagine new political realities, to stimulate regional identities. *Prydain* echoes their zeal in both subject and form. 'Text was shouted through megaphones, whispered in ears, scrawled on walls and floors, inscribed on the naked bodies of the performers, set on fire' (Roms, 2004, p. 188). Both English and Welsh languages are used: half-heard, overheard, heard in fragments. Snatches of Gielgud's *Henry V* are sampled and deconstructed by Reuvival.

> The first performer began to cut off his clothes with a knife. While gradually exposing his flesh he was simultaneously revealing the markings of text written all over his body. He was then blindfolded, two open books were placed in his hands, and the books were set on fire. The performer began to move across the

space with his arms outstretched, balancing the two burning books in his hands, impeded in his movements by cold, darkness and fire. (ibid., p. 187)

Prydain declares itself a theatre-in-the-making, a work of construction with nothing to watch and everything to do. Within the half-lit, shifting maelstrom of activity, the participants are urged and cajoled into action, taught actions just minutes before they are presented. 'They carried out vital parts of the physical choreography of the work: they were asked to lift performers, move around parts of the set, join in a staged political process, etc.' (ibid.). They are led, instructed and incited: asked to pull, lift and demonstrate. Enfranchised to act. Any rehearsal is in view of the audience. Any one group of participants may be preparing whilst another is performing. The dramaturgy includes 'passages' involving performers and participants, and 'events' involving only performers. The 'events' are pre-rehearsed elements that punctuate and recover the performance into a semblance of order. Movements contrast horizontal – linear queue, procession, circular dance, assembly – with vertical – suspension, erection.

Here the spectator must negotiate his or her own presence moment-by-moment, deciding whether to follow, to keep up with a rapidly changing situation, demanding 'Who is who?', 'Whom do I listen to?', 'What's going on here?'. Standing, moving, running with, running away: necessitating choices within a provisional 'body politic'.

The final form came of necessity. Anything left in the building overnight was stolen, the full rigged amplification system twice. *Prydain* would be the last in a series of Brith Gof's productions for industrial spaces, the final moment in a project to examine the division of audiences and the dynamic interplay of two languages in performance.

'Welsh theatre can employ the Welsh and English languages in concert and in conflict, each language carrying different bodies of information without the need for translation, in a truer reflection of the linguistic composition of the nation', we conjectured. The experience of working in Cardiff, where audiences might include Welsh-speakers, non-Welsh-speakers and all shades of learner in between, led to new approaches to the collision and fragmentation of language in performance.

The performances of the *Arturius Rex* project paralleled contemporary conditions in the former-Yugoslavia with those in post-Roman Britain, and the breakdown in social order following the demise of both Arthur and Tito. In *D.O.A.* (1993), English-speaking performers struggled to speak Welsh, mirroring their desperate attempt to communicate the horrors of war. They scrawled on the black walls that suggested the Black Chapel of Arthur's death in chalk. The setting was a roofless room, a ten-foot cube. In this space were a metal bedstead, a bucket and a standing audience of fifteen. Above them, forty others peered down over the wall from a scaffolding walkway. Suddenly two men in filthy combat clothing rushed in, carrying disabled actor Dave Levett as the wounded Arthur, screaming and shaking in distress. Levett's wheelchair would never appear. Throughout, he was carried, assisted and positioned by his colleagues. Performing primarily prone on the bed, two different perspectives were available. In the room his torments were experienced at an oblique angle, in close-up. For those above, he composed graphic two-dimensional images within the frame of the bed.

In *Camlann* (1993) the audience was divided from the outset into Welsh-speakers and English-speakers, each group following different performers to different areas of the warehouse, where they were persuaded to take part in games of tug-of-war, in processions, in the creation of sound effects. The two languages were constantly heard over, through and in conflict with each other, particularly in periods of jingoist oratory and direct taunting. Only gradually did the two audiences come together, at which point they were invited to change sides if they wished. *Camlann* forsook built scenography, the installed lighting a conundrum for audiences. Did it indicate places to congregate or places to avoid?

Cusanu Esgyrn (1994), a Welsh translation of Euripedes' *The Trojan Women*, was staged in a modern, prefabricated barn. On either side of the central playing area were two parallel scaffolding walkways. The audience was divided into men and women, men viewing the performance from above, the women with the all-female cast on the floor below. The live soundtrack was for three electric guitars. The entire text was pre-recorded and played in performance, the performers speaking acoustically to accompany their own amplified voices when the rigours of the physical action allowed. The female audience were drawn into the action in certain moments of activity, and always on view, in their varying commitments and responses, from above. All objects used in the performance were contained in storage boxes stacked in the open scaffolding frameworks.

Arturius Rex (1994) again employed parallel scaffolding walkways, though now fronted by hardboard panelling. Audience members were given the option of viewing the performance at a distance from the action: from above or at ground level. In the open performance area, there were no formal divisions between performers and spectators. Welsh and English were spoken at the same time, each individual free to find and follow the voice of his or her choice. At the beginning, performers were seated or lying on a number of cast-iron beds in a scene reminiscent of a battlefield hospital, quietly relating their personal stories. The beds would eventually become cages eerily redolent of Guantanamo Bay, audience members forced to move at speed to avoid performers leaping at and up the walls.

Pen Urien, the 'Head of Urien', went unperformed. In a deserted forest clearing a performer would have disinterred his colleague. For the duration of the performance, he would have had to deal with an inert and unresponsive body in his explanations and emotional outbursts on the futility of war.

The *Arturius Rex* project was mounted in new, functional, nondescript buildings, buildings that nevertheless provided security and services – heating, lighting, power, toilets. Several productions entailed the construction and *emplacement* of a unique staging unit prior to the commencement of rehearsal. The performance was specific to this set of dimensions and characteristics of lighting, acoustic, surface, of wall and floor. Such continuity of conditions allowed the development of detailed choreography for a known and unchanging area, including speed and dynamism within known parameters, the presence and touch of proximate performers, extremes of activity for the known surface, and the devising of complex and detailed imagery and stage pictures for fixed arrangement of audience.

City: The Hayes, Cardiff

Image 3.9 Polaroid taken by audience member: Pearson/Brookes, *Polis*, Cardiff, 2002 (unknown)

A telephone kiosk. A group of people standing ...

It's 21 September 2001 and a cluster of people listens in on a conversation, as a figure they assume to be a performer speaks to directory enquiries, urgently and forlornly seeking the numbers of pubs that once stood in this area of the city: The Salutation, The Lifeboat, The Greyhound. The list is long as he tries to get purchase, but the encounter brief. Suddenly he is gone and they are left in the clamour of an urban Friday.

At 8.00 p.m. Mike Brookes and I had met an audience of forty in the studio theatre of Chapter Arts Centre in Cardiff. Twenty individuals immediately left us, setting out in five taxis, each group with a guide, in search of four performers, two men, two women and a photographer (Jeff, 2009), adrift in the city. At five separate locations – dockside, coffee shop, dancehall, bar, hotel room – each group came upon a performer often engaged with an unsuspecting public: serving in a cafe, dancing in a club. Their task was to identify the performer and to record their meeting for precisely five minutes on video and on Polaroid: different audiences doing different things in different places simultaneously. Required to negotiate their own presence in the various milieus – in places unfamiliar and disquieting, in places familiar but changed in nature in their nightly guise – they listened to pleas and protestations and promises, observed scenes of intrigue, mystery and provocation. Witnesses to chance happenings, events caught out of the corner of the eye. In the hotel room through which each performer would eventually pass, one group took no camera. Later, they would be interrogated for what they remembered there. A hole in the plaster seemed for them and for those whom they watched, a clue to past misdemeanour. Of a punch thrown in anger or frustration.

These twenty then returned to Chapter, groups arriving back at the same time with dubious bits of this or that – poorly shot videos, underexposed photographs – purporting to show that or this, evidence that something, perhaps momentous, was happening 'out there', slightly beyond our capacity to apprehend it. They came with tall tales, travellers' fables. They returned like righteous eyewitnesses or innocent bystanders or those 'helping us with our enquiries'. With descriptions of places visited, conversations overheard, half-heard, misheard: hard evidence or pure fiction, truth or illusion? 'As witnesses to and recorders of these events the spectators were figured as actual co-creators of the work' (Roms, 2004, p. 178). In the taxis on the homeward journeys they also recorded each other, responding to questions such as 'Describe the last time you were frightened' for later viewing.

We projected the videos that they had made simultaneously, four times on different walls of the studio theatre, each time amplifying the soundtrack from one piece of footage. The city as it was 'just now' now, present in the theatre. It slowly became apparent that the performers were linked in the same story: that their figures were in search of each other. With four separate encounters now brought together in juxtaposition, we saw them telephoning each other in different projections, holding up photographs of each other, leaving messages for each other. We also saw them shouting at strangers, collapsed in the street, playing darts in a club, intruding into the life of the city. Yet most of their actions, movements, reunions remained out of sight, off-camera. In times of tape rewind in the studio, we played the video diaries of personal stories from the taxis on four separate monitors. The audience members themselves become part of the polyphony of the city. And those from the hotel room *told* of what they saw.

All this was lost on those who had initially stayed in the studio, who had reminisced about Cardiff. They had already departed in the same taxis in pursuit of the performers who had now moved to new locations in the city, a series of fixed points, in continuance of their quest. To the kebab shop downstairs from 7 James Street where some at least knew that Lynette White was murdered. Sometimes to places marginal, sites unencumbered by such history, where claim and counter-claim could be made, where anything might be said or done, where old scores might be settled: multistorey car parks, taxi offices, garage forecourts, station ticket halls.

The same process was then repeated for over two hours, a constant coming and going of audiences, and the gradual accumulation of fragments – maps, scripts, photographs, videos, texts – that were laid out on five separate benches, one for each character, gridded and boxed in white adhesive tape, the only place where the story became available *in toto*. Different perspectives on the same story. How will they find each other, find solace in each other's arms, when all here is in movement: people, objects, geographies? They struggle to recognize landmarks now changed, working hard in their wandering and searching from maps of different ages, from street maps that have rapidly become outdated. But memory preserves portions of other maps, overlain, redrawn, wafer-thin, riddled with holes, occasionally brought to mind – at the flowerbed that was once the Custom House pub. They walk the city into existence, five separate trajectories, five destinies prefigured by squabbles about 'who did what, to whom and where'.

And a few audience members realized that they were witnessing the homecoming of Odysseus to Ithaca – a place that he barely recognizes, a place where he passes unrecognized, a place where he returns to the love of his life. Finally the lovers were downstairs in the bar in Chapter, reunited and being photographed. The eternal embrace of Odysseus and Penelope ...

We called it *Polis*: a multisite work, for one room and other places (Pearson, 2007a):

> the kind of sites that might be opened up within and alongside a city's spaces by a combination of low-grade technology, the choreographed spatial presence and absence of the performers and audience (who, by means of recording and replaying techniques, may not share the same spaces at the same times), and language that slips playfully between textual, performative and geographical spaces. (Wilkie, 2008, p. 98)

A provisional performance built from scraps, moments of revelation, morsels of opinion, from the experiences and contributions of those present, those who bothered showing up (see Roms, 2004; Pearson, 2007a; Wilkie, 2008).

'We will enable a number of things to happen simultaneously and provide a telescope for looking,' said Mike Brookes. *Polis* existed in a multitude of places, some of which may even be out of sight, in a work adjacent to the everyday and potentially as large as the city. It refused to coalesce, to make itself available for total scrutiny. There was no single place from which one could see it all. It was never one thing. It was *field* rather than *object*. And it was *forensic* or archaeological in aspect. The audience was charged with documenting performance, returning it as *evidence* of events from which others were absent. Our understanding of what is going on was reliant upon the skill of the performers to make themselves momentarily apparent in the public domain, and the ability of audiences to recognize and record them. Significantly, one order of *documentation* had already made its way back into performance, repositioned in the timetable as other than a 'post-' phenomenon. To understand its scale, let alone its narrative, the individual spectator pieced together documents and the recall of overhead conversations and interrogations in acts of *interpretation*: in the *reconstitution* of the past from its surviving fragments. Performance as constituting a single or linear narrative is put under pressure.

These are the kinds of question *Polis* raises:

> ▪ Where was it being generated: in one place or many places? Places from which performers and spectators were variously *excluded* or *absent*, where *co-presence* no longer seems a useful definition of performance, problematizing *live-ness* as an essential condition?
>
> ▪ How was it being apprehended: in one place or many places? Places where the potential to monitor response in a 'feedback loop' no longer seems like a useful definition of performance?
>
> ▪ How many audiences were there here: experienced by some individuals as a night-out at the theatre, by others as a momentary occurrence in the city?
>
> ▪ Where was the authentic story of *Polis*? Where is the optimal position of critical scrutiny?

For me as performer: long periods of improvised conversation with audience members on their reminiscences of Cardiff, on *local knowledge*. For Mike Brookes as designer and technical director: a repositioning from the off-stage of the lighting box to the floor of the studio, where all his equipment is evident. And all his expertise apparent, in his constant tuning of the assemblage of sound and image. Working with material of varying quality, never knowing what might return: confident in the robustness of a *concept* within which individual contributions could be slotted, yet ever mindful of the clock.

In *Polis* site-specific performance forsakes fixity and architectural enclosure. In the entwining of journeys and locations it becomes *peripatetic* and *transient*, pausing and moving on, indicative in both its story of return and choice of sites of a city in flux.

The telephone kiosk itself recently disappeared under the largest building site in Wales.

Landscape II: Snitterby Carrs, Lincolnshire

Image 3.10   Mike Pearson, *Carrlands*, Ancholme Valley, North Lincolnshire, 2006 (Mike Pearson)

A riverbank. You, standing ... And as you begin the walk from Brandy Wharf Bridge to Snitterby Lock, I speak in your ear.

So begins *Carrlands*, a series of three sound compositions inspired by, and set at, locations in the agricultural landscape of the Ancholme valley in North Lincolnshire, and created in collaboration with composer John Hardy (Pearson, 2007b). These audio works – integrations of spoken text, music and effects, with subtle invitations to action and instructions to users – offer direction at places infrequently visited, but which have their own unique characteristics, qualities and attractions. They accompany a series of walks, guided tours of nowhere in particular. Available for download as MP3 audio files from a dedicated website, each has a distinct tone, character and instrumental voicing, and is further divided into four fifteen-minute *movements* reflecting an aspect of the location – its history, its flora and fauna, agricultural practices, notable events.

After download, the listener is free to choose how, where and under what conditions of time, season and weather to access the material, either at site or elsewhere. If listened to at a distance, a number of photographs are available in the online gallery to provide visual reference and orientation, though the listener is encouraged to picture the landscape in the mind's eye. If the works are be taken to the actual locations on a portable player, the listener is at liberty to select the time, season, weather, personal mood and social conditions – alone, in a group – of their encounter. Movements may be listened to consecutively or with pauses between them. Sites are readily accessible and routes for walking are recommended, though in the main these follow paths on the riverbank. None of the texts is either prescriptive or precise in its address to topography, and participants are free to roam the surrounding landscape. And none is remorseless. Musical passages repeatedly punctuate the narrative. Technology plays a significant and transformative mediating role in the response of art to the environment: performance as a medium that can precipitate and encourage public visitation.

The Ancholme Valley was long a water-world, its peaty fenland soils effectively drained only in the early nineteenth century. It is a shrouded prehistoric landscape. In places there are substantial quantities of prehistoric bog oak, and occasionally spectacular Bronze Age relics emerge: boats, rafts, piers. It is essentially a man-made landscape, highly administered and maintained now through relentless pumping out and pumping in. Simple, flat, frequently deserted, it lacks conventional scenic heritage, those monumental features that might draw the gaze. It does not easily reveal itself. Few Xs mark the spot. There are no blue plaques to record famous personages. But this was once a populous place. Monastic communities worked the land piecemeal. Victorian women and children laboured here in large gangs. Its big skies resounded to the noisy transits of Second World War bombers. Its banks were places of communal recreation for villagers until the mid-twentieth century. And anglers once arrived by the coach-load. Only recently has it seemed empty, frequented only by dog-walkers and passing pleasure craft. Become a place of suicide and infanticide.

The composition of *Carrlands* involved conventional library and archive research, drawing upon the reports of the Ancholme Inland Drainage Board, Environment Agency flood assessments and M. C. Balfour's late nineteenth-century *Legends of the Cars*, an extraordinary evocation of the predrainage landscape of fogs and fevers, of shattered bog oaks, apparitions, ague and opium eating (Balfour, 1891). It also drew upon on-site fieldwork to examine and explore details, marks and traces of human activity: the ruins of the farm rented by my father's uncle. It also included interviews, undertaken at site when possible: with disciplinary experts; with regional specialists and enthusiasts, including ornithologist, museum curator, water bailiff; with village history groups; and with local inhabitants, family members and those who have lived and worked in the carrs – dwellers perhaps (see Ingold, 2000, pp. 189ff.). Those who don't require maps to get around, farmers in the main ...

The aim is to elicit insights from archaeology, geography, natural history and folklore, and combine them with the detailed and first-hand experiences, opinions and memories of local people. There is a purposeful blurring of personal, expert and popular sources: to help illuminate, explicate and problematize the multiplicity of meanings that resonate within and from these landscapes, to espouse their imbricated nature. The attempt is to demonstrate the intimate connection between personal biography and the biography of landscape, between social identities and a sense of place, through concatenations of local observation and critical academic discourse.

Sometimes interviewees are quoted verbatim, but *Carrlands* is primarily achieved in a solo voice: to ensure one level of cohesion and to lessen technical problems of equalization. A voice that can seduce and reassure, surprise and inform. The recorded text forms a single layer within a sonic *stratigraphy*. The musical components are built up *beneath* the recorded text, emerging more demonstrably in verbal pauses. *Above* the voice there may be more ephemeral features: *effects* – birds calls, aeroplane engines – and *echoes* of the interviewees speaking their own words slightly out of phase with my voice. From moment to moment the music itself may further evoke or disrupt the atmosphere of these seemingly uninhabited lands. It includes instrumental, vocal, orchestral and electronic, and processed strands. Sampling from archival sources: Percy Grainger's folk-song recordings from the turn of the twentieth century, the voices of Italian prisoners-of-war. Effects that recall former sound-worlds in these places: Merlin aero-engines. And within the matrix, the highly modified, unrecognizable voices of interviewees provide musical textures or, when digitally analysed, the notation for instrumental composition. Become part of the landscape ...

In form, *Carrlands* employs and extends a methodology familiar from artistic projects such as Janet Cardiff's seminal *The Missing Voice (Case Study B)* (1999) at Whitechapel, Graeme Miller's *Linked* (2003), and contemporary museum trails. It is a form of *remote*, doubly remote, site-specific performance. The listener is cast not only as an audience of one but also as active participant in meaning creation. Negotiating complex shifts in time and subject matter; bringing their own physical experience, phenomenological encounter even, to the stories and information embedded in the compositions. Working with imagination in a landscape lacking authoritative viewpoints. Shifting from optic to haptic apprehension. Betwixt and between ... earth and sky ... land and water ... me and them.

All three vectors in play – place, performance and participant – are generative and in a dynamic relationship. Landscape is *constitutive* rather than merely scenic backdrop. Not only are other occupations apparent and cognitively active, it may also change its nature instantly. A sudden shower disrupts the listener's emergent interpretation. *Carrlands* involves an invitation to action, repositioning spectatorship as participation. In its unchanging texts and its recommended walks, it can appear *programmatic* – directing and choreographing as it informs. But the participant is free to wander, with body and imagination.

There are no startling vistas in the valley. Only the river bridges offer purchase in the level expanse. A landscape then for doing, feeling and contemplating as much as for looking, and for performance that avoids either pointing to or pointing out. The admonitions are not then to move or look here or there, but rather 'Picture this', 'Imagine this'. There is work to be done: walking, looking, musing, imagining, in acknowledgement of growing perception that as visitors to heritage sites our threshold for data is surprisingly low. And that a plethora of historical information can overwhelm us and sully the experience.

Carrlands is intended to enhance and stimulate public appreciation, understanding and enjoyment of landscape through active engagement. It draws attention to and illuminates the historically and culturally diverse ways in which a place is made, used and reused. It proposes performative approaches to acts of interpretation, for anyone who may choose to engage with them.

These are the kinds of questions that *Carrlands* poses:

> - How and why does this place come to be as it is?
> - What struggles, natural and human, lie behind its benign facade?
> - Can we regard it as much as a network of related stories and experiences as the outcome of particular processes of human intervention, as a collection of topographic details?

Participant responses fold into the project as *feedback*, through a questionnaire on the website. But they are not asked to make a qualitative judgement on the artwork. Rather, they are invited to contribute their own observations of these places and how they themselves might describe and interpret them. Drawing on knowledge from other academic disciplines, from local understandings and knowledge, from hearsay. Adding expert observation, personal memoir, biographical detail, poetry, fiction ... Stimulated by the compositions of *Carrlands*. To elucidate better the entangled nature of land, human subject and event, the contested relationships between landscape, experience and identity in this place, and to acknowledge the close link between culture and subjectivity within a given region.

Site: Exercises

In which the reader is invited to undertake research at a particular location: to develop narrative from such enquiry and to engage in a practical and physical exploration at such a place.

As ways of telling ...

In preparation for a site project *Strasse(n)wecken* (2006) at the Johannes Goethe University in Frankfurt, Germany in July 2006, students were asked to undertake the following exercises that included (a) individual fieldwork and (b) weekly group meetings that should not be longer than ninety minutes and could be informally convened (see pp. 154–5).

> There are no correct procedures. Truth and fiction, lying and romancing, the fragmentary, the digressive, and the ambiguous may always be included. The object is to find pleasure in telling, and in listening too.

Week 1

Meeting. Introduce yourself to a colleague by: (a) describing your shoes; (b) emptying your pockets and describing the contents; (c) showing and telling about any scars you have; (d) describing a personal accident; (e) relating your earliest memory. Do this as individual anecdotes lasting not less than two minutes each. Don't interrupt each other!

Week 2

Personal research. Site: visit a gallery, museum or other public building. Later: (a) what details do you remember most clearly? (b) write a postcard, describing the place in five words; (c) write one sentence to describe the experience; (d) prepare for exercise (c) below.
Meeting. (a) Describe a familiar room: somewhere you can revisit in your mind's eye; (b) describe a favourite place from your childhood; (c) for not more than five minutes, describe your visit to the gallery. Do this as individual anecdotes. Don't interrupt each other!

Week 3

Personal research. Site: stand or sit in a public place, a street corner or square for fifteen minutes. Pay attention to detail. Later: (a) eyes closed, mentally reimagine your visit; (b) from memory, draw a map of the place – include significant features; what symbols are you using? (c) write five things that would make this place better; (d) prepare for exercise (b) in the meeting to follow.
Meeting. (a) Describe a journey; (b) for not more than five minutes, describe and demonstrate your visit to the public place. Now you can interrupt with questions and respond with answers.

Week 4

Personal research. Site: try to overhear a conversation in a cafe, bar, station. Later: (a) can you remember a complete sentence? (b) can you remember a single gesture used? (c) what was the most memorable thing said? (d) prepare exercise (d) below.
Meeting. (a) Describe a grandparent: his or her appearance, quirks, foibles, stories; (b) describe the 'black sheep' of your family; (c) describe your family traits: hereditary features, details of physiognomy, posture, gait, accent, behaviour; (d) for not more than five minutes, tell about your overheard conversation. Show the gesture you observed. Interrupt; respond.

Week 5

Personal research. Site: observe an event, occurrence or incident in a public place. This may for instance be a departure at the station and it may not be very protracted. Later: (a) imagine who the people were who were involved. What was their story? (b) prepare for exercise (c) below by developing a story around your observations.

Meeting. (a) Bring an object and tell about it: a toy, a tool, an item of clothing; (b) bring a photograph and describe it: who? where? when? what is the main point of attention? (c) for not more that five minutes, describe the event you observed: (i) what happened? where did it occur? who was involved? what kind of sounds were happening? what kind of smells? (ii) show something of what happened: a movement perhaps.

Week 6

Personal research. Site: hold a conversation with a stranger. Later: (a) recall the details of what he or she told you: what kinds of things were revealed? (b) in preparation for exercise (d) below, devise a fictional portrait of the person you met.

Meeting. (a) Describe an entrance or exit that changed your life; (b) describe the last time you were frightened; (c) describe an incident of jealousy; (d) tell the story of the person you met.

Week 7

Personal research. (a) Site: research the history of your neighbourhood; (b) look for archive photographs and descriptions of the area, newspaper cuttings, maps, plans; (c) take two photographs to represent your neighbourhood; (d) look out for marks of human habitation. Later: prepare for exercise (c) below.

Meeting. (a) Describe how you got here today; (b) begin a story with the words 'When I was in ...'; (c) tell a short, fictional story around the details you observed in your neighbourhood. This can refer to the photographs you have taken.

Week 8

Personal research. Site: research your apartment. Talk to the landlord. Try to discover the identity and personality of former tenants. Did anything unusual happen? Later: (a) who lived there before you? (b) did they leave traces? (c) prepare for exercise (c) below.

Meeting. (a) Talk about a close friend; (b) talk about a pet; (c) tell a story from your apartment.

Week 9

Personal research. Site event 1: through talking to different local inhabitants, try to identify a single, significant event that happened in your neighbourhood.

Then (i) seek out different opinions on the same event, from press, police, shopkeepers, etc.; (ii) find one person willing to tell this story to camera, video it if possible. Later: prepare for exercise (b) below.

Meeting. (a) Describe an 'inciting incident' in your life: a change of consequence: a birth, a death, a sudden shift in biographical direction, orientation or emphasis; (b) tell the story of your neighbourhood event.

Week 10

Personal research. (a) Site event 2: interview a shopkeeper in your neighbourhood about the most significant event that has happened there; (b) ask the police about the most serious crime that has happened in the neighbourhood. Later: write an account of the neighbourhood event in five texts of fifty words in preparation for exercise (c) below.

Meeting. (a) Tell a personal anecdote involving embarrassment; (b) describe the worst smell you can remember; (c) distribute your texts to five of your colleagues and ask them to read them aloud. If you are unhappy with the reading, ask them to repeat this after giving them instructions on how it should be done.

Week 11

Personal research. Prepare an account of an event from someone else's texts, rephrasing it and elaborating it as if it were your own.

Meeting. Relate the event to your colleagues as dramatically as you desire.

As ways of doing ...

In a plain setting, begin by creating choreographic sequences of simple movements:

For solo performer: beckon, walk, stride, jump, kneel, fall, crawl, spin, roll, shout.

For two performers: mirror, copy, lead, embrace, push, lift, carry, drag, throw, whisper.

For a group of performers: jog, run, crush, tangle, catch, link, copy, climb, collapse, sing.

Individual movements should be precise and repeatable. They can be integrated in any order into fixed sequences or used as the constituents of an improvised *language*.

Next *articulate* any movement in sequence or improvisation in the following ways: by using more or less time to complete it, by using more or less energy, by making it bigger or smaller, by applying tension, by eliding one with the next without break, by enacting a percentage of the original, by repeating it, by reversing it, by distorting it, by using a different part of the body to complete.

> - Which articulations are more feasible with which movements?

Next *mediate* either sequence or improvisation in the following ways: by confining it to a particular ground area, large or small; by confining it to a particular volume of space, beneath a table for instance; by restricting the capacities of the performers, through blindfolding or the wearing of constraining clothing; by completing it within or over set periods of time; by adding and integrating objects such as wooden pallets, chairs, umbrellas, newspapers, luggage.

> - What are the repercussions?
> - How does such mediation enhance or compromise the tenor of the physical work?

Next *relocate* either sequence or improvisation to a variety of sites.

> - What is the effect of placing the work in relation to, or confined within, a naturally occurring architectural or natural feature: a flight of stairs, a balcony or corridor, a tree or sand dune? Or of changed environmental conditions, surface or climate: working on a pebbly beach, a grassy slope, in a swimming pool, in a downpour or a snow fall? Or of social situation: in a stationary car, in a toilet cubicle, in a lift?
> - Can it exist, covertly, at a low percentage in public: in a fast-food restaurant?
> - Can it be variously congruent with, indifferent too, in conflict with, the site?

Next *recontextualize* either sequence or improvisation at site: by the addition of soundtrack, narration, script and lighting. By altering the background ...

> - How might such increments accord with or problematize the architectures and narratives operative within the site?
> - Can we regard these exercises as the equivalent of Tschumi's 'programmes', as active experimental practices to test multiple correlations of event, movements and space?
> - What does performance reveal of site, and site of performance?
> - What specificities of the one impact upon the other?
> - What is the ergonomic relationship between body and building?

▦ What is physically possible, and what ill advised?

▦ And what options become apparent for the dispersal of audiences and for the provision of alternative viewpoints? Performance seen at a distance, in close-up, from an oblique angle, from above, approaching, passing.

Site: Project: Trace:, Cardiff

Image 3.11   *Trace: Dis-placed*, National Eisteddfod, Cardiff, 2009 (Tim Freeman)

In which a site and series of engagements are described. The reader is invited to conceive performance for the same location.

Site

Trace: Gallery is situated in a terraced house in Cardiff, the home of performance artist André Stitt (Trace:, 2009). The two front downstairs rooms have been knocked into a single space, a common arrangement in Cardiff, and the plain walls painted white. Each winter since 2000 Trace: has hosted a programme of performance events. Each month an artist is invited to create work in response to the characteristics and qualities of the space and its immediate context. This has included both short-term interventions and longer engage-ments. Towards 6 p.m. on a Saturday, a small audience gathers: standing, sitting on the floor, occasionally moving to see better, or to avoid the action, sometimes even remaining outside peering through the glass doors as in 2001 when Canadian artist John G. Boehme struck six hundred golf balls against an aluminium sheet hanging on the wall. Over the succeeding hour, artists present autonomous performances, sometimes a reconfiguration of existing work, or bring the processes of durational works to conclusion. The remains of the per-formance stay in the gallery, either as planned installation or informal detritus, for the following month, before being cleared and the walls repainted.

Each artist is invited to address the same site. Memorably, Eve Dent was nowhere to be seen as the audience entered. Only gradually were they aware of a tiny fall of soot in the cubic opening that was once the fireplace. Dent was standing vertically in the chimney in 'an interplay between hiding and being seen, mimicry and merging the body with the environment' (Trace:, 2009). 'In the creation of my body/architecture hybrids I seek to animate the hidden poetic life of a space' (Dent, quoted in Rees, 2003, p. 27).

> We are left in our comfortless waiting, broken only by an occasional colloquy of thumping and soot-falls, until we notice her blackened fingers. They have crawled slyly into the room, clinging like ivy, curled as if to lift the wall away. Then toes peep, a filthy leg, a body twisted in negotiating this threshold, until at last she emerges. Wearing a simple white dress and a disposable breathing mask, her clothes and skin are stained with ashes. She appears as something other, alien. She is *das unheimliche*, that familiar stranger, becoming so by becoming visible. (ibid.)

A performance recalling at once Victorian child labour and women's bodies, hidden, built into houses ...

Traces of work inscribed on the walls, hacked into the floor, are painted and plastered over but not erased. They become part of the site itself: the blood from Kira O'Reilly's 'cutting' performance, the text that Marilyn Arsem wrote in pencil, circuit after circuit, for twenty-four hours. Extreme actions in a domestic setting. The audience gathers in the kitchen, their perception infused with memories of other times, other events in this one place.

In *[The Noise of] The Street Enters The House/ [The Noise of] The House Enters The Street* (2004) Roddy Hunter included a mattress, a pink coat and a dead bird all found in the streets around. And a lightbox with slides of an abandoned housing project for phosphorous miners and their families in Kazakhstan. 'We wanted the room to be cold, really cold, but an industrial air conditioner cost £180 per day and we couldn't afford it' (Hunter, 2007, p. 130).

> So, here's what happened. I rolled up the blinds and opened the windows to let the sound from the inside meet the noise from the outside. I'd waited for the room to go quiet. I rolled the blinds back down so we'd think more about aural

rather than visual concerns and because I was probably going to take my clothes off later … I opened the window, chalked a crack from the window across the floor, sit at the lightbox, look at slides, wear elastoplast, take temperature, go to mattress, take the temperature of the bird, wear elastoplasts on my eyes, so I can't see, undress/dress in old coat, ask for hammer and masonry chisel, make a new crack across the floor with a hammer and masonry chisel, return/dress, take thermometer, place on lightbox, chalk line on crack and close the windows. (ibid., pp. 129–30)

Brief

- What performance would you conceive for Trace:?
- How might it reference (a) the local context and (b) previous performances in the gallery?

Trace: itself has recently become itinerant. For the National Review of Live Art (2008) a full-scale, free-standing replica of the gallery was constructed in the large, former carriage hall at Tramway in Glasgow. Contributing artists were invited to work in response (a) to this new structure, a pristine white box, form without resilience; and (b) to their recollections of previous performances in Cardiff. A second manifestation of *Trace: Displaced* was presented on the field of the National Eisteddfod in Cardiff in August 2008, amongst the stalls, stands and pavilions of Welsh cultural and political organizations. Here the replica was in brown chipboard, with grass floor and ceiling open to the elements, somewhat incongruous amongst the white tents and awnings. Whilst maintaining a degree of structural integrity, it resembled rather a full-size *maquette* or more shadowy *simulacrum*.

Four performative interventions of three hours' duration were planned, in which 'references to locations in and around Cardiff are displaced and relocated'. Both interior and exterior spaces and walls were available. Outside, André Stitt posted photocopies of Cardiff street scenes in emulation of bill-posting to advertise fringe events on the field. Inside, Lee Hassell rendered the walls with areas of building plaster. Recollecting imagery from Roddy Hunter's early performance, I worked with a repertoire of objects sourced from local charity shops: ten men's suits, ten pairs of shoes, ten books in Welsh. In each intervention I introduced a new element, positioning them, manipulating them, animating them: suits, shoes and books carried, thrown, worn, combined, cut, shredded. At the end of each session, they were hung as part of an accumulating installation and in juxtaposition with the work of other contributors. Lee Hassell nailed the remnants of shoes into a formal frieze of plaster rectangles. On the final day, it poured with rain. As a handful of visitors hurried past, I pinned together a suit from fragments of other suits, and Hassell plastered me against the wall, a figure of abjection. And as we decided enough was enough,

Eddie Ladd began a complex, improvised dance sequence amongst the debris of performance, alone and unwatched in the downpour.

- What performance would you conceive for *Trace: Displaced*?
- Within this specific context, how might it reference other locations in the city?
- What constraints might working in the public domain place upon the work?
- What materials would you use?
- How might the work respond to, or be mediated by, the various surfaces available?
- Where else might the replica be located?
- How else might the replica be orientated, and built from what fabric?
- How does the replica sit within the existing social or architectural context?
- How might the existing environmental conditions inform the work conceived within it?
- How might the characteristics of the replica, its dimensions, textures and degrees of robustness, mediate performance?

Imagine a single figure in the room moving, then several figures. Then figures with objects ...

4

In which ten sets of geographical, architectural, social and cultural conditions and formulations are described as they inform or impact upon the conception and exposition of site-specific performance.

Landscape

Image 4.1   Simon Whitehead, *Tableland*, Mid-Wales, 1998–99 (Martin Roberts)

In the early 1790s on the Hafod estate south of Aberystwyth Thomas Johnes began to fashion the landscape according to William Gilpin's principles of the *picturesque*, a concept based on variety, intricacy and partial concealments in order to excite active curiosity (see Cumberland, 1996 [1796]). Gilpin acknowledged the active role of environmental engineering even if this entailed building waterfalls. He specified the need for foreground side-screens, with middle and background of differing shades. The ruins and humble cottages and farm animals that functioned as focal points were regarded as more picturesque than monuments. Elements of roughness and wildness were essential, though always tempered by moments of beauty. Johnes constructed paths that directed the visitor to a sequence of contrasting scenes or perfected pictures. There were dynamic contrasts between sheltered paths in the riverside meadows and beside the dark, gloomy depths of the overgrown torrents. The Ladies' and Gentlemen's Walks followed different routes. As foreign travel during the Napoleonic period grew increasingly dangerous and internal communications improved, 'picturesque tourism' developed and Hafod became an important locale on the 'grand tour' of Wales. Walkers become significant figures in a theatricalized landscape, its ordering akin to the scenic conventions of the contemporary stage, though elsewhere they sought the *sublime* – natural features that inspired awe and unsettling fear or astonishment – as illustrated and promoted in Richard Wilson's paintings of mountain scenes in north Wales.

Such large-scale modelling was an extension of the eighteenth-century taste for landscape, the contemplation of which became a cultivated pursuit involving much screwing up of eyes and moving to and fro to get the view right: to see the scene as if through the eyes of painters such as Claude and Poussin. The 'Claude glass', a dark mirror, enabled the viewer to manipulate perspective and condense the landscape into an idealized image. It was only a short step to begin to shape the land itself.

Landscape escapes with difficulty this durable and pervasive formulation as a piece of scenery, a visual phenomenon and a pictorial prospect from a select point of view. 'Understood as a way of seeing, landscape is embedded within the perspectival traditions of Western art' (Wylie, 2006, p. 522). It becomes 'a unit of visual space': a 'visual image of cultural meanings' (Wylie, 2007, p. 91), 'indissolubly associated with a conception of depth' and 'spectatorial epistemology' (Wylie, 2006, p. 522).

Not that these were the only examples of wholesale landscape reorganization in that period. The parliamentary enclosures produced the small fields and hedges still evident today in parts of lowland Britain. A landscape surveyed, measured and quantified, to be laboured in as much as looked at. In Britain there is no wilderness, no untouched natural landscape. Every metre is the product of human intervention.

Landscape is at once a piece of land, a scene, a way of looking, a vista, a thing seen, a form of representation: 'nature, culture and imagination within a spatial manifold' (Cosgrove, 2004, p. 69). Each separate definition might inspire and orientate performative engagements: *distance* and *size* are vital aspects. Where is the work located in relation to those watching it, and how big is it? In Robert Wilson's *KA MOUNTAIN AND GARDenia TERRACE* (1972), giant cardboard cut outs moved slowly across the hillside. In her graduation performance (2000) at Dartington College of Arts, Sally Watkins provided the audience with telescopes to view distant performers. In the late 1960s Cardiff student Frank Triggs planned to colour a one-kilometre square in the Brecon Beacons the same as the Ordnance Survey map, with blue streams, brown contour lines, yellow roads. In *Half Life* (2007) Scottish company NVA built a henge monument in timber and cut geometric viewpoints into the plantation (Farquhar, 2007). In choreographer Sioned Huws's *Cor Meibion* (1997; Huws, 2009) her home landscape in north Wales is internalized, its features represented by shifting arrangements of male singers, female clog-dancers and playing children.

Does performance reach to the horizon? If not, how is it delineated? In Wrights and Sites *Pilot: Navigation* (1998) audience members held up empty rectangular frames 'and composed the sunset they saw' (Turner, 2004, p. 381), focusing on one aspect and disattending to the other elements of the scene.

But 'landscape is not just a way of seeing, a projection of cultural meaning' (Wylie, 2005, p. 245). Neither is it purely a setting for performance. Beyond its primary features of *horizon, atmosphere, ground, things*, it is also a *sensuous display*: 'a variegated scene of perception and action' (Casey, 2001, p. 418). It is a 'domain of experience': 'a charged background of affective capacities and tensions acting as a catalyst for corporeal practice and performance' (ibid., p. 236). It is a locus of affect: 'an intensity, a field perhaps of awe, irritation or serenity which exceeds, enters into, and ranges over the sensations and emotions of a subject who feels'; 'affect thus denotes the shifting mood, tenor, colour or intensity of places and situations' (ibid.). 'By attaching materialities to affectivities, and perceptions to places, the landscape does not structure a subject but orients "a way" of living. Landscapes engender investment not by having or, much less, by "naturalising" meaning but by gathering other narratives, practices, and encounters around them' (Rose, 2006, pp. 548–9).

'Therefore landscape might best be described in terms of the entwined materialities and sensibilities *with which* we act and sense' (Wylie, 2005, p. 245). There is no separation of self from scene: 'the self has to do with the agency and identity of the geographical subject; body is what links this self to lived place in its sensible and perceptive features; and landscape is the presented layout of a set of places, their sensuous self-presentation as it were' (Casey, 2001, p. 405).

'Body and environment fold into and co-construct each other through a series of practices and relations' (Wylie, 2007, p. 144). Performance as a mechanism of involvement, an interpenetration of materialities – landscape as 'a concrete and sensuous concatenation of material forces' – and motilities, 'styles of occupying and traversing' (see Wylie, 2002, p. 251), comportments and competencies. Landscape occasions attentive, performative responses. 'To walk is to pay attention' (Roms, quoted in Whitehead, 2006, p. 4).

Walking appears as a ubiquitous aesthetic activity, 'in resistance to the postindustrial, postmodern loss of space, time, and embodiment' (Solnit, 2000, p. 267). 'To walk; to get oriented; to get lost; to err; to submerge; to wander, to penetrate, to go forward' (Carieri, 2002, p. 18). 'The journey is of less importance than the walking itself' (Wunderlich, 2008, p. 132). And in walking corporeal rhythms are juxtaposed with visual events. Landscape becomes 'a *milieu* of corporeal immersion', 'counterposed by a visionary moment of drama and transfiguration' (Wylie, 2005, p. 242). However, it is affected by 'predispositions, life-world experiences and past–present histories' (Campbell and Ulin, 2004, p. 98).

'There are only varieties of walking, whether these be discursive registers (pilgrimage, courtship, therapy, exercise, protest), or particular modes of engagement (strolling, hiking, promenading, pacing, herding, guiding, marching)' (Wylie, 2005, p. 235). In its forms and attitudes aesthetic performance might emulate Wylie's propositions. The options: to walk, to accompany others on a walk, to experience, to enable others to experience affects, to relate experiences after having walked. The approaches: purposeful, discursive, conceptual, preconsidered, choreographed.

Simon Whitehead's many perambulatory projects (see Whitehead, 2006) result from his learning to walk again after spinal injury. In *Walks to Illuminate* (2005–06), staged at the Yorkshire Sculpture Park, energy harvested by daytime walkers wearing solar hats was used to power lights in the shoes of nocturnal ramblers. In *Lake Guitar* (2005): 'particularly in snow storms, I can often be heard before I am seen'. 'These acts and experiments are made as homage to the place, the meeting of cultures and natures and the resonance of one within another (ibid., pp. 72–3). To be 'in' the landscape may also to be up against it: 'to be dogged, put-upon, petulant, breathless' (Wylie, 2005, p. 240). Conversely, 'to haunt a landscape is to supplement and disturb it' (ibid., p. 246).

In their project 'The Art of Walking: An Embodied Practice' Dee Heddon and Cathy Turner (2009) challenge walking as masculine – 'dizzied by extension and expanse' (p. 235) – and the inherent dangers of valorization of individualism and subjectivity.

Landscape may also be a scene of familiarity for those who dwell there: 'meaning is immanent in the relational contexts of people's practical engagement with their lived-in environments' (Ingold, 2000, p. 168). 'The countryman, the peasant, is someone whose occupation is the country and the land. He occupies it and takes care of it, and he is occupied with it: that is, he takes it in hand and is taken up by it' (Nancy, 2005, p. 55). Landscape becomes embedded with memory. For individuals, daily passages through the landscape become biographical encounters as they endlessly recall previous events and see traces of past activities. Certain places are visited recurrently, along paths that become well worn. Familiarity informs an art, a right way of moving around in the landscape that becomes like a series of known or named locales, linked by paths, movements and by narratives. Paths link familiar places and bring the possibility for repeated actions. Walking then is a spatial acting out, a kind of narrative, and the paths and places direct the choreography. This regular moving from one point to another is a kind of mapping, a reiteration of narrative understanding. Different paths enact different stories of action for which landscape acts as a mnemonic.

'There is some peasant in anyone who belongs and who is taken up with time-and-place, in anyone who makes his own some corner of the here-and-now' (ibid., p. 55). Performance as a pagan activity ...

In Cliff McLucas's final theatre performance *Draw Draw yn ... (On Leaving)* (2000), he laid out the ground plan of Johnes's demolished mansion at Hafod in marble chips on the floor of a large hall in Lampeter. The Hafod Trust is currently renovating Johnes's 'walks' on the estate.

Cityscape

Image 4.2   Pearson/Brookes, *Carrying Lyn*, Cardiff, 2001 (Paul Jeff)

On Saturday 2 June 2001 Pearson/Brookes presented *Carrying Lyn*, the first of its multisite performances in Cardiff. As the audience awaited videotapes ferried by cycle couriers from performers on the street, short theoretical and critical textual reflections on the contemporary city were available for perusal on a long, gridded table, and as audio recordings. They outline perceptions of the city within which *Carrying Lyn* is enacted:

> The city is a congregation of strangers. We can never know more than a fraction of our fellow inhabitants and we can never know the whole geography in any kind of detail.

> The city is a place of diversity and multiculturalism. In order to orientate ourselves, we may be drawn to live in the city with others of our kind in a particular

neighbourhood: our own race, creed, language, religion, background. We may indeed be denied permission to live anywhere else. And here we may attempt to preserve a particular identity through social practice and custom, through our diet, through our calendar celebrations. And all this may give a particular ambience to the neighbourhood – Chinatown, Little Italy.

In the city, we can be anonymous. This perhaps increases our freedom of action. We can be who we want to be, without the pressure of communal sanction. We are free to create the identity we desire through our choice of clothing, insignia, behaviour ... We may do this to indicate our allegiance to a particular sect, gang or place of origin. Or we may adopt different identities for different arenas. But the interaction of strangers is fraught with danger. It has to be policed more rigorously.

Although we may come to know one area of the city in detail – our street corner, local market, recreational facilities – the rest we will only know as isolated locations strung together by journeys. To move around we may even need maps – an A–Z, the Underground plan – and we begin to rely on others, on public transport, to get us there.

French anthropologist Marc Augé uses three simple spatial forms to map social space: line, the intersection of lines, and the point of intersection. In the city, they correspond respectively to paths that lead from one place to another. To crossroads and open spaces where people pass, meet and gather and which are sometimes large in order to satisfy the needs of economic exchange as with markets. And thirdly to monumental centres, places of institutional complexity – town hall, seat of government, palace, cathedral. Routes, crossroads and centres: whilst they may be found elsewhere, they are all found in the city. The notions of itinerary, intersection, centre and monument begin to describe the urban space. Thus individual itineraries in the city are constantly drawn towards centres, where they intersect and mingle. Augé suggests that there is then the possibility for polyphony, the interlacing of destinies, actions, thoughts and reminiscences.

But there is also an absolute separation of public and private domains. Power – bureaucratic, monarchic, economic – accumulates in the city and it may want to protect its practices from prying eyes. We are surrounded by buildings to which access is restricted or denied to us because of our status, because our actions may be against the common good – buildings of government and legislation.

In other places, our presence might be less prohibited than undesirable. For across the city there are places of factional interest – chapels, mosques, Masonic Halls.

In cities, history accumulates. Many live on their rubbish, their debris endlessly accreting beneath the feet. Not only does waste gather but buildings are also repeatedly knocked down, and others erected on their site. Most cities are multi-temporal. The remains of the past are all around us. Architecture survives. Here a Georgian town house exists next to a modern designer home. Some buildings are thought worthy of preservation and restoration. And some fragments of buildings become integrated into others as if they are half-digested: stratifications of past occupations, repairs and constructions, the superimposition of different time-scales. Other buildings are repaired, their function changes. A chapel becomes a disco. Their identity is unstable. And in certain places we may have an uncanny feeling of the auras of the past.

In public, we may require a kind of physical restraint, a kind of decorum that allows the mass to function. Even in fifth-century Athens, the sign of temperance was 'doing all things in an orderly and quiet fashion – for example, walking in the street'.

The city is too complex an organism for us ever to fully know it, consisting as it does of endlessly intersecting narratives. A famous Situationist map of Paris demonstrated that most Parisians only ever moved regularly between three points in the city, their entire life circumscribed by a triangle – home, work, shop. We may not feel so constrained but we do tend to stick to particular routes, creating for ourselves a cognitive map of the city, enabling us to get around.

But if we are to make work in the city how might we begin to sensitise ourselves to its nature and make effective use of it? For instance, if the dominant theme of the city is trade and commerce, what might the sub-themes be? If we call Cardiff 'The City of Rugby' can we begin to make performance which enhances this theme and which defines our essential role within it?

■ How might we deal with the fact that the city is often designed for the able-bodied, middle-aged?

■ Can we create projects with the disabled, the young and the old that begin to question this middle ground?

■ Can we, for instance, create environments which are only accessible by wheelchair, lifts which are four feet high and which occasion the so-called able-bodied to squat and bend?

■ Can we begin to draw maps that take different focal points, creating projects for instance which only operate literally within the sound of Bow Bells?

■ Can we begin to alter the nature of the city itself by planting gardens on derelict sites as has been done in New York, raising questions about environmental degradation?

■ Or in keeping with traditions of street trading can we try to sell food in a way that is other than simply holding it in the hand?

▨ Can we open a different kind of museum or perhaps a zoo featuring 'urban man' as its prime exhibit? Or perhaps provide an alternative tour of an existing museum, drawing attention to overlooked details or creating fictional histories and usages for familiar artefacts and exhibits?

▨ Can we imagine performance for the transport system where potential spectators are available for the longest periods of time? Or over the tannoy of a tour bus? Or in a parked car?

Well can we? Or has the city become such a potentially dangerous environment that any deviance from normal patterns of behaviour might be enough to attract unwarranted attention. Good enough reason perhaps to try.

▨ What kinds of site does the city offer?

▨ How might performance be located on its grid of streets, in its piazzas and squares, in its shops and hotels, in its locales of special interest – museums, galleries, public buildings?

▨ What is the nature of its intrusion?

As Royal de Luxe's *Elephant* (2006) walks across London and La Machine's *Spider* (2008) crawls through Liverpool it is at the scale of institutional parade – military march past, state funeral or religious observance. As Sophie Calle (Calle *et al.*, 2003) follows strangers in the street, with no other purpose than to give direction to her daily life, or audio walkers listen to Janet Cardiff's *The Missing Voice (Case Study B)* (1999) in Whitechapel, performance is barely perceptible in the urban flux. Does it stake its claim to the hurrying mass at a regular pitch in the tradition of the Victorian street performers in Henry Mayhew's *London Labour and the London Poor* (1985 [1861]) or at a site of media attention in David Blaine's spectacular stunts? Is it as fleeting as Krzysztof Wodiczko's projections or Janet Cardiff's texts on electronic advertising hoardings?

▨ What might be said and done in public? At Speakers' Corner? Or behind closed doors, or somewhere between? In the 1970s the performances of Squat Theatre and their audience in the company's shop in New York were observed by passers-by in the street.

▨ Does it draw attention to the contrasting nature of the city in the day and at night, when a place of business and commerce becomes the scene of entertainment and pleasure? Or to other maps of the city, as in Platform's tour, making plain the relationship between companies and institutions involved in the oil business (Platform, 2009)?

▨ Does it utilize inherent systems of transport and circulation? Or those engaged in delinquent practices that challenge architectural order – skateboarders, free runners? Does it draw attention to the common good, as in Goodcopbadcop's breaking of inane and archaic by-laws in Cardiff?

▨ And does it evince archaeological and historical *depth*, drawing attention to that which is hidden, as in the Platform 'lost rivers' project in London, or that which is indistinct, that which has left no trace – sites of vernacular events, scenes of crime?

Environment

Image 4.3   Stan's Café, *Of All The People In The World*, 2005–present (Ed Dimsdale)

Early in 2005 the University of Illinois staged a 'protracted symposium' entitled '*Walking as Knowing as Making*: A Peripatetic Investigation of Place'. Several American delegates spoke of wilderness and the solace of the wild, of one-to-one encounters with wild animals. But Jack Turner, author of *The Abstract Wild* (1996), retorted that Yellowstone National Park is the most mapped area in the USA and that every single large mammal there wears a radio transmitter. In *The Wild Places* (2007) Robert Mcfarlane visits isolated, uninhabited and inhospitable places in Britain where nature holds sway. But there is little that is 'natural' and untouched by human hand on these crowded islands with a long history of occupancy. Any notion of wilderness is difficult to sustain here.

At the Illinois symposium, set in the midst of the so-called 'Jefferson Grid' of plots one mile square, in 'what was once a vast expanse of tallgrass prairie and what is now a relatively homogeneous landscape dominated by corn and soybean, the apotheosis of modern industrialized agriculture' (Brown, 2005), the long-term impact of human intervention was self-evident.

> Far from any traditional destinations and lacking all but the slightest topographic variation, walking in central Illinois often seems an anomaly – acutely out of sync, both spatially and temporally, with our lives, the land, and our expectations for how the two should interact. Given its history this region does however offer fertile ground for any consideration of the relationship between ways of knowing and ways of making. The prairie, perceived by early European settlers to be nothing more than a stubborn impediment to progress, was eventually tamed by the application of an unwavering grid and the invention of the stainless steel plow and steam engine. It is precisely from the vantage of these signature products of the Enlightenment and Industrial Revolution that we can begin to understand the present day configuration and composition of Illinois. (ibid.)

But on disused inter-urban railway embankments the plants of the prairie return, in a microcosmic glimpse of the past: human and natural forces in on-going, dynamic interplay.

In 1985 Bedwyr Lewis Jones published a short but influential article entitled 'Cynefin: The Word and the Concept' (Lewis Jones, 1985). '*Cynefin* is an untranslatable word' he begins, and goes on to consider its cultural specificity. But he does usefully locate the human instrumentally within the environmental: 'it is the totality of the *loca* where one belongs, a *loca* conceived in a much more familiar way than in the terms environment and habitat' (ibid., p. 121). Beyond '*ardal*, the immediate neighbourhood' and 'those ill-defined but well-recognised cultural areas which we call *bro*', *cynefin* is 'that area we feel we belong' (ibid.). 'For most this is the place where we were brought up, the surroundings which impressed themselves upon us in the formative years between five and fifteen' (ibid.). In admitting 'deeply felt ties of familiarity and identification', his formulation is redolent of essentialism and the nostalgia of a Welsh professional class for a lost rural past, and disregarding of contemporary experiences of migration and forced dislocation. 'But then we are country-people for the most part.' But Jones stresses that one can acquire another *ardal*: 'it becomes their adopted *cynefin*'.

There is no distanciation here with regard to scenery. Attachments are 'more homely, more localised':

> our appreciation is not confined to the features of landscape and terrain. We are always aware of the men and women who have lived in these parts and the history which they have shaped.
> *Cynefin* is more than landscape and scenery. It is a piece of earth where a community has lived. (ibid., p. 122)

Jones emphasizes the bond and role of language, of local argot, as 'a storehouse of the transmitted legacies of experiences and imaginative constructions of those particular parts' (ibid.). Tellingly he suggests: 'local speech is a treasury of sensitive response to a total environment of land and sea, weather and seasonal change, animals and birds, flowers and trees, husbandry and craft, and human behaviour' (ibid.).

In this he alerts us to the total composition of environment and all contributory aspects that might orientate site-specific practices. He espouses the local and particular, and traditions of relationship, over more abstract definitions. And he attends to the historical dimension: 'land and language are two strands that tie the Welsh-speaker to his *cynefin*. There are other links such as remembrance of things past' (ibid.). Human history and agency become part of the *loca*, 'a tangled web of tradition'. He concludes with a warning to conservation activists:

> They need to take a man-centred view of habitat – to see the land of Wales as an interlinked quilt of *cynefinoedd* where men and women have lived and talked, where they have worked and suffered and dreamt dreams, where fauna and flora are the background to the drama of human life! (ibid.)

Increasing environmental awareness and growing concerns over degradation and climate change will doubtless impact upon site-specific performance, encouraging practices directly empathetic, or politically demonstrational, or proactive in espousing the recycling of materials and moves towards carbon-neutrality.

The training in Tess de Quincey's 'Bodyweather' project (de Quincey, 2009; Grant, 2006) has antecedents in Japanese *butoh*. It aims to enhance sensitivity to environment: 'exercises in which the performers observed intensively an element of the natural world around them (a cloud, a rock, even a blade of grass) and, through this concentrated attention, attempted ... to emphasise on a cellular level with the chosen element' (McAuley, 2000, pp. 4–5). McAuley notes that what is produced is not 'a body of work, but a body of experience, an exploration of that place through the performers' bodies' (ibid., p. 6). In this assertion of direct, causal links between experience and its rendering as aestheticized movement, analysis through visual or narrative optics may prove inadequate.

In *Home of the Wriggler* (2006) by Stan's Cafe 'the lights and sound are all powered by the cast, giving the show a strange intensity and immediacy'. The company's *Of All the People In All The World* (2003) uses large quantities of rice piled in a mountainous landscape, 'to bring formally abstract statistics to startling and powerful life'.

> Each grain of rice equals one person and you are invited to compare the one grain that is you to the millions that are not. Over a period of days a team of performers carefully weigh out quantities of rice to represent a host of human statistics: the populations of towns and cities; the number of doctors, the number of soldiers; the number of people born each day, the number who die; all the people who have walked on the moon; deaths in the holocaust. (Stan's Cafe, 2009)

Recently, the notion of *cynefin* has informed the design of 'a sense-making framework' (Kurtz and Snowden, 2003, p. 468):

> The name *Cynefin* is a Welsh word whose literal translation into English as habitat or place fails to do it justice. It is more properly understood as the place of our multiple affiliations, the sense that we all, individually and collectively, have many roots, cultural, religious, geographic, tribal, and so forth. The name seeks to remind us that all human interactions are strongly influenced and frequently determined by the patterns of our multiple experience, both through the direct influence of personal experience and through collective experience expressed as stories. (ibid., p. 467)

The 'Cynefin Framework' addresses situations of complexity and informs decision-making, strategy, and policy-making. It aims to help to understand the operation of formal and informal communities and the interaction of both with structured processes and uncertain conditions within a particular context, such as a zone of conflict. From *cynefin*, it acknowledges the existence and potential influence of a wide range of affiliations in a situation. It reflects a paradigm shift in organizational structure and culture in contemporary society, challenging conventional assumptions of order, rational choice and intentional capability. Their model includes three ontological states – order, complexity and chaos – and five domains. Within the ordered vector are the known and knowable. Within the unordered, the complex and chaos. At the centre, disorder. Too detailed to examine fully here, it does drawn attention to the manifold factors, the multiple differing opinions and perspectives, the conflicting knowledges and claims to ownership that might be revealed by, and at stake within, the total environment of site-specific performance. Not only those of site and its inhabitants, but also amongst the artists and their practices.

Kurtz and Snowden's pedagogical process is distinctly dramaturgical. It begins with *contextualization* and the collection of representative *items*: 'communities, products, actions, motivations, forces, events, points of view, beliefs, traditions, rituals, books, metaphors, anecdotes, myths, and so on: they are any items that are important to the sense making process' (ibid., p. 471) – sufficiently diverse 'to allow multiple perspectives to emerge'; concrete enough 'to move away from existing abstract beliefs'. These are appended by 'relevant stories surrounding the issue, drawn from oral histories, collected anecdotes, published reports, historical documents, and the like' (ibid.), drawn from a *narrative database*. Subsequent *convergence methods* include the construction of *composite fables* from anecdotes and the creation of *alternative histories*. The resulting sense-making items are then placed within the framework and the area of possible disorder described.

Focus finally shifts to the boundaries between domains and how the movement of items might effect or lead to asymmetrical collapse, imposition, incremental improvement, exploration or liberation – therein informing policy. Again attention is drawn to the heterogeneous range of items, 'broad but not infinitely so', that might be in play in site-specific performance, and the possible aesthetic and social implications of their inclusion, juxtaposition and movement.

Heritage

It is 3 July 2003 and members of the Centre for Performance Research's Summer Academy stand on a hillside at the head of the Afon Lwyd river in south Wales. To our left are the remains of an early ironworks, across the valley the pithead winding gear of a mine:

> The area around Blaenavon bears eloquent and exceptional testimony to the pre-eminence of South Wales as the world's major producer of iron and coal in the 19th century. All the necessary elements can be seen, including coal and ore mines, quarries, a primitive railway system, furnaces, the homes of workers, and the social infrastructure of their community. (Blaenavon Industrial Landscape World Heritage Site, 2009, *Coity Tip Trail Leaflet*)

We reflect upon creating performance in this 'relic landscape', a former place of mineral exploitation, manufacturing, transport and settlement, and upon the notion of 'site' itself. For, in 2000, all before us was designated a UNESCO World Heritage Site, with the ambition of increasing cultural tourism and assisting economic regeneration. In the combination of all phases of early industrial production here, the nomination document claims *uniqueness*, *integrity* and *coherence*:

> The Blaenavon landscape was the product of the human creativity of many individuals, entrepreneurs, technologists, engineers and workers, over several generations. It is an outstanding example of characteristic forms of human settlement and the exploitation of mineral and energy resources associated with the coal and iron industries in the first phases of the Industrial Revolution. (Blaenavon Industrial Landscape World Heritage Site, 2009, *Nomination Document*, p. 19)

The site is clearly *demarcated*. It is confined to 'land historically leased or purchased to provide minerals, energy and infrastructure for the Ironworks'. However, 'the boundary has been modified where appropriate to conform to identifiable landscape features or to exclude areas of land which have suffered loss of original features'. 'Site' is defined as much by contemporary ambitions and pragmatism as by the extent of historical occupancy.

Within the nominated area are twelve scheduled ancient monuments, eighty-two listed buildings and four sites of special scientific interest (SSSIs). In 'scheduling', nationally important sites and monuments – 'not always ancient, or visible above ground' – are afforded legal protection against disturbance and damage. No work can be undertaken without consent. In the 'listing' procedure, buildings are graded for their architectural and historic significance.

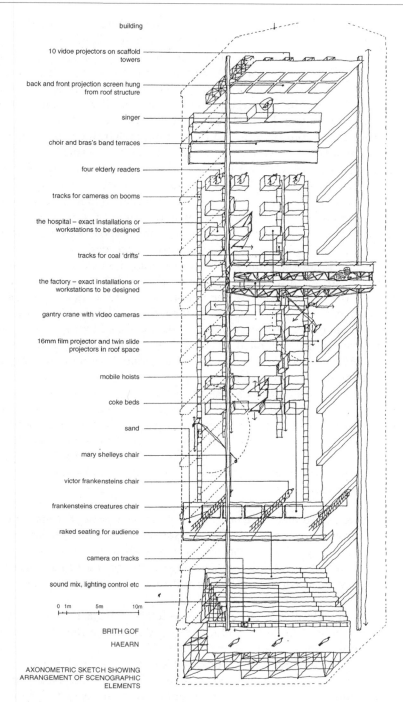

building

10 vidoe projectors on scaffold towers

back and front projection screen hung from roof structure

singer

choir and bras's band terraces

four elderly readers

tracks for cameras on booms

the hospital – exact installations or workstations to be designed

tracks for coal 'drifts'

the factory – exact installations or workstations to be designed

gantry crane with video cameras

16mm film projector and twin slide projectors in roof space

mobile hoists

coke beds

sand

mary shelleys chair

victor frankensteins chair

frankensteins creatures chair

raked seating for audience

camera on tracks

sound mix, lighting control etc

0 1m   5m   10m

BRITH GOF
HAEARN

AXONOMETRIC SKETCH SHOWING
ARRANGEMENT OF SCENOGRAPHIC
ELEMENTS

Image 4.4 Axonometric projection: Brith Gof, *Haearn*, disused iron foundry, Tredegar, South Wales, 1992 (Cliff McLucas)

Whilst they can be altered, extended or even demolished, consent has to be officially obtained. 'SSSIs are the country's very best wildlife and geological sites'; 'it is an offence for any person to intentionally or recklessly damage or destroy any of the features of special interest of an SSSI, or to disturb wildlife for which the site was notified' (Natural England, 2009). In addition nearly half of the area is within the Brecon Beacons National Park, adding a further level of statutory control. Each of the above provides a regulatory definition of site, setting conditions of access and prescribing what might be done there. Site-specific performance will have to adhere closely to the rules.

There are two major sites 'in state care': the Ironworks, where three blast furnaces were constructed in 1789, and the surviving coal mine at Big Pit. Until 1975, when a programme of 'excavation, consolidation and repair' commenced, the Ironworks were in a ruinous state. Now in the care of Cadw, 'materials and methods appropriate to the character of the monument have been used throughout'; 'wherever possible all conservation measures are designed to be reversible' (Blaenavon Industrial Landscape World Heritage Site, 2009, *Nomination Document*, p. 50). Whilst claims are made that 'value has been placed on authenticity', the key here is *consolidation*: presentation abides by current health and safety regulations, decay suspended, the building neither how it was nor otherwise might be. Such sites are easily distinguished by the limits of their manicure. Access is strictly limited, the conditions of entry listed in accompanying by-laws. Again any performance must be negotiated within tight strictures.

An application is a commitment not only to protection and preservation but also to presentation and promotion: 're-enactment of nineteenth century work, living conditions and play will be considered' (ibid., p. 56). In October 2007 BBC Wales broadcast the first series of the living history television series *Coal House* (BBC Wales, 2009). Three families lived in original cottages in Stack Square close to the Ironworks for several weeks, as if it were 1927. The production team took great care to ensure that as much of the experience was as authentic as possible:

> However, we realise that there were certainly some aspects that may not have been exactly right for the period. This was sometimes due to 2007 factors such as health and safety rules. Feather, horsehair or even straw filled mattresses do not comply with modern fire retardant regulations, so we couldn't use them. I think that we've managed to create an authentic look on the whole.

After filming was completed, one cottage was left fully furnished 'to allow visitors to see the living conditions endured by the families in the series', though not, one supposes, those 'endured' by families in 1927.

Abandoned in the early 1980s Big Pit was taken over and run for fifteen years as a tourist destination by former miners. It is now the National Coal Museum. Although the unique underground tour of historical workings remains a popular interpretive feature, the script now contains fewer firsthand experiences and barely suppressed allusions to industrial injustice.

Such sites emerge through vagaries of survival, differential preservation, statutory designation and protection, and contemporary agendas as much as their inherent attributes. They gain additional value by being narrativized in works such as Alexander Cordell's novel *Rape of the Fair Country* (1959), set in Blaenavon against the Chartist uprising of 1839. Rumour has it that the Ironworks were saved from demolition in 1959 only by the prospect of filming the book with Richard Burton and Stanley Baker.

But as we look on Blaenavon it is difficult to know where natural and man-made landscapes begin and end. Although substantial working practices were protracted here, we may need the word of others, in guidebooks and on maps, to direct us to the exact sites of extraction and manufacture.

Sites of more fleeting or transitory occurrences are identified and maintained through sectional interest, albeit for the common good. On Ordnance Survey maps a pair of crossed swords with a year beneath symbolizes a site of battle. Although no physical remains may be apparent, a location is marked and distinguished from its surroundings in perpetuity, the event commemorated. Despite their nondescript nature and lack of definition as a momentary gathering of forces from other places, such sites animate the imagination of enthusiasts. They are enlivened by irregular visits from battlefield re-enactors. And sometimes a whole industry can be built around the event – at Culloden where the battle lasted one hour (National Trust for Scotland, 2009). Or in east London on 'Jack the Ripper' tours where 'You will visit the site of "Prostitute Island"', 'You will see the actual doorway on which Jack the Ripper may have scrawled a sinister message' (Ripper, 2009). And in the absence of obvious traces, the shortfall might be made up by narrative speculation and invention.

Other sites are indicated by a cross or by Gothic lettering: 'Castle', 'Abbey'. These may denote standing relics. Otherwise they are qualified: 'Village (site of)'. Roman antiquities are marked in bold – '**ROMAN SETTLEMENT**' – invariably followed by '(site of)'. Whether remains are apparent at the surface or not, they are all differentiated and cut out of the topographic continuum, identified as sites of interest if the scale of the map allows.

Recent Ordnance Survey series cater for specialist audiences, directing attention to sites of special interest. On the Landranger series the properties of the National Trust and the Forestry Commission are clearly delineated as well as camp sites, picnic sites and selected places of tourist interest and viewpoints. But such distinction seems confounded by satellite navigation systems that prioritize the route without attending to sites on either side.

Many of the disused industrial buildings within which Brith Gof performed in the 1980s and 1990s have not survived. They didn't make it as heritage sites. They didn't get onto the map as a '(site of)'. They were single purpose buildings, annexed in their final moments. They stood within compounds: within systems of barriers, fences and monitored thresholds. They were sites of work, of restricted practices, of site security. They were bounded, defined by enclosure, with distinct insides and outsides. In the 1980s Brith Gof had created 'large-scale events devised for special locations and occasions' (Pearson, 1985, p. 2). Unsurprisingly, the term 'site-specific' appears at this point.

Performance resembles a form of industrial production or *process design*. Process design can involve the design of new facilities or it can be the modification or expansion of existing circumstances. Design commences at a conceptual level and culminates with the creation of plans for construction.

Place

Image 4.5   Polaroid taken by audience member: Pearson/Brookes, *Polis*, Cardiff, 2002 (unknown)

> Place is space in which important words have been spoken which have established identity, defined vocation and envisioned destiny. Place is space in which vows have been exchanged, promises have been made and demands have been issued. (Brueggemann, 1989, p. 26)

In practices biographical, relational and intimate, site-specific performance in the 2000s has reflected the 'placial turn' in disciplines such as geography and anthropology. In reaction to enduring notions of emplacement and essentialism, place is currently regarded as that actively worked, that brought into being:

> what is special about place is not some romance of a pre-given collective identity or of the eternity of the hills. Rather what is special about place is precisely that throwntogetherness, the unavoidable challenge of negotiating a here and now

(itself drawing on a history and geography of thens and theres); and a negotiation which must take place within and between both human and nonhuman. (Massey, 2005, p. 140)

In Walter Brueggemann's formulation then it is the words and promises that constitute place rather than being contained within it.

Older definitions acknowledge investment: 'beyond clothing, a person in the process of time invests bits of his emotional life in his home, and beyond the home in his neighborhood' (Tuan, 1974, p. 99). Place as 'a portion of land/town/cityscape seen from the inside … entwined with personal memory, known or unknown histories, marks made in the land that provoke and evoke' (Lippard, 1997, p. 7). Marc Augé has recently stressed protracted familiarity: 'a place is a space where relationships are self-evident and inter-recognition is at a maximum, and each person knows where they and others belong. Therefore place is also interested in time' (Augé, 2000, p. 10). But other commentators have acknowledged an essentially performative aspect. For anthropologist Tim Ingold, places are knots in multiple and interlaced strands of wayfaring – the basis of dwelling – rather than nodes or containers in a static network. 'The wayfarer is continually on the move' (Ingold, 2007, p. 75). 'Wayfaring, in short, is neither placeless nor place-bound but place-making' (ibid., p. 101).

> To get some measure of control in his wandering he's constantly drawn to familiar places: significant places, memorable places, hidden places, nondescript places. To places where things, important things, have happened but of which only he has the barest inkling. To favourite places: the market stall where the fish are still arranged in floral bouquets. His patch is small and he walks it tirelessly, routine holding him in place, whilst all else is in flux, countless, tiny journeys intertwining and mingling. (Pearson/Brookes and Thomas, *Raindogs*, 2002)

Beyond providing a metaphor for social process, aesthetic performance might itself be place-making. At undifferentiated or indistinct locales within a landscape, it might bring together heterogeneous elements in a moment of absorption, in intensifications of affect: alluding to, referencing, pointing to, summoning and bringing into play memories of people, events and things, and personal, local and disciplinary knowledges. Highlighting previous occurrences here, becoming a constituent of future memory for those present. Complexity is revealed in mundane circumstances: 'the local is also unavoidably heterogeneous' (Heddon, 2008, p. 94).

> He has decided that he will become a street-greeter, welcoming visitors to the city, a city that only he knows. Here on this spot for instance he will tell them, Captain Scott paused on his way to the civic dinner, feeling an icy blast from far south suddenly scour his heart. He knows a thousand such places, unmarked, invisible to those whose feet grind away the streets each day. And these he will reveal: he will become a revelator. (Pearson/Brookes and Thomas, *Raindogs*, 2002)

An important component is the audience itself: 'place as formed out of the specificity of interacting social relations in a particular location' (Massey, 1994, p. 168). At such places, performance engenders a provisional and contingent communality in the here and now. 'At the same time as places are dynamic, they are also about proximities, about the bodily co-presence of people who happen to be in that place at that time, doing activities together' (Sheller and Urry, 2006, p. 214). '"Here" is an intertwining of histories in which the spatiality of those histories (their then as well as their here) is inescapably entangled' (Massey, 2005, p. 139).

In *Way from Home* (2002–08), her work with refugees and asylum seekers in Plymouth, Misha Myers invited participants 'to make a map of a route from a place they called home to a nearby special place that they had visited often. Following these maps as a guide, the mapmaker took a walk in Plymouth, transposing the landmarks of the city to their map of home' (Myers, 2006, p. 213). Working with particularities rather than generalizations, involving significant places and details in a 'self-contained process of self-characterisation', the performance avoids confessional and traumatic revelation.

> The instructions for the walk seemed to offer an opportunity for a more subjective inscription of place through a peripatetic process promoting discourse, dialogue and exchange.
>
> Creative agency is released to the walker through the instructions and does not rely on my presence, which becomes activated more as a catalyst, ally and/or witness. (ibid., p. 217)

Thus 'those co-existing and multiple narrative contexts, histories, journeys and bodily efforts that are involved in the finding and founding of place' are animated by, and find a place within, performance.

There are particular Welsh apprehensions of place, albeit with ill-defined borders. *Y filltir sgwar* is the square mile of childhood: that patch we know in detail, the location of formative events and experiences, but which are ever expanding and without firm edges. As I indicated places of personal significance in my own square mile in *Bubbling Tom* (2000), so performance acted as a mnemonic, 'inspiring animation and reinvention' (Heddon, 2008, p. 101): for the local audience of their own recollections of these same places at other times, and for visitors of other analogous times and places. 'Spectators become equal participants in the performance event and in the performance of place, charged with replotting and reshaping it' (ibid.). Neither exclusive nor exclusionary the square mile is overlain and interpenetrated with the personal maps of others that may include moments of convergence and mutual recognition.

As I showed body scars, mimicked familial physicalities and re-enacted youthful activities, I echoed Edward Casey's axiom: 'the body is the heft of the self that is in place' (Casey, 2001, p. 416).

The body not only goes out to reach places; it also bears the traces of the places it has known. These traces are continually laid down in the body, being sedimented there, and thus becoming formative of its specific somatography. (ibid., p. 414)

Casey notes that we are forever marked by places, tenaciously and persistently: 'we are subjects of place or, more exactly, *subject to place*' (ibid., p. 415).

What you will see, if you look carefully, is the small scar above my right eye where I fell whilst carrying a large bottle of 'dandelion and burdock'. 'You weren't used to carrying pop bottles, that's why you fell. Knocked your teeth back in. Upwards. Nan and me had to hold you down while Topin stitched you,' says me Mam. I've no memory of the event, though of course others remember for me. The scar is still there. And the body begins to bear the marks of its history: the skin a map of accident, injury, labour. Some reassurance maybe that time has passed. (Pearson, *Bubbling Tom*, 2002)

Y fro is neighbourhood, region, *heimat*: the place where we profess to come from. *Brogarwch* the affection it might inspire.

Around the idea of settlement, nevertheless, a real structure of values has grown. It draws on feelings: an identification with the people amongst whom we grew up; an attachment to place, the landscape in which we first lived and learned to see.
But I know, also, why people have had to move … it can become a prison: a long disheartening and despair, under the imposed rigidity of conditions. (Williams, 1973, pp. 84–5)

Whilst *y fro* might, in rural areas, be defined by topography or range of social relationships, between *residency* and *dwelling* there might be an uneasy tension. In 2001 Mike Brookes and I were commissioned to create a performance in a village close to the Czech/Polish border, in the large baroque church undergoing restoration after five decades of abandonment (Pearson, 2006a, pp. 75–9). Situated in the former Sudetenland, the German population had fled the village or were forcibly removed at the end of the Second World War. Czech settlers quickly occupied the empty houses. This history is contentious and still has currency. To draw attention to it, even through valorizing the church as a place of interest, could have proved divisive. So we decided to bring other places of the village into the church as video footage. In one sequence we recorded inhabitants, in the fields, gardens, streets, pointing to where they thought the church stood in relation to their present position. Some had only a vague idea. The church was absent from their mental map. It played no part in their wayfaring, in how they got around. Our performance was their first occasion to visit. To see themselves projected onto the ceiling …

Scenography

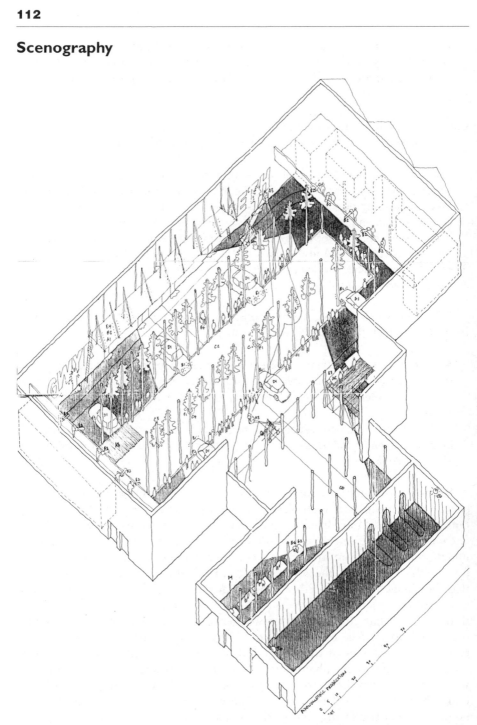

Image 4.6 Axonometric projection: Brith Gof, *Gododdin*, Tramway, Glasgow, 1989 (Cliff McLucas)

In Brith Gof's large-scale, site-specific performances (see pp. 150–6) scenography took the form of construction at the *scale* of the host architecture, though in asserting its distinct identity not necessarily on the same *orientation*. It reached the walls.

In unpublished notes for a lecture presented at Roehampton University (McLucas, 1998) Cliff McLucas reflects upon his approach to the design of *Gododdin*, staged in the machine shop of the disused Rover car factory in Cardiff in December 1988, a space 290 feet by 132 feet with 20 feet of clearance. Included here, at length, it demonstrates his approaches to scenic construction.

First it was suggested that I might think about bringing the outside inside. Second, I might think about breaking the massive space up and that a promenade audience might be moved from scene to scene around this building – rather like a series of outdoor tableaux. I was excited by the first notion but decided to ignore the second!

On my first visit to the site I was struck immediately by the size of the building and it seemed to me that this was the location's most powerful characteristic. Architecturally, this was impossible to deny, but theatrically – from the point of view of the performer, who thinks automatically of having to fill the space – its size was deeply threatening. I decided that this issue – a strange choice between the concerns of the performer and those of the audience – should be addressed and that the 'tableaux' model would have to be replaced. Architecturally, the building was a simple shed structure with roof lighting, a number of structural steel columns, a low building at one end and two big roller shutter doors at opposite ends of the space. There was also a factory clock suspended from the roof space off centre in the huge room.

I decided that the audience should be given the experience of the building's massive 'non-theatrical' scale and so decided that they would enter at one corner, through one of the big doors. Given this first view of the location, I wanted to create the longest perspective possible and so I decided to place an avenue of trees from corner to corner. This meant that the audience could not ignore the immense dimensions of the space, and the avenue also had the benefit of defining three new spaces – a triangle to each side of the avenue and the long thin corridor within the avenue itself.

Next I wanted to suggest to the audience – who, we had decided, would be free to move around the building – where the focus of activity in the room would be and I chose to create that most democratic of arrangements for viewers – the circle. A simple calculation of circumference and audience numbers, together with the logic that nobody beyond three rows back will see anything on the flat, made it clear that we needed to make a big circle the width of the room.

The circle was a circle of sand edged with concrete blocks. Sand was chosen as an active material – it can be made perfect by raking like a Japanese sand garden, it can be transgressed by performers, you can easily move it, bury things in it, throw it, fall onto it and so on. It also carries the marks – physical memories if you like – of what has happened there.

The circle was reinforced by the reorganisation of the industrial fluorescent light fittings in the factory – into a massive circle around the edge of the sand. In addition, a significant water supply on site meant that it would be possible, during the duration of the performance to gradually flood this arena thus converting it from dry, clean sand, to wet ankle deep mud and then of a 'lake' of water – thereby offering a range of implicated physicalities for the performers.

All of this created the impression that the performance would take place in the circle – when, in fact, the spaces 'left over' at both ends of the room would also be used and the 'breaking out' of the circle by performers was seen as a scenographically transgressive act – implicating audience members and allowing and encouraging them to follow and engage with the action.

I needed at least one other element to bridge between floor and ceiling as the trees had done and I decided that the factory clock should be taken as the centre of a 'mountain' of sand. The image of sand falling through an egg timer was in my mind I guess.

Finally, I wanted another scenographic element that ideally should be mobile and, in view of the buildings previous use, I decided to try to get fifty old cars that could be driven around and rearranged into new configurations to define new performance areas. The fact that all cars came with their own built in lighting – their headlights – was a big plus for me. A distaste for theatrical lighting at this point led me to want to work with only the factory's own fluo-rescents, car headlights and four powerful mobile follow spots. (McLucas, 1998, pp. 5–7)

McLucas goes on to explain the practical problems of working at the level of civil engineering: using mechanical equipment to handle the sand, drain-ing the car engines and filling them with water. In the television documentary of *Gododdin* (1990) he explains the significance of the existing architecture: rows of columns and roof lights inspiring the avenue of trees, albeit at a dif-ferent angle. He adds that the perfect circle of sand will by the end of the performance become a perfect circle of water. Such formality pays little heed to the incidental requirements of the performers. Instead it sets the *material conditions* in which they go to work. Although the construction stands in the same space as, and adjacent to, the audience, it may subtly bring about discrete effects.

It may be possible to construct an active environment – of wind, rain, snow, excessive light – in which surface and climate may change from moment to moment and in which irrevocable acts such as flooding the performance area can occur. (Pearson, quoted in Pearson and McLucas, no date, p. 6)

The adoption of a dynamic and creative approach to site and to the creation of an active environment was invaluable in determining what the performers might do – and offered a new set of creative frameworks from which to generate work – frameworks outside the performer's body. (McLucas, 1998, p. 8)

In *PAX* (1990–91) the wind blew. In *Prydain* (1994) drummers played frenetically in their own rainstorm. Significantly in *Gododdin*, an elegy for those fallen in battle, there was no adversary. As they climbed rope nets in jets of water, as the circle filled with water, the performers were overcome by the increasingly arduous conditions, collapsing finally in exhaustion. Whilst performance lacks durability, the ghost has substance.

Gododdin was subsequently reconfigured for staging in a quarry in Italy, a crane factory in Hamburg, Germany, an ice-hockey stadium in Leeuwarden, Friesland, and the hall of Tramway in Glasgow. Given the complexity of the construction – effectively three-dimensional project design – each version was accompanied by a *workbook* giving full details of how to build the scenography at a specific site, with attendant drawings, plans, sections and diagrams, in subsequent projects computer generated. In addition to floor-plan and section, site and construction were represented by *axonometric projections*, looking down from an angle of forty-five degrees. The workbook for Leeuwarden notes that the 8,000 sandbags forming low hills and increasingly distinct islands, reflecting the local landscape in which villages stand above the drained fenland on man-made features or *terpen*, should be 'laid in such a way as to provide a highest point towards the rear of the hill' to accommodate the audience; also that the layer of sand should be seventy-five millimetres deep and 'red/yellow rather than grey/white'. And of the ten disused cars, that 'they will not go back to their owners in the same condition in which they arrive' (McLucas, 1989, pp. 13–15).

In reflecting on his design for *Tri Bywyd* (1994), McLucas reveals his architectural proclivities:

> I had also been concerned with the unplanned use and transformation of buildings – industrial lofts to apartments, streets to processions, hospitals to offices and so on – and had tried to develop a set of attitudes that would bring together built and conceptual architectures, and implode use and enclosure. (McLucas, 1998, pp. 13–14)

He also reveals the growing perception of his role: 'the demarcation of labour in these works had to be quite different to other theatres – and the role of scenographer/director began to merge as a key discipline and as a clearly necessary role' (ibid., p. 8).

Materiality

Why make theatre in eccentric locations?
A. A range of techniques, materials and phenomena (such as cars, fire, rain, wind, large volumes of water and so on) immediately become possible.
These techniques or materials may be of the nature of the site (an iron foundry, a garage, a railway station) or they may not. This may or may not be important.

Image 4.7   Brith Gof, *Rhydcymerau*, Disused cattle market, National Eisteddfod, Lampeter, West Wales, 1984 (Dorian Llewellyn)

> In theatres they would either be impossible (for legal, safety or 'aesthetic' reasons), or they would appear perverse. (McLucas, 1993, p. 3)

The lack of seemliness at site, its non-pristine nature, may allow, or necessitate, the use of resources, substances and working practices unseen or even illegal in the auditorium: the unusual, the imprudent, the downright dangerous. Animals, machinery, vehicles, trees. Site may supply significant amounts of power and other utilities. Its plumbed-in facilities may require expert and specialist management. It may permit the inclusion of equipment and apparatus not conventionally considered part of the expressive repertoire of theatre, confounding audience expectations and upsetting patterns of critical apprehension: 'real trees, real oil drums, real cars and I think that introduces into the heart of the theatrical discourse, a whole array of questions about reality and pretence' (McLucas, quoted in Morgan, 1995, p. 46). In their regular and eccentric motions, such phenomena may augment the kinetic momentum of performance. In *Gwynt, Glaw, Glo a Defaid* (*Wind, Rain, Coal and Sheep*) (1992) rocks rattled round in a cement mixer as a white-clad maiden from a Noh drama walked slowly across a floor of coal. In the third version of *Los Angeles* (1992) two large industrial fans lift the newspaper that covers the floor, sending 'waves' into the audience.

The sixth of Haearn's architectures is that of The Grid. In contrast with the sophisticated and continuous 3-D space generated by contemporary robotics, the key mechanical components of the Industrial Age such as the wheel, the track, the pulley, and the lever all generate limited and reduced movement in three dimensions – up and down, left to right, forwards and backwards. All movements in Haearn arise from this mechanical agenda. (McLucas, quoted in McLucas and Pearson, no date, p. 11)

If the stage is by nature *synecdochic*, a part representing a whole, then site is often a scene of *plenitude*. If theatre is characterized by *omission*, then site-specific performance exists within a *plethora* of phenomena, all competing for attention, all potentially meaningful: a concatenation of that *at* the site and that brought *to* the site.

In a real site there is very rarely the plain backdrop favoured by most modernist art forms – the white gallery for showing pictures, the black theatre for creating clear outlines. The removal of clutter and the suggestion, through framing, that events and objects may be separable and visible in high contrast to each other against their bleached out context, is a difficult strategy to sustain in a contemporary cultural landscape. (McLucas, quoted in McLucas and Pearson, 1995, p. 1)

Performance may include materials in exceptional quantities, ratios and configurations, such as 8,000 breezeblocks in Station House Opera's *Bastille Dances* (1989):

Everything follows from the simplicity and mobility of the blocks. Gesture, imprisonment, release, support, removal of support, enclosure, shelter, concealment, exposure, entombment, resurrection, bringing together, splitting apart, are simple functions of performers moving blocks in relation to each other. (Maynard Smith, quoted in Kaye, 2000, p. 172)

Their handling and manoeuvring might blur 'the distinction between work and performance' (Pearson, 1985, pp. 3–4), their engagement and manipulation generating dramaturgical material. Performance may however be ill-equipped or under-resourced to deal with them, needing modes of engagement with the same element of risk of health and safety as to the original workers. And 'bodies can and do become overwhelmed' (Thrift, 2008, p. 10). 'Only when a block is dropped is the weight understood. Only when a wall collapses is danger apparent' (Maynard Smith, quoted in Kaye, 2000, p. 181). And in addressing the materials of site: 'the action of performance may emulate or mutate previous activities and behaviours at site: the physical manifestations of the processes of work, play and worship' (Pearson, quoted in Pearson and McLucas, no date, p. 11).

In performance diverse objects without natural affinities of origin, provenance and type can be drawn into heterogeneous, hybrid *assemblages* that include the juxtaposition of the historical and the contemporary in forms of purposeful *anachronism*. This may proceed through processes of *accumulation*, the gradual identification of what is needed to achieve this or that. Or by *imposition* of a design concept that prescribes a closed *repertoire* of items that must fulfil all functions. The choices are of similarity and difference – only red things, one thousand spoons. The assemblage may achieve coherence in its evocation of setting. Or it may be wildly eccentric, a separate reality, existing only in the special world of performance.

Performance is not discrete and may combine found objects, those appropriated from everyday life with those fabricated and made for the task that coexist in this special world in extra-daily combinations and conjunctions. If found, an object may be chosen for its intrinsic characteristics and qualities: its appearance, patina, texture, feel or size. It may need to be appropriate to a particular period, location or governing idiolect. Always redolent of other times and places it renders the assemblage *multitemporal*.

It may also be selected for its *fit*: its ergonomic potential – feel, balance, weight and dynamism in usage. For in performance the object is *double*. Within the dramaturgy it may serve overlapping functions of representation, in the creation of character identity and social situation. It is also one of the 'tools of the trade' of the performer. It enables him or her to go to work, to function *in* performance. During the period of rehearsal, it may be invested with value and meaning by the performer. It may then function as an aide-memoire for that state of mind and body necessary to complete the task of performing. On an operational level, it may become the locus of nostalgia, reliable old friend, providing orientation, performance after performance, through the familiarity and the superstitions this often engenders. In this, it may resemble a fetish. Its loss in transit can cause personal and artistic crisis. And it serves as a talisman, tying each performer back to the months of research and rehearsal and the gradual clarification of intent and meaning, some tangible proof of hours worked and of a process now made manifest and at risk in performance.

If *fabricated*, an object may be a *replica* of its everyday equivalent, though made in different materials, to different dimensions and at different scales. It may be unable to stand the rigours of quotidian usage, of weight and force, and may necessitate alternative ergonomic engagements. Or it may be a work of *invention*, provided for a specific purpose or as a fantasy of imagination, but present only within this special world.

Fabricated objects are frequently designed, conceived and constructed to a governing artistic, stylistic or aesthetic concept or tradition. Such conventions set the parameters for the assemblage, limiting, for instance, the range of materials and techniques of fabrication to be used and the hierarchies of scenic arrangement to be employed. It may exist as a proactive strategy or as a list of prohibitions.

Objects stimulate action, facilitating interaction and exchange: 'in addition to "determining" and serving as a "backdrop for human action", things might authorize, allow, afford, encourage, permit, suggest, influence, block, render possible, forbid and so on' (Latour, 2005, p. 72). Objects have agency: '*any thing* that does modify a state of affairs by making a difference is an actor – or, if it has no figuration yet, an actant' (ibid., p. 71). Objects and actions adhere: 'things become part of hybrid assemblages: concretions, settings and flows' (Thrift, 2008, p. 9).

Performance might favour certain things for their ostensible semiotic potency and flexibility. Irit Rogoff notes the rhetoric of luggage, 'suspended between an unrecoupable past and an unimaginable future' (Rogoff, 2000, p. 39). Others because of their ability to transform:

> And who will forget the use of sawdust to create the outline of the trees on the stage, and the secret of the sack of bones which grew into an animal's skeleton, there on the same floor where animals were bought and sold for generations. (Rogers, quoted in Pearson, 1985, p. 15)

Objects are inherently unstable, serving representational, decorative, functional, fictive or cognitive purposes, moment by moment. Their identity and meaning may be only partly controllable.

At site, it may be difficult to distinguish what is in play. Anything that has passed the boundary into performance may be assumed to be significant. However prosaic or banal, nothing will remain neutral or simply decorative. And the audience will search for, and generate, meaning in everything they see. Whatever the nature of the assemblage, its animation may resemble a work of *bricolage*, an improvised response to an environment of fixed resources, a way of making sense with the materials at hand.

> Use one (or multiples of one) basic article of furniture within the performance area.
>
> 1) Use it (them) functionally: e.g. sit on the chair.
> 2) Use it (them) for space delineation: e.g. standing on a rug constitutes immunity from performance laws.
> 3) Use it (them) for their properties: e.g. making a sculpture out of tables. (Howell and Templeton, 1976, p. 71)

Virtuality

Image 4.8   Composite image: Eddie Ladd, *Stafell B*, Aberystwyth, 2004 (Jamie Andrews)

In their introduction to the *new mobilities paradigm* Sheller and Urry consider pervasive computing and connectivity 'on the go': the appearance of machines 'miniaturised, privatised, digitised and mobilised', 'closely interwoven with the corporeal' (Sheller and Urry, 2006, p. 221). The effect they suggest is to produce 'novel and "flickering" combinations of presence *and* absence of peoples, enemies and friends' (ibid., p. 222). As screens proliferate in cameras, laptops, telephones, there are enhanced opportunities to record and transmit imagery. What now constitute everyday practices were only recently at the edge of technological experimentation.

In 1995 Brith Gof created a work-in-progress entitled *Estronwyr* (*Strangers*) with Catalan company La Fura dels Baus. After a period of rehearsal in Barcelona, I returned to Wales. During the performances a small audience gathered in the Trade Centre in Cardiff where we could witness events in Spain relayed to us – though often highly pixilated and at no more than one frame per second. We could also send images to the performance – colour pictures of Patagonia, of weapons – from a mounted camera, and then witness them projected in the performance on the video returned to us. This early example of video conferencing known as Integrated Services Digital Network (ISDN) required equipment operated by the Spanish telephone company and two separate phone lines, one for sound and one for vision. What is now a commonplace was only feasible in a special suite. Whilst mobile telephony has been increasingly adopted in site-specific performance, less attention has perhaps been paid to the television screen *as* a site of performance.

In 1989 Channel 4 television broadcast *A TV Dante: The Inferno Cantos I–VIII* by Tom Phillips and Peter Greenaway (Greenaway, 2009), a series of short films that superimposed recordings of actors, narrators and commentators, and found and sampled visual material, including natural history footage and the animated photographs of Eadweard Muybridge:

> The eight Cantos of the film are not conventionally dramatised, rather they are illuminated with layered and juxtaposed imagery and a soundtrack which comments, counterpoints and clarifies. There are visual footnotes delivered by relevant expert authorities, and these often perform the function of narration as well as illustration.

The result is a dense overlay of references, symbols, allusions, people, events and animals. Much of the found footage is manipulated and degraded. At one point there are, by repute, thirteen layers of imagery. Experts – historians, biologists, behaviourists – appear in small boxes inset into the overall composition of the frame, to comment upon moments in both the text and the constructed visuals. Again, the orchestration of sound and image was, at the time, achieved through the application of computer programs available only to broadcasters. Today such editing is possible on a domestic laptop. *A TV Dante* directly inspired a series of televisual works by Cliff McLucas responding to and taking advantage of the opportunities offered by regional broadcasters BBC Wales and S4C.

A Oes Heddwch? (1990) was created for the Welsh-language music video programme *Fideo Naw*. Named after the appeal made to the audience as a large sword is opened and closed above the head of the winning bard at the National Eisteddfod – 'Is there peace?' – it addressed the then contemporary campaign of house burning by Meibion Glyndwr. And it established the keynotes of McLucas's signature style: first that the screen is a physical site and material can be arranged and composed over the whole area within its borders. Second, that different orders of visual material can be simultaneously superimposed and 'boxed'. Third, that all words spoken are present on screen as printed text that can be scrolled both up and down and from side to side. Fourth, that both visual and aural components can contain original, sampled material: voices and events from the past can be made immediately present.

A Oes Heddwch? is bilingual. On screen the Welsh text in red is confined to a column on the left, scrolling bottom to top, the English in blue to the right. Samples are taken from political pronouncements of the past forty years including Saunders Lewis's radio broadcast *Tynged Yr Iaith* (1962) that stimulated the birth of the Welsh-language movement. Those in English include an aggressive interview with activist Helen Prosser by Jeremy Paxman. The words 'Fe godwn ni eto' ('We will rise again'), in white, scroll right to left recurrently. But the video sequences are not mimetic, showing rather a complex doubling and repetition of suspended figures and conflagrations against a pounding electronic soundtrack. Controversially, it ends with a fictional telephone conversation between Meibion Glyndwr and a police duty officer that was assumed, in the context, to be an actual recording: 'You couldn't speak English could you? I'm terribly sorry I just don't understand you at all'.

PAX TV: Y Fam, Y Ddeaear a'r Angel (*The Mother, The Earth and the Angel*) (1992) reworked motifs from the large-scale work *PAX* (1990–91) surrounding the lonely death of an elderly Welsh woman whose son is an astronaut. Eleven minutes long, it was filmed in a house in Devil's Bridge outside Aberystwyth and broadcast by BBC Wales.

Again all text in the soundtrack is present on screen, travelling from right to left. But with four voices potentially in competition, each is always confined to the same horizon. At the top, the soprano voice of the angel. Then the son as he describes the earth, and the appearance of heavenly creatures. Next the woman speaking her doubts and fears. And finally the scientist, explaining processes of global warming. The words move at the speed of their speaking, creating a sense of on-screen dynamism.

Again imagery is placed in boxes that themselves travel and then haemorrhage into the full screen, though slightly out of sync. Motorized cameras attached to tracks gave a down-facing view of the bedroom and the woman's collapse, extending out through the windows into the yard and over the road as an aged tractor passed vertiginously below. As the camera flew in and out of the room and time-frame, all edits were on the window-frames. Prior to recording, the bedroom was redecorated and a replica ceiling built in the village hall.

Suspended through this ceiling as the angel, I could appear to hover in the room when videoed from a track below.

Y Pen Bas, Y Pen Dwfn (*The Shallow End, The Deep End*) (1995) was originally conceived as a live performance for a swimming pool and video wall that proved financially prohibitive and technically too complicated. Reconfigured as a fifty-six minute work for television, it involves two worlds: below the water historical events relating to the flooding of Cwm Tryweryn by Liverpool Corporation and, above the water, the story of Robinson Crusoe that 'embodies all the wealth, power and certainty of the English coloniser'. These worlds meet literally on screen, as it is split horizontally. In the upper section, two Crusoes are shipwrecked and take refuge on a floating pontoon. In the lower, performers in breathing apparatus rebuild their community from the flotsam – house, chapel, post office, school. Recorded with extreme difficulty and necessitating framing a sequence in only half the viewfinder, it included startling underwater scenes. But the action was again schematic. The complexity came in the mix of voices on the soundtrack reading Defoe and accounts of Tryweryn from library sources and specially convened interviews with political activists. For long periods a female voice recites the names of drowned farms.

John Rowley played Robinson Crusoe. His own video work in collaboration with director/cinematographer directly references site-specific performance. In *Sound Effects of Death and Disaster* (2001) his distracted and dishevelled figure wanders deserted streets in Sheffield. Occasionally his short choreographies, quickly conceived in relation to elements of architecture, such as a doorway or lamp post, are accompanied by extracts from a 1960s BBC 'Sound Effects' record, often used in amateur theatre. The recordings set durations rather than suggesting actions: in 'Collapsing Mine Shaft 28' he balances on a handrail in an underpass, face pressed against wall. In the final 'Three Men Screaming 8' he plunges into an inspection pit full of water.

In *Lost Sounds of Wales* (2001), made for the BBC Wales 'Double Yellow' arts programme, he returns short recordings made in the 1950s and 1960s to the sites of their registration. As Sally Jones of Tregaron relates how her corgi is named after Miss Wales in 1961, Rowley stands mainly out of focus under an umbrella in a chapel graveyard.

In *You Are My Favourite Chair* (2004) a couple, alternately frenzied and lethargic, inhabit rooms in the disused St Pancras Hotel, using its furniture and fittings. She almost drowns him in the bath. He photographs her vomiting on a sofa. The opera singer heard distantly on the soundtrack is in the room next door. In *Dark Sounds for the City* (2005) Rowley returns to sound effects. At different sites in Cardiff, performers are asked to undertake actions for precise durations without knowing which library recording will subsequently be added – as an elderly woman tries to drink tea from a rattling cup in a new show house, the wind blows. And as I stand shirtless in the distance, on the roof of a council-owned tower block, the tallest building in Cardiff Bay, flood waters rise.

Connectivity

Image 4.9   Eddie Ladd/Cliff McLucas, *Lla'th* (*Gwynfyd*), Felinfach, West Wales, 1998 (Cliff McLucas)

In May 2001 BBC Wales holds a one-day conference in Cardiff on new technologies. The event includes an early experiment in live *streaming* but, as I begin speaking, the *feed* switches to happenings in another room, a moment that demonstrates the irreconcilable gulf between the highly regulated practices of broadcasting and the potentially profligate freedoms of the desktop. For my presentation commences with a short video downloaded from a website prepared by Mike Brookes that shows a man apparently being put to death, stabbed in the neck. I then reflect on the nature of this fragment and upon all those who might also be watching, elsewhere:

1) Load and play.

1/1 What the ...? (silence)

1/2 What is it, this four-second clip, extract, sample, file? Free-floating, without label or credits or signature. Documentary footage or fake? Absolute truth or total fabrication? Verisimilitude? Fiction?

And is it already too late in the day to say or to care, one way or the other?

1/3 And if this is what I think it is, what is it for, and where does it come from? And how did it get into my house, so swiftly, so easily, or is that already an anachronistic, rhetorical question?

1/4 And *if* this was, then *who* was this? The one with hair cropped close, from vanity or necessity or obligation; the other gloved, red-sleeved, from duty or desire.

1/5 And if this was, then *where* was this? And is it regret for a failure of international will or nostalgia for faded youthful beliefs that makes me want the snowy, rocky backdrop to be in Kosovo?

1/6 And if this was, then *why* was this? As a good deed, a punishment, an act of benevolence, a simulation or a drama?

1/7 And if this was, then *when* was this? Ten minutes ago or yesterday or thirty years ago or just now ...?

1/8 And if this was, then *why* is it bereft of context: all detail of person and place and time, of the effect on other lives, once lived in hope and now in grief, once in plenitude and now in loss?

1/9 And if this was, *why* do we see only this single action – cropped, clipped – and nothing of what happened before and after, much before and much after? Or at the same time ...?

1/10 And if this was, is this the first person I've ever seen – apart from grainy wartime footage – being purposefully put to death, on camera, in close-up, clinically, for my benefit, in the knowledge that I'm watching, whoever I am? And why can I not avert my eyes? And why does it draw me back again and again even though I know how it turns out?

I go on to consider the onset of the *digital*, directly referring to, though without referencing, Zygmunt Bauman's notion of *liquid modernity* (Bauman, 2000). How does it unsettle all three terms in play: site, specificity and performance? What new forms of creative activity does it anticipate? What are its salient features?

First, that all data can be rendered as the same code: as combinations of 0s and 1s, as 'on' or 'off'. That all is now potentially of the same order of signification: as contemporaneous *equivalence* in the homologization of information – personal, academic, military, demographic, genetic. Whether on screen, in mixing desk or adrift in virtual environments, everything is potentially a *sample*, thus problematizing questions of origin, authorship, status and authenticity and enabling the convergence and interpenetration of knowledges, once regarded as having no natural affinities, into new arrangements and leading to new approaches and attitudes to the notion of 'source material', and to history itself.

Then, that the spatial notions of 'solid modernism' collapse: Cartesian concepts of near and far, here and there, inside and outside, of distance as a unit of time, are confounded. Old polarities of centre and periphery, regional and national, rural and urban are challenged. And on the Web, itself already a limited two-dimensional notion, there is no limit to the *depth* of our enquiry.

That we enter the *post-panoptical*: by definition, the Web and the Net are not *places*. They offer no favoured viewpoints or perspectives from which to scrutinize the terrain. They are not available for visual representation as maps. They are constituted rather as interaction.

That this leads to *deterritorialization*: geophysical boundaries are permeated and compromised. Capital and power become increasingly extraterrestrial. Labour becomes disembodied. Call centres can be anywhere. Notions of strategic or defensible space lose there usefulness ... or perhaps become more poignant. We know the theatre of war is no longer spatial, but do the civilian casualties know that? And, ironically, there are increased opportunities for surveillance.

That information flows: the essential metaphors of the digital are of liquidity, fluidity, porosity. No institutions are sacrosanct from pollution or cleansing. Our chief anxiety here might be of disorder, for no one seems to be in control.

That as anything can become a *sample*, so cultural resources can be activated and animated as never before, resonant voices from the past *re-presented* in contemporary contexts. Whilst the movement of such free-floating signs and their juxtaposition and integration can lead to new and startling dramaturgies, such reordering is not simply aesthetic. It is also political.

That the twin dangers of cultural (mis)*appropriation* and *commodification* of the past are thus ever present. The ethical responsibilities of the artist become ever greater. The attendant questions will be of *origin* and *authorship*: what material is being used, where from, for what purpose, on whose behalf?

That as data is rendered contemporaneous and contiguous, there is the potential for disciplinary and genre breakdown: challenging old monopolies of representation. Data from art/science/pedagogy and the practices of auditorium/museum/lecture theatre can meet in new contexts, in new taxonomies, as new genres. What commenced as the movement of knowledge in academia, money in international banking and coordinates in the military can now draw together phenomena with no previous or natural affinities.

That place no longer solely defines identity: we become members of multiple communities, of shared interest and value. We are at liberty to create our own electronic identities: out there, we are disembodied, depersonalized. In worlds beyond the optical, our anonymity is assured. This might aid democratization in eradicating distinctions of race, colour, ethnicity, gender, age. A fixed address no longer defines our citizenship. And as the relative values of inner (here) and inter (there) offer no advantage if both are instantaneous, we might be tempted metaphorically 'to leave home'.

What might be the implications, practical and metaphorical, physical and virtual, for site-specific performance? First, the opening of new kinds of representational space: *temporary autonomous zones*, strips of activity where positionalities are redrawn and where meaning is negotiated into temporary and contingent existence, with constant oscillation of fragmentation and integration, where no prior judgements as to the suitability of dramatic material are made and where there are no predetermined solutions, no guaranteed happy endings, no crisis resolution, no closure: radically unfinished work.

The reconfiguring of the performance *object* as *fluid field*, and as *encounter*: as interaction and negotiation. Moving from *ostension* to *interlocution* with the emergence of the *dialogic*. To the *blurring* of disciplinary, originary and informational boundaries – between art and science, creative and critical, academic and professional. To the *deterritorialization* of *practice* that becomes unstable as it moves across *platforms*, equally appropriate in auditorium, museum, theme park, lecture theatre, on website, digital television, crime scene reconstruction. To the reordering of *hierarchies* and *taxonomies* of significa-tion within the dramaturgical matrix. To the idea of a *general public* replaced by multiple communities of *shared interest* and value, rather than of location, within which new identities might be created and espoused. Within such inde-terminacy, the main questions may be:

> 10/2 Can I still take a stand, offer a point of resistance, a shunt, a point of capture, without need of empathy or compassion or understanding or affinity or pity or sympathy or the taking of sides?
>
> 10/5 Can I demonstrate my ethical purpose, this condition of being-for, this pro-found and consequential 'responsibility for' the other, without any good cause or hopes of reward or for change?

In Cardiff, I conclude:

> 10/9 Can I open a new kind of representational space to create contemporary meaning, like this one, without the need for any of us – you, me, him – to throw ourselves into a lovers' embrace, into the clinch of drowning men?
>
> 10/10 And what was it, this thing Pearson and Brookes just did? Was it a lecture, or a performance, or a demonstration?
>
> Of this I'm certain: someone was killed and however many mail groups and chat rooms and streamed conferences we participate in, as Goya notes in a caption to one of his 'Disasters of War' series of etchings: 'this always happens'. (see Hofer, 1967)

Inaccessibility

> At least we didn't have to eat the dogs. (Ron Shields, *On Ice* participant)

It is 9 April 2003 and a group wearing crampons halts on the Franz Josef Glacier:

> a blinding white expanse, water running every direction over the ice into bot-tomless holes of deep blue, brilliant turquoise ice pockets, the sound of liquid always moving beneath the surface. After spending a half hour alone on the ice, each of us devised an activity, an action, to share with the group. (Marilyn Arsem, *On Ice* participant)

Image 4.10 *On Ice* workshop, Franz Josef Glacier, New Zealand, 2003 (Marilyn Arsem)

We are towards the end of *On Ice*, an itinerant workshop held during the Performance Studies international conference PS9 at the University of Canterbury, New Zealand.

For three days we travelled together by minibus, seeking out traces and relics of, and sites related to, the 'heroic era' of Antarctic exploration (1895–1917), aiming to highlight the historical significance of Christchurch, and to appreciate the role of organizations and institutions situated there in polar research. We were drawn into interdisciplinary encounters with local academics, curators, experts and artists in lectures, presentations and guided tours. We visited museums, archives, heritage sites and tourist attractions. We got a feel for the ice on mountain and glacier.

Our joint ambition was to develop provisional expertise in polar matters: 'an ability to talk expertly with experts, to get beyond the basics, to get into the minutiae, devilish detail and puzzling pieces that provided the bread and butter of our research. We pursued facts, and around these wove creative speculations' (David Williams, *On Ice* participant). To work creatively together, in reference to our new and expanding collective knowledge. To consider related matters – the nature of site-specificity – and how our specific visits and meetings might provide inspiration and subject matter for performance. We focused upon issues of masculinity and heroism, imperialism, tales of exploration, shortfalls in polar narrative, historical and contemporary mediated representations of Antarctica, improvisation in extreme circumstances, heritage management and museology, tourism, ecology, 'polar theatre' and expeditionary entertainments (see Pearson: 2004; 2005a; 2009).

In preparation we read works of polar literature. During long hours on the road and in late-night bars our talk was incessant. We met the director of Gateway Antarctica, who showed us a woman's 'urine director'. The retired curator at Canterbury Museum, who showed us Amundsen's pocket knife. Archivists in the museum collection, who showed us the book Shackleton's crew printed. Guides at 'The Antarctic Attraction' who described the effects of cold on human physiology, and the problems of cleaning brushes for artists. And the chief executive of the Antarctic Heritage Trust, who showed us a DVD of Shackleton's hut. We went to Lyttleton Museum and Akaroa, birthplace of Frank Worsley, and to the Banks Peninsula. We rode a 'Haglund' snowmobile around the International Antarctic Centre at the airport, and drank at Bailie's Bar, as had Scott's crew. We related favourite polar tales and personal experiences of site work. We devised individual performances for the 'Snow and Ice Experience', a room filled with forty tons of real snow that we entered in polar clothing. And as we couldn't go south, we went up, up the Franz Josef:

> by the time I was climbing the glacier with my team of fellow explorers, my head was filled with images of human endurance in the least hospitable conditions on earth: running noses with mucus immediately turned to icicles by the chill-wind; men amputating another's frostbitten toes; eating their own fingers in the delirium induced by winters of total darkness; men shaving for photos in absolute survival conditions; cross-dressing; subsisting on whale blubber and Emperor penguins ... or each other! (Gretel Taylor, On Ice participant)

This was essentially work by proxy – dream work – work in relation to, and in evocation of, a place inaccessible for most of us: though in 2007 David Wheeler of IOU became British Antarctic Survey artist-in-residence (IOU, 2009). But site-specific practices, conceptual and practical, may yet illuminate pressing issues of interpretation in Antarctica itself.

In the Ross Dependency are five wooden buildings, the expeditionary bases of Borchgrevink, Scott and Shackleton, with many of the provisions still intact. Scott's Terra Nova hut contains 8,000 inventoried items – clothing, food, utensils, scientific apparatus, furniture, animal carcasses. Ordinary objects in extraordinary settings, in deposits that extend across the immediate terrain. Although these prefabricated buildings were intended for occupation over only one or two winters, they have survived in the exceptional circumstances of isolation and of preservation: unvisited for forty years, the Terra Nova hut gradually filled with ice, becoming in the words of the New Zealand based Antarctic Heritage Trust (AHT) a 'frozen time capsule'. The AHT is currently engaged in a project to survey, stabilize, conserve, restore and reconstruct these surviving, and powerfully evocative, places, and their contents. It is further charged with displaying and interpreting them for growing numbers of tourists.

These are fragile places. Accumulations of snow annually threaten the timber frames. The salt-laden atmosphere bleaches wood. High winds disperse loose objects and blast scoria against outer surfaces. Higher temperatures and humidity, occasioned by visitors, increase rates of biological decay and metal corrosion. Tourists' boots abrade the floor. At the Nimrod hut, it is Adélie penguins that trample the site and coat it with guano.

And they are complex places: all here is not what it seems. The interiors are not just as they were left as if for our future apprehension, a unique glance of the past just as it was. What survives is incomplete. It is that which was not consumed – that which was surplus to requirements or had served its purpose. That deemed of neither further use nor value, not worth bringing back by expeditions always in financial straits. That left, altruistically, for future parties. In the interim, the sites have been repeatedly entered. During the 'heroic era' itself, huts were visited and inhabited by each successive expedition. They foraged, scavenged and raked over remains, reordered internal layouts, moved stores from one site to another, reused materials. Each hut is a *palimpsest* of Edwardian expeditionary activity.

More recently, objects have been pilfered, stolen, removed for safekeeping or exhibition elsewhere. In the 1960s American sailors bulldozed surrounding 'rubbish' into the sea. There have been well-intentioned attempts at clearing, tidying, restacking: scattered and rotting stores regarded as threatening 'the cohesion and visual unity of the site'. Visitors have repeatedly repositioned artefacts to dramatize the locations, or to make them accord with period documentary photographs and written accounts. All this leads to uncertainties of sequence and chronology. Claims of authentic restoration using the material at hand might be regarded with scepticism.

At the Nimrod hut the AHT plan involves rebuilding lost features, reconfiguring the original layout, removing subsequent additions, replacing and even replicating iconic artefacts, the original ambition to reflect better its main period of occupation, as if the men had just walked out in 1909 (AHT, 2003). The intention was to recreate, or more properly create, a particular historical moment. But such restaging risks becoming a *simulacrum*: a perfect replica, including replicated objects, of something that never existed in the first place. It is admitted however that contemporary arrangements resemble 'a set for tourist photographs'. If so, what alternatives do site-specific practices offer?

Explorers wrote about themselves and their companions, both human and animal, in diaries, published accounts and scientific papers. Men were filmed and photographed at work and play by official photographers. Less formally, they recorded each other. Surviving objects are pictured *in situ*, and men and animals stand in places still discernible. Text and image allude to and illustrate objects and events that are observable in both museum collections and in the on-site archaeological record: documents and artefacts mutually reference each other. There is here an exceptional opportunity to draw together people, places and things. Close scrutiny of the material record, in combination with the recovery of the day-to-day experiences of explorers from documentary record, might inform the standing arrangement and exhibition of an interior. Drawing together objects into contiguities and discordances of type, function and appearance that confound simple attributions of period and provenance, as in Peter Greenaway's projects to reorder museum collections (see Greenaway, 1991). Or Shimon Attie's projected realignments of original photographs of prewar Jewish buildings and population on the same surviving architecture in Berlin (Young, 2000, pp. 62–73).

The use of recorded media might make present 'absent' performers. For example, multiple audio guides employing different, synchronized tape sequences instructing various audiences to visit dispersed locations where certain kinds of conflicting or contradictory historical and topographical information is made available. In so doing choreographing the visitors themselves. Recent work on combinations of GPS, locative media, web-casting and mobile telephony might make available performance being created at locales *remote* from the huts themselves.

But given their parlous state, perhaps they are best left unvisited. The conservation reports of the AHT contain full structural plans and inventories (AHT, 2003; 2004a; 2004b). The Trust's website includes a three-dimensional photographic impression of the interior of the Nimrod hut (AHT, 2009). What might be achieved elsewhere: scenographic and mediated overlays of different periods and accounts; or virtual, three-dimensional simulations of interiors in a Cave Automatic Virtual Environment?

In the final moment of *On Ice* we gather at Kathleen Scott's white marble statue of her husband in Christchurch. What, we wondered, would a commemoration of Shackleton's stranded crew look like? We pose with expressions of abject terror.

Context: Exercises

In which a number of applied and tested explorations of site are listed: to inspire and stimulate practical initiatives by the reader.

Micro walks

Micro walks/remote instructions for the group:
Solo exercise. Using A4 paper, take one minute to draw the house you grew up in (eyes closed, non-dominant hand) (after Whitehead, quoted in Savage, 2004).

On another sheet of A4 paper draw a plan of your route from home to work. What have you included and excluded? How are features, identified as significant, represented? Does the plan fit onto the sheet? Can a colleague decipher it and if not, why not?

Island, forest, disused steelworks

Upon visiting an island, or a forest, or a disused steelworks:

- Use your own body – stride, orientation, range of sight and hearing – as a device of measurement for surveying the location. What is recorded, what excluded?
- At five points write texts of fifty words to describe the place: topography, sky, flora, fauna, weather.
- Take two photographs. What do you choose to record?
- Recover one object.
- Use the data gathered to create a map of the location in another medium at another scale elsewhere. What is its symbolic order?
- How might you describe the location for an audience, using the records generated if desired?

During the KnoWhere Project on Lundy Island 2000–01 the remit of participants was 'to engage with the natural light in this island landscape with their differing sensory capabilities and to develop material for their collaborative artwork' (Warr, 2001, p. 8). Partially sighted artists used heightened aural and olfactory sensitivity, tactile experiences and 'bodily and facial resistance to wind and weather' (ibid.) to inform later creative practices. Felix Mood's photography was 'not distracted by a plethora of detailed visual information' (ibid.).

> A map is a kind of diagram but unlike other diagrams it does not reduce, it represents and abstracts space but retains coordinates for imaginative engagement with a place – through its colours, shapes, place names, representation of materials and forms. (ibid., p. 11)

During the Centre for Performance Research Summer Academy (2002), back on the mainland after a day on Ramsey Island off the west Wales coast, one group made an edible map, eating their way through it whilst describing both topographic features and their experiences of the visit.

A site that can only be entered once

Upon visiting a site that you can only ever enter once, or under special conditions of time or access:

- What might be achieved within the limits set?
- What are your strategies for remembering?

- What would you have remembered had you gone without a camera?
- How can you tell about it elsewhere, particularly if it is a place of desertion?
- How can you reproduce it elsewhere at a different scale?
- Conduct a guided tour at a place you have never visited before.

Later, elsewhere, relate the same tour: describe what happened, show what happened, then show more slowly. Recreate the experience for not more than five minutes and at a smaller scale.

Studio space

In a studio space, conduct a guided tour of the house in which you live, somewhere that you can visit, in detail, in your mind's eye.

- What do you point out?
- How do you show and tell?

Watch and listen to the tours of others. After a time, undertake their tour.

The square mile of your childhood

Using the square mile of your childhood, describe favourite places, the best places for this or that activity, the places where you heard this or that and where significant things happened.

Public domain

In The Arcades Project artist Jennie Savage proposes multiple engagements with the late Victorian and Edwardian shopping arcades in Cardiff whose viability is jeopardized by recent adjacent retail development: 'exploring the place between public spaces, town planning, constructed landscapes and the human story: the lived lives and personal narratives connected to those sites'. 'Working through a process that uses archiving and intervention she seeks to map the other life of a place or community in order to reveal a complex situation, a micro-structure or simply an unheard voice' (Savage, 2009). The Portable Cinema, housed in an empty shop, programmed films such as William Raban's trilogy *Under the Tower*, shot around Canary Wharf and recording the changes in London's East End as it was transformed into a major financial centre. In the documentary web-based archive project *Multiple Voices* Savage outlines the following research process:

Getting started:

1. Choose a subject from the list below and start thinking about how you might respond to this.
2. Book a one-to-one session with me and the technical manager to discuss your ideas. Bring along any preliminary notes, pictures, sketches. We will be available on Fridays and one weeknight per week. Please email to arrange a time. During this meeting we will put together an action plan and also discuss the ways in which we can help you with your ideas.

Subject headings:

These subjects could be responded to photographically/using film/mobile phones/writing fiction/observational or site specific writing/using sound/drawing ... etc. (basically anything which can be made into a digital format – e.g. drawings that can be scanned, etc.).

- People: 1. People who work in the arcades; 2. Shoppers; 3. Arcade characters; 4. Portraits of people and their shops; 5. Arcade observations.
- Space/place: 1. Design/motifs; 2. Architectural details; 3. Space/volume; 4. Movement through the space; 5. Entrances and exits; 6. Materials.
- Shops/stalls: 1. People/shop keepers/shoppers; 2. Goods on display; 3. Window displays; 4. Fashion; 5. Exchange.
- Time/change/transformation.

Notes:

1. Anyone can take part. Your commitment could be one afternoon taking photos or writing notes in the arcade through to the production of a feature film. All contributions will be very gratefully received.
2. All work submitted will be included in the archive and credited to its author; you will also retain the copyright of your work and are free to use it in any other context.
3. However, I reserve the right to contextualize your contribution in whatever way I feel best suits the project.
4. We cannot supply equipment or help with money to cover materials, however we can supply technical support and computer based back-up.

Add performance to Savage's list of approaches. Given that the arcades are privately owned and that permission for expositional performance is unlikely to be forthcoming what might be attempted covertly, or achieved elsewhere? Try repeating Savage's project in another context.

During the first workshop of the Arts and Humanities Research Council network 'Living in a Material World: The Performativity of Emptiness', participants spent two days in Bristol Temple Meads railway station, pursuing individual and group projects to reveal the nature of the site (see p. 23). How the active engagement with and practising of space creates our material experiences of place. The presence of absence, the plenitude of emptiness ... In preparation for the subsequent symposium, network organizers Jo Carruthers and Angela Piccini collaborated with discussant J. D. Dewsbury to ask the following questions that might be applicable to the visits above:

1.
- What is the direction behind the enquiries you made of the site?
- Is there an agenda – in terms of pedagogy, ideology, practice or philosophy – behind what you set out to do there?
- What do you believe in (in terms of why you investigate such sites in the way you do)?

2.
- In what ways was the body central to your enquiries into place and space?
    - the ways in which you are drawn to the affective locations and ecologies within the site?
    - the visceral impact of the space itself and the flesh of other bodies (including the wear and tear left on the material fabric of the site)?
    - the experience of the duration of the workshop (e.g. in terms of emotions and the relations with other participants)?
    - the perspective and orientation of the senses?
    - the question of animal and non-human presence (e.g. bricks, electrical cables, plumbing, electromagnetic waves, etc.)?

3.
- For your investigations on the day, what was the present time, the enacted 'now', of the emptiness of the site?
- Were you aware of trying to avoid the dangerous attraction of memory and the erasures enacted by remembering?
- What are you re-animating or is it more an animation of the site?
- Are there 'present' ghosts or traces of 'absent' past inhabitations?
- Are the material traces of past occupations loss or an affirmative force?

Questions for the symposium on the day:

- What are the products of the weekend investigations – do all participants *accept* the products of the others (the objects of text, idea, thought, image, action, event, trace, etc.)?
- To whom are these investigations addressed – what kind of *subject* is the audience?

In a creative address to place Miranda Tufnell and Chris Crickmay suggest:

> Making a place
> In an empty space ... choose a spot

Collect ingredients
three chairs … four bones … a newspaper
a reel of cotton … twigs … feathers … red paint
Make a 'place' with the elements you have collected
Move … write … view with a partner
To explore the stories of the place you have made.
(Tufnell and Crickmay, 2004, p. 227)

Miniature performance

Create a performance for a very small area such as a table-top or a part of your anatomy (Howell, 1999, p. 180).

Context: Project: FIBUA, SENTA, Sennybridge

In which a site and its current usage are described. The reader is invited to conceive hypothetical addresses to the same location that might further reveal or critique the particularities and complexities of its existence and of its unique potentialities.

Image 4.11   Training facility: FIBUA, SENTA, Sennybridge, Mid-Wales, 2007 (Mike Pearson)

Site

The ranges of SENTA, the Sennybridge Training Area, cover 24,000 hectares of the upland landscape of mid-Wales, with Mynydd Epynt to the north, and a series of streams and small rivers running south to the Usk. In a process repeated elsewhere in Britain as part of the national need and war effort, it was requisitioned in 1940, and a population of 219 individuals from fifty-four homes were moved out, never to return. There were no nucleated settlements here but this was a populous place of scattered farms, crossed by drovers' roads, with a school and chapel on its southern fringe. The eviction was swift. Farmers were given only fifty-seven days to sell their livestock (Hughes, 1998). There was a deal of political clamour. Both activist and pacifist Saunders Lewis and the young Gwynfor Evans, first Plaid Cymru MP, addressed public meetings. The population never returned. The British Army has occupied this landscape for the past sixty-eight years as they have other parts of Britain (Wright, 1995).

The remains of the chapel are still visible, though it has been taken down to knee-height for reasons of safety. Behind it are the ruins of the farm Tir Bach, setting for T. C. Thomas's short drama *The Sound of Stillness* (1959) in which ejected farmers plan to defend their homes. A plaque marks the site of the school. There are Bronze Age cairns and the bridges, culverts and painted murals of Italian prisoners-of-war. But the army's presence is everywhere now evident. They have a long-standing relationship with the place. They've named it – Burma Road, Canada Corner, Range D, Albert Square. Mapped it with their own unfamiliar symbolic system. Altered it, positioning and regularly renewing targets that become points of focus in a fairly simple terrain: a timber and canvas village here, an armoured car there. And modelled it purposefully: creating plantations with ready-made clearings to facilitate firing artillery 'out of cover' in years to come. Essential to this bond are the ways in which they recurrently reimagine it: training for the jungle in a pine forest, for the desert on a Welsh moor land. Move through it: orientated by admonitions to start and finish, large signs bearing the letters 'S' and 'F'. Perceive it: as always 'going forward', to another point, point to point, at speed; as generic, as nowhere in particular, as potentially anywhere. Experience it: frequently head down, in close up – as sustained attention, as moments of intensity, as moments of self-hypnosis, 'go in, go in'. Engage with it: 'blending in', 'deadly still'; then, 'springing forth'. Regard it: as a place where someone is always trying to kill you.

In the south of the range stands FIBUA, Fighting in Built-Up Areas, a set of buildings that purportedly replicates a German village, from an era when the Third World War would be fought on the plains outside Hanover. In fact it was built in the early 1990s, from the plans of an existing mock community on Salisbury Plain. Once, it might have been Northern Ireland, today Afghanistan or Iraq. But lacking windows, it resembles rather a deserted community in Bosnia *after* the conflict: burned out tanks. Or windows shuttered, a sink estate, awaiting demolition: burned out cars. Its *emptiness* is profound. This is a place where grave stones have neither names nor inscriptions, where darkened rooms have trapdoors and creeps, where the barn bear no trace of agricultural labour, where there is no plumbing. Where there is the odd pile of spent cartridges, an emplacement of ammunition boxes, scrawled graffiti hinting as ad hoc constructions of homeliness but not a single bullet hole or sign of domestic decoration. The living would be tough indeed here, and always on-view, from the control room in the church tower, via multiple video cameras.

First memory. On a grassy patch, they had laid out coloured tapes, each empty rectangle representing a room, conjoined rectangles, a floor. Here, in full sight of the instructor, they learn the *choreography* that will ensure best practice – survival – once inside the darkened interior of a house: rehearsing individual and group dispositions until they become second nature.

Second memory. Behind one building, we encountered a small infantry group, in ear-protectors, preparing to enter. In a looping line, they moved from one side of the door to the other, at an unhurried tempo. 'Ah,' said the range commander, 'they're going in *slow-time*.' They were 'marking it through': that procedure we use in physical theatre when developing a choreographic sequence, without the need to expend excessive energy. And then in they went. The couple of desultory bangs didn't impress him much.

Third memory. On a slight rise, there is a house that has no front: opposite, a small grandstand. A place to watch two flows simultaneously – attackers/defenders, pull/push, give/take – in cut-away. Enactments, simulations, *scenarios* …

This landscape is ever expectant. It is the visiting units that decide what they will at SENTA: topography drives tactics. The nature of the exercises is not random. Each has particular objectives, specific sequences and desired outcomes, *dramos* even, of the most elemental form. And in this, they resemble the theatrical *scenario*, a term the military itself has, of course, annexed. Scenarios enable the army to think through situations, to test for weaknesses. Whilst the scenario is enacted locally, it is presented as universally valid. Its outcomes will hold good anywhere on the world stage, though of course it is only as powerful as the biases that drive it. The danger surely here is that subject to the will of the scenario, anything might be possible: a suspension of human responsibilities to the prerogatives of the plot.

FIBUA silently waits. Units put together scenarios from a known repertoire of elements, whilst acknowledging the need to make something different happen: to counter complacency, the risk of mishap; instilling vigilance against enemies unseen, anonymous, and, ironically at FIBUA, absent. The ordering and reordering of structural moments as a kind of dramaturgy …

These empty spaces, little more than architectural drawings, resemble Tschumi's 'pure spaces' with the intrusion of troops as the 'simple body movements' he imagines to animate them. Military scenario as *programme*, variously congruent with, indifferent to, in conflict with the architecture: an experimental space where the military might test the strategic and operational significance and efficacy of articulations of place and occupancy. The houses as places of shelter, as locations where danger lurks, as somewhere to be simply traversed: action and spaces generating meaning, revealed in the detail of the encounter – frame after frame, episode after episode, in moments of fear, mutual reliance, solace.

Brief

In light of the information above:

- How might performance inhabit the various spaces at FIBUA?
- How might it emulate the military scenario in its dramaturgy, in the distribution of its scenes at site, in its conventions and protocols?
- In what ways might it annex the technologies of the army: its hardware and paraphernalia, technologies of lighting, vehicles, field kitchens, etc.?
- Does the audience arrive in army trucks? Are they separated into smaller units? Are they cast in a role? Do they move from one locale to another in the village?

If military scenarios are inevitably imaginary and predictive, what results from their implementation and aftermath in theatres-of-war? Consider stories returned from Bosnia and Afghanistan and Iraq, from Guantanamo and Abu Ghraib, of combatants, insurgents and civilians alike. The domestic in the military rather than the military in the domestic ...

- What narratives might be invoked here, what haunts the place: those of the original inhabitants, of the processes of dispossession and dereliction, of political response, of nascent nationalism, of lingering local discontent, of the defence of just causes, of heroism in adversity, of misjudgement and war crime?

At the house with no front, for an audience seated in the grandstand, imagine a performance:

- How do the dimensions of individual rooms prescribe what might happen there? How are they linked? Is action simultaneous or sequential?
- How are the bare spaces furnished, the grey breezeblock walls decorated? What effects might be plumbed into this architecture?
- Given the resilient fabric of the building, how might water and smoke and other effects, inadvisable in the auditorium, be employed?
- What is happening outside as well as inside the house?
- How are the minutiae of intercourse relayed to the audience – the voices of performers, their facial expressions?

It may help to draw the house in outline as a template.

At the centre of the SENTA range, on Mynydd Epynt itself, is the so-called 'impact zone', a no-man's land fired *into* for sixty years, its soft soil absorbing the shells without forming craters. Under normal circumstances this is the most dangerous place in Wales, shrouded in taboo and superstition, where even the army fears to tread. A place resistant to either *scenario* or *programme* and perhaps susceptible only to *concept*: to the truly hypothetical, to the *projection* of speculations and dreams and performative imaginings *onto* a place we can never visit. A place that problematizes site-specific performance as the easy occupation of a benign locale.

5

Scenario: Dramaturgy

In which a cumulative series of conceptual and applied practices in making site-specific performance is described and examined.

Event: the nature of performance

Image 5.1 Brith Gof, *Gododdin*, Kampnagel, Hamburg, 1989 (Friedemann Simon)

> Projects that implicate action, place and viewer can only help to suggest that things are, indeed, more complicated than we might like to think. (McLucas, quoted in McLucas and Pearson, 1995, p. 1)

Any outline of the characteristics of site-specific work might usefully begin with suppositions concerning the nature of performance itself: regarded here as *bracketed activity*, as *special world*, as *sensorium*, as *field*, as *site of cultural intervention and innovation*, as *utopia*, as *heterotopia*.

As bracketed activity, performance has a demarcated beginning and end, describing a fixed period of endeavour. At site and within the continuum of the everyday, it may need to work hard to distinguish itself, to indicate that it has come into being, that it should be attended to, that it has now completed its business. Sometimes it will announce itself, unequivocally publicized and scheduled to take place in a certain location at a certain time, or make its presence felt through the intensity or scale of its intrusion. As La Machine's giant mechanical spider walks across Liverpool European City of Culture, all eyes turn. It may be evident in the levels of rhetoric employed by performers, though this may be difficult to tell apart from social histrionics, in the differential levels of *energy* articulated against *time* (using more or less energy over more or less time than might be anticipated for a similar activity in everyday life): in *modifications* of physical and vocal resources, in the *transformation* of recognizable activities of work, play and worship. It may require degrees of cultural competence on the part of the audience 'to know it when they see it'. At other times, it may slip imperceptibly into the cracks in the urban fabric, apparent only to those 'in the know'. Brackets may appear suddenly. They may be of varying strength and durability. And since site persists through time, its features are always in play. The brackets are already there in the moment of the audience's arrival.

As special world, performance is set aside from everyday life by contractual arrangements and modes of behaviour. It is conceived, organized, controlled and ultimately experienced by its varying orders of participant. At site, it is superimposed onto and implanted within the real world where it may function as skewed optic or irritant.

As sensorium, performance works with and on all the senses of the audience. The visual need not take precedence. In any moment it may favour one or other sense. At site, it may offer an audience new sensual experiences. It may also struggle against persistent factors of noise, heat, odour ...

As field, the constituents of performance are ordered topographically. At site these mingle with, and are inseparable from, extant and cognitively active phenomena.

As site of cultural intervention and innovation, performance is a place of experiment, claim, conflict, negotiation, transgression: a place where preconceptions, expectations and critical faculties may be dislocated and confounded. A place where things may still be at risk, such as beliefs, classifications and identities. At site, in places unmarked by the conventions of the auditorium and social decorum, performance may have enhanced opportunities to do this.

As utopia, performance envisages the righting of wrongs and the nascence of a new social order. At site it may do this at the very locales of that which is under critique – on a street corner, in a council chamber.

As heterotopia (Foucault, 1986), performance resembles a counter-site site that can call upon, make present, represent, contest and invert all the other real sites in a culture. At a real site, it gets complicated!

In a series of unpublished documents and lecture notes from the 1990s, Cliff McLucas posits programmatic definitions of site-specific performance. Informed by experiences of conceiving building-based work at that time, his insights may still have resonance and inspire further initiatives in practice.

> At their best, works of the nature of *Haearn* – works that fold together place, performance and public – have no natural edges or frame to hold their identity discrete, no clean backdrop against which their outlines might be thrown into crisp focus, and they do not rely on containment for their identity and their integrity. A 'bastard' theatre, it is theatre 'to the horizon'. (McLucas, quoted in Pearson and McLucas, no date, p. 12)

> Such works have the characteristics of a complex living thing – (how is it being done? and by whom?) – and therefore feel 'real' and 'natural'. A whole world can be created and peopled. This 'naturalness' might create the impression that the work came easily into the world, or even that it was always there waiting to be revealed. This is not true. (ibid., p. 13)

> Such works – operating in three dimensions and time – have the characteristics of the 'field' rather than the 'object'. They are enigmatic, inasmuch as any one viewer may pay more or less attention to any one event in such a multi-focus field of material. For the viewer, they are inherently non-hierarchical – any one of the work's components may, at any one time, provide the 'centre' or 'datum' round which other materials are working, but the responsibility for fulfilling this role is not carried by any one 'prime' component (as for instance does the script in a piece of orthodox, narrative theatre). (ibid., pp. 13–14)

> Such works bring together a gathering of interpenetrating, but discrete, discourses jostling to create meaning. They take on the characteristics of a hybrid. As a hybrid the work's parts will never fully coalesce – and it will contain irreconcilable 'differences' within its field of material. (ibid., p. 14)

> Three
> Some key characteristics of Brith Gof's site specific theatre works.
> This new definition of 'the work' in site-specific pieces of theatre has a number of characteristics and implications.

> 1. The work is a broad field – operating in three dimensions and time – a constellation of materials of different natures such as text, sound, physical action, image, etc.
> 2. It is highly sophisticated and probably not pre-conceivable in all its detail (but each detail is a part of a network and its effects may cause ripples through many other details).
> 3. It is only controllable (once up and running) in fairly crude ways 'after the fact'.

4. It is enigmatic – inasmuch as any one viewer may see something different to others within a multi-focus field of material. Watching an audience watching such work is not like watching an audience watching tennis. That is, their heads do not all turn in unison, and more often than not, within any close group of audience, individuals will be watching different things.

5. This work raises the question of definition – what and where is the work? How is it pinned down? How is it approached? Analysed? It is difficult to think of many other art forms that will allow, and even encourage, such a multiplicity of readings.

6. The 'work', therefore, tends to escape definition, description and photography – there being no 'outside' vantage point on which to stand. The only tactic is for particular sets of details to be gathered and re-arranged in an effort to encompass or 'hold' the work for consideration.

10. It may contain irreconcilable 'differences' within its field of materials, and tends not to constitute a single, unified 'ideal audience'.

11. At its best, it is not possible to separate out or 'disentangle' different elements, since the tactical, day to day bleeding of the one into the other is an important process in the life of the work.

12. And so on, and so on.

13. Can we say, therefore, that pieces such as Brith Gof's large scale, site-specific theatre works, inasmuch as they generate a work that is an integrated hybrid of performance (the ghost), place (the host) and public, are formally discrete from other theatres? (McLucas, 1993, pp. 6–7)

Significantly he would add retrospectively (on *Haearn*):

> Site as a term was beginning to include meaning and historical part narrative as well as the formal built architecture, and place began to feel like a more useful term than the more abstract term site. (McLucas, 1998, pp. 12–13)

Context: the influence of location

> *Haearn*'s host, Tredegar, is constituted in a complex network of History (World, British, Welsh, and Local), Politics (Socialism, Internationalism, Communism, Nationalism), Culture (Language, Work, Community) and Economics (Iron, Steel, Coal). (McLucas, quoted in Pearson and McLucas, no date, p. 3)

At site, social, cultural, political, geographical, architectural and linguistic aspects of *context* may inform or prescribe the structure and content of performance. They may constitute a *brief*, recommending or requiring particular modes of engagement: to unlock the site, to reveal the multiplicity of its constituent narratives, historical, architectural and environmental. And to use it as resource as well as source in contemporary acts. Performance may directly

Image 5.2 Eddie Ladd/Roger Owen, *Unglücklicherweise*, Barn, Maesglas Farm, St Dogmael's, West Wales, 1994 (Jesse Schwenk)

reference such aspects, or it may unwittingly rouse them. Any encounter with site is potentially divisive, recovering that which was thought lost – reawakening memories, stirring emotions, mobilizing causes. Disputes over ownership, over the proprietorship of interpretation, will surely follow. In its engagement with history and politics, issues of 'ownership and occupation, individual and group identity, power, boundaries, rights of inclusion and exclusion, memory' (McAuley, 2007, p. 7) may recommend circumscription. Context is ever-present, unavoidable. Performance may need to tread carefully, or at least accept responsibility for what it might disturb.

It is 11 September 1998 and delegates of the Centre for Performance Research 'Peoples, Places and Pasts' conference are at Maesglas Farm near St Dogmael's in Carmarthenshire, for a second time. Earlier, Roger Owen had presented an audio tour of the outbuildings of this, the site of his upbringing. In three separate sheds, taped accounts of childhood memories played. One recounted superstitions and terrors, of the demon tongue that will lick your finger as you put it through the circular hole to lift the latch on the cow-byre. A second invited the audience to regard a range of objects – tractor, bailer, agricultural implements. Only gradually was it apparent that most were absent, that Owen was describing the scene and familiars as it appeared in the mid-1970s, through a filter overlaying the extant and neglected architecture. Now, delegates are directed to the former milking parlour where, standing in the stalls, each is invited to don a simple, cardboard Friesian cow mask. Maesglas was once a dairy farm located in a thriving regional industry, now much diminished by European Union quotas and over-production elsewhere. Over the next hour Owen's sister Eddie Ladd leads the herd along paths difficult to discern that were once walked four times every day by cattle, almost of their own volition. What could have been ridiculous becomes a poignant evocation and commemoration of past practices. As the figures plod silently, or gather to chat, or stand apart trying to get some purchase on the event from an external viewpoint incidentally drawing attention to them, they highlight the condition of a landscape once populous, now emptied. The knowledges in play here are personal, familial and local, but the resonances of interventionism broader.

Roger Owen has plans to map the stands where milk churns once stood for collection, at the end of farm lanes throughout the region. And to conceive for these small elevated platforms a short *anterliwt* (interlude) after the popular dramatic form of the late eighteenth century. He aims to reveal not only overlooked and often overgrown features of landscape but, incidentally, the economic and political policies and pressures at a variety of scales, regional, national and international, to which their abandonment might be attributed.

Maesglas has provided the inspiration and setting for several of Ladd's performances: 'there's nowhere that's going to let you stick in six tons of corn and leave you to it for 6/8/12 weeks or whatever so we did it at home in the potato shed' (Williams, 2005, p. 6). In *Unglücklicherweise* (1994) she emulated sequences from Leni Riefenstal's film of the Berlin Olympic Games *Olympia* (1936), diving in a cone of barley ringed by straw bales. In her long concern with tensions and elisions between greater and lesser narratives and fascination with Brian de Palma's film *Scarface*, Maesglas recurrently appears. In the video *Miami: West Wales* (2000) her choreography, based on Al Pacino's performance, is located in bedroom, wagon shed and yard. In an extended studio version of *Scarface* (2000) her live movements are simultaneously superimposed on projected imagery of house interiors and landscape by 'blue-screen' technology (Ladd, 2009).

On 17 June 2001 artist Jeremy Deller restaged one of the most violent confrontations of the 1984 miners' strike that occurred between police and pickets outside a coking plant in the village of Orgreave in South Yorkshire on 18 June 1984 (Deller, 2009). Close in date and giving an impression of the weather in which miners had sunbathed and played football and police become overheated in their uniforms, in a field close to the now-demolished plant and finally in the village streets, Deller's main conceit was to collaborate with historical battlefield re-enactors to reimagine an event within living memory. Enthusiasts played police on foot and horseback. Miners were drawn from surrounding communities. Whilst the details of the various events and skirmishes of the day – notably the appearance of NUM leader Arthur Scargill walking in front of police lines – were drawn from documentary sources and the oral testimony of those originally present, the choreography and rules of engagement taken from the conventions and practices of re-enactment, clearly demonstrating the artifice of the event. Each of the various cohorts of police was formally introduced to the crowd: those with round Perspex shields, those with long shields, used for the first time in mainland Britain at Orgreave. And a commentator described 'the intricacies of various police formations' (Roms, 2001, p. 125). 'There were groups of people everywhere telling each other how they remembered the events of June 18, 1984. This was the project's greatest achievement: that it conjured up the shadows of the past in the resurrection theatre that is our memory' (ibid., p. 126). Inescapable amongst the shadows lurked the Thatcherite project, the dismantling of British heavy industry and the enfeebling of unionism.

In 1968 Robert Kennedy undertook a two-day tour through impoverished communities in Kentucky. In September 2004 John Mapede restaged the visit, on site, with local performers, 'in order to hold an historical mirror to present day issues and ideas':

> Local citizens, some of whom saw Kennedy as schoolchildren in 1968, will play national figures; children will play their parents; today's political and community leaders will play their past counterparts. The construction of memory and commemoration is one context; environmental sacrifice and economic self-determination another; federal policy promises and failures yet another – the project exists to reveal both the imbalances inherent in our society and the extraordinary work and workers attempting to expose and rectify them. (Malpede, 2009)

However, as Gay McAuley observes and tacitly cautions:

> Locally based spectators experience an enhanced kind of creative agency in that their knowledge of the place and its history may well be deeper than that of the performance makers, and they will continue to frequent the place after the performers have left. (McAuley, 2007, p. 9)

In June 2001 playwright Ed Thomas and I began a conversation. For eighteen months we met at 4.30 p.m. every Friday afternoon. Initially our talk rambled. It was the schedule of discussion that was significant. Eventually we focused upon Cardiff's bid to become European City of Culture 2008, the slogan for which was taken from Thomas's play *Songs from a Forgotten City* (1995): 'Take me somewhere good'. As the city, once the major port of the south Wales coalfield, now capital of Wales and seat of the Welsh Assembly, seeks a post-industrial identity, hurriedly disguising or dismantling its past, large parts of the dockside have been redeveloped as leisure amenities though, in a failure of civic will, Zaha Hadid's winning design for a new opera house went unbuilt (see Crickhowell, 1997).

How might the bid, in its extravagant, politically driven espousal of the role of art, provide the context and set a timetable for artistic endeavour? Might it provide a platform, an officially sanctioned platform, whilst in its inherent myopia admitting the critical and the dystopian? Over a seven-year period, during which one of us might conceivably die, we planned to reimagine the city. What if we hired an office for seven years without knowing what we would do there? What if we persuaded a newly built hotel in Cardiff Bay, as the docklands have been renamed, to give us the same room every Friday night for seven years? Could we make a myth from a ritual by inviting 364 individuals to stay there, each recording their dreams of Cardiff the following morning in a video diary – celebrities, artists, taxi drivers, local residents? Could we construct exact replicas of several locations in the city on a sound stage – restaurant, accident and emergency unit? At the original sites we would record conversations with citizens, overtly with chosen guests, covertly on CCTV cameras. On set, performers would present the recorded encounters and texts, using dramatic devices to reframe and reorientate the action, to retime events, to involve others, to remix elements, to achieve different outcomes. Original and replica would then be presented side-by-side in performance or broadcast. Could we record barely rehearsed performances in the public domain? A Greek drama filmed within the setting of a rugby international, performers working in and with the crowd ...

Cardiff's bid failed. Our project stalled at the stage of concept.

Concept: governing ideas

Image 5.3   Brith Gof, *Cusanu Esgyrn*, empty barn, National Eisteddfod, Neath, South Wales, 1994 (Pete Telfer)

This is a chord, this another, this is a third. Now form a band. (*Sideburns* fanzine, December 1976)

It is 16 January 1999 and a group of people stands in a disused garage, hung with heavy black drapes, in Aberystwyth. They feel the movement and hear the voices of eleven student female performers amongst them. But they see nothing, for all here is in pitch darkness. The performance is entitled *Angels*. Its texts are drawn from the visionary writings of Emanuel Swedenborg, from accounts of near-death experiences, from the partial testimonies of serial murderers Frederick and Rosemary West, who between 1967 and 1987 killed twelve young women, and from the stories of their victims.

The performers have rehearsed for several weeks, first to get a physical measure of the site, then in blindfolds to inculcate moving in space without fear or hesitation, and finally to create group choreographies, with an imaginary audience, in the blackout. They have prepared strategies, learned how best to go on here. Only in performance will their efficacy be tested. They work in three horizons. Below the waists of the audience, crawling on the floor, creeping between their legs. Face-to-face with them, occasionally disconcertingly close. And above their heads, through rehearsed lifts and carries. They struggle, literally, to keep in touch, to concert their efforts without visual cues to commence or respond. The audience of forty is embraced and caressed, gently shepherded and roughly jostled in set patterns of movement: voices far away, coming closer, ascending. Performance as an encompassing ambience, a place of suspension and limbo, without here and there, without them and us: from which there is no escape. From which the performers are, at the end, absent.

The central questions here: how theatrically to represent fabulous creatures, and how to bring into any kind of representation the torments suffered in that cellar in Gloucester? The answer: to suspend the visual and to perform in the dark. And from this single *big idea*, all else proceeds: the physical and vocal techniques employed, approaches to rehearsal, the attitude to and handling of audience. Whilst appearing a self-imposed restriction upon, or obstruction to, creativity it focuses attention in a devising situation in which anything might be possible.

In this instance, *concept* is an over-arching notion or set of notions that orientates and informs structure and content and that has practical implications and repercussions for all aspects of the performance, aesthetic *and* technical. A decision 'to bring the outside inside', to perform underwater, to undertake a guided tour, to use cycle couriers, anticipates all else, setting the broad parameters within which detail will be generated. Concept may fix a governing aesthetic or set of organizing principles or procedures to be pursued: Matthew Bourne uses male dancers in his production of *Swan Lake* (1995). Lars von Trier films *Dogville* (2003) on a sound stage with the town represented as a plan of the white outlines of buildings on the floor. Mabou Mines situates *Oedipus at Colonus* (1988) within the conventions of a gospel service.

At site, concept may be inspired by, or derived from, the characteristics of the place. Site might offer:

(a) a particular and unavoidable history (for example, Auschwitz); (b) a particular use (a cinema, a slaughterhouse); (c) a particular formality (shape, proportion, height, length or disposition of architectural elements, etc.); (d) a particular political, cultural or social context (a prison, a shop, museum, a hospital); (e) a particular kind of 'halfway house' for event and audience to meet (a workplace, a meeting place, a street, a church). In other words, deciding to create a work in a 'used' building might provide a theatrical foundation or springboard, it might be like 'throwing a six to go', it might get us several rungs up the theatrical ladder before we begin. (McLucas, quoted in Pearson and McLucas, no date, pp. 5–6)

Site may be directly suggestive of subject matter, theme, dramatic structure; it will always be apparent as context, framing, sub-text. (Pearson, 2007c, p. 7)

Its usage, or former usage, may directly inform the dramatic structure: the 'hand in glove' *congruence* of performance *about* war-wounded in a hospital, with the audience sitting around performers in beds. Or constituted as a religious service in a chapel, or as a political meeting in a council chamber.

But performance may equally impose a concept on site, their relationship *incongruent* or *paradoxical*, including orders of material unusual, inappropriate or perverse here: a sixth-century battle elegy in a car factory, an oratorio in a railway station. Despite their apparent dissimilarities, they begin to bleed into each other. In *Gododdin*, the decision to work in a car factory provided a range of resources for the performance: lit by headlights, the warriors carrying bonnets as shields. And the performance, as metaphor, highlights the sense of industrial defeat inherent in the empty building.

Such a reading onto may be extremely dogmatic and uncompromising. In an event planned to celebrate the opening of the Department of Theatre, Film and Television in the Parry-Williams Building of Aberystwyth University, Mike Brookes decided to do two things in a large studio theatre: first to install so much lighting that it would be impossible to see the walls in the brightness; second to make it rain indoors. Once this was achieved we would then decide what to put in it, from the poetic works of Thomas Parry-Williams.

It may even be constituted as *dogma*, as a series of adherences and prohibitions inventoried in a manifesto. In a short item entitled 'How to Make a Peter Greenaway Film' (*The Late Show*, 1989), made by film director Nick Broomfield, the viewer is advised first to get him or herself a Michael Nyman soundtrack and then to employ a group of English stage actors, stand them a long way from the camera and encourage them to talk very loudly.

Within performance, *concept* also denotes a singular proposition or imperative: a task undertaken to completion, rules to be adhered to, instructions to be followed. It foresees and prescribes what will happen without necessarily settling how. As a statement: 'this is what I shall do'. In this it is closely akin to practices of conceptual art and practices in associated fields: from John Cage's *4'33"* (1952) to Yoko Ono's *Cutpiece* (1965), from Richard Long's *A Line Made by Walking* to Gillian Wearing's *Signs that Say What You Want Them to Say and Not Signs that Say What Someone Else Wants You to Say* (1993).

Given the difficulty of rehearsal or the scale, duration or nature of the endeavour, concept becomes a crucial aspect of landscape performance in the form of a stated ambition or the setting of conditions of time, place or approach. It is a recurrent feature of Simon Whitehead's work. For example: '*Tableland* (1998–99): "I carry a kitchen table along the roads that encircle the Llanaelhaearn uplands, Pen Llyn. Placed at intersections, in fields, a domestic object becomes part of the landscape. An act of belonging"' (Whitehead, 2006, pp. 28–9). In *Stalks* (2000–01) he trailed animals across Barcelona, 'with the intention to be led into relationship with a city unknown to me. I follow dogs and their owners, feral cats and pet shop hamsters, creating an experiential map of routes and encounters of particular areas of the city, night and day' (ibid., pp. 44–5).

In *2mph* (2002) he pushed a stuffed goose in a hand cart along the old cattle drovers' roads from West Wales to Smithfield Market, covering the 300 miles in twenty-three days, showing the notebooks he kept on the journey at the Nightwalking Festival (ibid., pp. 10–11).

As his contribution to the Centre for Performance Research 'Mapping Wales' project, *Source to Sea* (2001), Whitehead walked the full length of the River Ystwyth, from its origins in a bog in the Cambrian Mountains to its mouth close to Aberystwyth Harbour with American artist Rachel Rosenthal. The journey took three days. Along the way they talked and collected objects. In a subsequent performance they laid a strip of white paper across a studio and placed the gathered objects upon it at regular intervals. They then retraced their journey using the objects as mnemonics to recall memories of their mutual experience (ibid., pp. 40–1). In a forthcoming project he plans not to use motor transport for a whole year.

It is 27 March 2009. During a wine reception at The Presence Project international conference 'Performing Presence: From the Live to the Simulated' at Exeter University, Mike Brookes brings me a chair from the adjoining room, then two microphones, then a music stand. I sit and begin to cut my shirt with a knife, the sound greatly amplified next door, where the image of a blazing car is projected onto one wall. Follow a cable outside and there is the car, a toy six inches in length. Follow another cable upstairs and a microphone rests on a plastic container full of crickets. Quietly, I begin to read a text of absence and loss occasioned by personal experiences of dementia, gradually shredding my suit. Some people stay with me, an increasingly abject figure. Others accompany Mike Brookes as he mixes sound and image from various sources. And others still seek out the origins of these samples. We call the performance *Something Happening/Something Happening Nearby*. 'Digital thinking realised with string and plastic cups,' retorts Mike Brookes.

Devising: practical applications

The practical aspects of devising are as follows:

Image 5.4   Brith Gof, *Gododdin*, disused Rover car factory, Cardiff, 1988 (Brian Tarr)

- Begins with a process of *research*, frequently interdisciplinary research: into site and subject.
- Continues with an *audit*: of personal abilities and material resources.
- Involves the *identification*, *selection* or *rejection* and *accumulation* of concepts, actions, texts, places and things that are composed in space and time according to sets of governing aesthetics, ideologies, preferred techniques and operative technologies. In this there are two basic phases: *selection* and *orchestration*. Both are susceptible to forces of *desire* and *necessity*: the tension between what we want to do and what we ought to do here.
- Its work is often with *fragments* and *traces*: in acts of *assemblage*. Such assemblage is characterized by *omission* – it only includes a certain range of things – and by extra-daily *juxtaposition*: as like and unlike – without natural *affinities* or *linkages* – are drawn together in a new *taxonomy*.
- May be of limited scope or range of means. But at site there will always be *leakage*, of features of site into performance.
- May be pursued within the practices and approaches of a *genre*, such as *bodyweather*.
- May *annex* the conventions of another genre: as flamenco.

- May have distinguishing traits that constitute an *idiolect*, working recurrently from conventions of film acting.
- May start with the establishment of a certain *look* or with the institution of a shared training regimen or gathering of materials to be included.
- May be generated through trial and error, through improvisation and the testing of proposals over a protracted period.
- May be formulated as a *game plan* – as sets of rules or mutual understandings that give direction, purpose and pattern, if not plot, to the activity – or as *strategies* for action: engaged *tactically* in rehearsal and performance.
- May exist as storyboard, shooting script or *scenario*, within which detail is developed: as a rough sketch gradually refined.
- May include texts of different orders, making no value judgement on their inherent suitability.
- May work from two-dimensional visual sources, regarding them as an *arrested* moment that might be physically copied, deconstructed and projected backwards and forwards in time.
- Devised performance is a work of *project design*: its outcomes may be prototypes or production articles.
- Requires attention to the *visual* and the *aural* frame: to what goes where, to background as well as foreground. To *timbre*, *texture*, *rhythm* and *space* as much as character and story.

A surviving document, a typescript covering three and a half sides of A4, entitled 'Gododdin Scenario' appears partly to outline physical action and partly to document it. Whichever, it is extremely schematic. In each section there is a list of tasks or movements:

(5) BERSERKING

(a) Transformations:
    (i)   Moving without pause.
    (ii) Isometrics against the body.
    (iii) Bits being pulled off.
    (iv) Walk, throw, tense.
    (v)   Flying.
    (vi) Attacking the self: slaps etc.
    (vii) Slow change to animal characteristics.
    (vii) Mutate to animal/warrior.

(b) Berserk:
    (i)   Work with barrels: pushing, throwing, etc.
    (ii) Work on cars.

The preceding *Disasters of War* series of performances had enacted the postures and interactions of Francisco Goya's etchings to inform their physical action, with moments of formal emulation. In *Gododdin* these terse instructions provide the basis for improvisation. Set against a driving, live percussion soundtrack of six minutes, they may be accomplished in any order, with varying degrees of intensity, for durations decided by the performer. The only requirement is continuity: that the one segues into another. What is hidden here is the sight of performers throwing themselves into the air and writhing in water, diving onto cars, smashing windscreens with thrown barrels, as they incarnate the frenzy of Celtic warriors in their battle preparations. Although the 'what' is decided, the 'how' is reliant upon and emerges within the maelstrom of performance. It is informed by the pre-existing skills of the performers and a mutual appreciation of the requisites of dramaturgy at this point.

(9) LAMENT
(a) Individuals falling in tightish group.
(b) All group falls twice in car headlights.
(c) Work in pairs:
    (i) Carry, collapse and change over.
    (ii) Carry, collapse and drag.
    (iii) One collapses down standing partner. Reverse.
    (iv) Collapsing together.
    (v) Lying in water.

Elsewhere, it is 8 November 2002 and Welsh playwright Ed Thomas, Mike Brookes and I are performing *Raindogs*, 'a performance work for the city of Cardiff', at the Chapter Arts Centre.

The devising process began when Ed and I challenged each other to write a series of ten one-minute texts, poetic fragments and character sketches that we assigned to ten close collaborators. The actors, five chosen by Ed, five by me, and several well-known for their television work, never appear on stage however. They are present in performance only on video. Raindogs – a group of men, similarly besuited, who have lost their way home, in places from which the theatre audience is *absent* or *excluded*.

Five were recorded travelling through the city by car, train, bus, boat. Five others were asked to stand in the street and do nothing for several minutes until a CCTV camera located them. They had only the vaguest notion of when they would be recorded, and from what angle. The cameras found them immediately, for their stillness is a provocation to the flow of consumption. They are not participating. They must be loitering-with-intent. Pausing whilst all around them was in motion, their stillness deflected attention towards fellow inhabitants and architecture. All were subsequently videoed in close-up with their eyes closed. And also speaking directly to camera for precise periods of time: three minutes, four and a half minutes. Yet in shooting this material they were held apart, never party to what each other was doing, preventing temptations to bring dramatic coherence, homogeneity of expression, to ten separate biographies glimpsed in fragments and being played out in the city: on the fringes of our ability to apprehend them. Convergences of time, narrative and location – the figures' similarity in appearance, the interlocking nature of their stories, their simultaneous presence in the same landscape – were only apparent in performance, through the ordering and juxtaposition of footage.

After viewing the recorded material, Ed and I wrote further texts, developing the fragmented stories of these men. The texts interpenetrate fiction, with allusions to vernacular details of place and particular moments in civic history. Later reflective texts also sought to translate certain theoretical insights of Luce Giard, Michel de Certeau and Situationist International, and notions such as 'archaeologies of the contemporary past' into material suitable for public performance.

Our actors were asked to survive, often in the public domain, without precise direction or the support of rhetorical devices, often never quite sure when and from where they were being observed. The presence of a group of damaged men, both haunted and haunting, and played by uncertain actors, served to present recognizable places in unfamiliar ways, from unexpected viewpoints, and to reveal unfamiliar places, rarely visited but adjacent. The arrangement of the studio theatre – asymmetrical in the seating of audience and the distribution of monitors, projections, sound sources and live performers – offered varying, though partial, views. It conspired in its disorientating layerings and juxtapositions of oblique views both to evoke our city and to render it uncanny.

In performance these various short segments of video, totalling seventy-five minutes, were projected in parallel with other views of the city – a forty-five minute night-time tracking shot from a car for instance – and accompanied by a soundtrack of timed phases commissioned from composer John Hardy. Within the texts that took the form of poetic stanzas, proper psalms, personal narratives, descriptions, confessions and testimonies, there was no composite narrative, though the soundtrack conjures increasing tension and a final sense of resolution.

Site-specific performance as a *purposeful assemblage* of fragments created elsewhere, at some other time, from viewpoints unavailable to the audience, such as the control room of South Wales Police: forsaking the *architectonic* concerns of the 1980s. And with significant implications for the performer: what is forfeited here are all those mechanisms that ensure coherence, continuity and direction – character, motive, plot, crisis orientation.

Strasse(n)wecken (2006) (see pp. 83–6) was a multisite street work created with eight students of Frankfurt University, mapped onto the grid-like street plan in a scissor-like manner. On a street corner the whole group related the arrival of an immigrant into the city in a short poetic text and as a dumb show. The group then split into two smaller units each taking half the audience. Pausing on opposite corners of the block they then recount moments from their research and fieldwork in that locale: its history, significant events and stories of its inhabitants culled from interviews. On one corner notorious for drug-dealing, the group tells of previous experiences here from inside a cash-point room. All then reunited for the second instalment of the story at the next corner, and so on across the neighbourhood: diverse mode of expression here, from storytelling to mimetics, in a performance barely perceptible to the uninitiated.

Space: as organizing principle

Image 5.5   Brith Gof, *Arturius Rex*, industrial unit, Cardiff, 1994 (Jens Koch)

It is 29 October 1992 and Brith Gof is performing *Haearn* in Tredegar, south Wales: 'a large theatre piece about the creation of Industrial Man – a new human forged in the workshops of the Ironmasters and in the operating Theatres of the new Physicians of the Industrial Revolution'. It is staged in the windowless central hall of a disused iron foundry, a building 100 metres long and twenty metres wide (see Kaye, 1996a, 209–34). The audience is seated on a rake at one end. Directly in front of them are three high chairs constructed in scaffolding from which a female performer in increasing states of disarray will successively speak the words of Mary Shelley, Victor Frankenstein and Frankenstein's creature. Beyond that extend rows of matched pairs of brick benches, those to the left representing the hospital, to the right the workshop. Between them run two specially laid tram tracks. Facing them in the distance is a tiered platform upon which singer, narrator and orchestra are situated: one of the design conceits is that of 'The Valley' (McLucas, quoted in Pearson and McLucas, no date, p. 8). On the far wall is projected a documentary film of industrial production, intercut with footage of the two performers who appear as Man and Woman.

At this site, two effects difficult to achieve in the auditorium become possible. First, activities of different orders and intensities can be placed at different distances from the audience, stretching away from them in a scenic *depth*: in close-up, far away. Here backgrounds may appear active, perspectives false, scale confounded. Second, activities can approach the audience and recede. Railway trucks and wheeled hoists are pushed towards them. Performers mounted upon and suspended beneath the twenty-ton gantry crane that runs the full length of the hall are whisked away – 'actors continually change size' (Thrift, 2008, p. 17). The crippled god Hephaestus, wearing a swivel-harness that allows him to twist and somersault and breathe fire whilst travelling, flies towards the audience. From their fixed position, they peer into the darkened hall where sudden flares of light illuminate actions in the manner of the paintings of Joseph Wright of Derby, whilst the film flickers in the background. They look up and diagonally out to Mary Shelley. And they rock back in their seats as the gods hover directly above them.

The main spatial questions for site-specific performance are:

- How does it *disperse* itself within and in relation to a particular architecture or environment?
- How is the space delineated and formalized and how does this affect the type, nature and quality of the activity and its reception?
- Where is the audience positioned, and what *viewpoints* or modes of apprehension are thus conspired?
- How does spatial closure or confinement affect the expressive capacities of performers?

This necessitates working conceptually in three dimensions. Locating performance in both horizontal and vertical axes.

In a hypothetical model addressing these questions, imagine a crowd of people standing in an empty space, on a street corner, in a shed, in a field. No formal arrangement of performers and audience. No preordained performing areas. No framing devices. At site, there may be many interesting and unfamiliar things to look at – architectural features, the machinery of unfamiliar practices – but no clues as to what to watch. Emptiness is an illusionary category and performance may have to work hard to assert itself. *Size* is already a conditioning factor. The experience for ten people standing in a toilet cubicle is different from that in the nave of a cathedral. And *climate* too: they may be huddling together for warmth. And *atmosphere*, as they sniff the fetid air.

And then something happens, an action, a few words. The crowd steps back, withdraws, to give the activity space, a distinction is drawn between *watchers* and the *watched*, though this relationship may be subject to change. They take up the best position for watching, often a circle. A temporary, provisional playing area is created, sufficient to the task and constantly redefined by the erratic movements of the combatants. On Boxing Day in the crowded streets of their village, the Marshfield Mummers repeatedly make space for their six-minute drama (Pearson, 2006b, pp. 136–48). They process in single file. At particular points they suddenly loop to inscribe a circle. As they come to rest equidistant around the circumference, they face the centre, holding open the area as the crowd gathers behind them. Each will step in to speak his lines, walking in a circular fashion or standing at the centre and turning. Although *unmarked* these places are not random, but prescribed by tradition: in front of the Victorian almshouses practice and architecture can appear *conterminous*.

And then something else happens, either *sequentially* or *simultaneously*. In a series of *sequential* actions, the attention of the audience may shift, and rapidly. They may have to decide whether to move to see better, or indeed to escape. If they stand still, then they will doubtless see some activity in close-up, some at a distance, some half-hidden and some from behind. If simultaneous, it may be impossible to see everything at the same time, or at least making decisions upon what to focus upon within the range of possibilities. Either will impact upon *dramaturgy* and its *reception*.

Performance may be uncompromising in its need for space, clearing a path through the unswerving focus of performer or through the inclusion of tasks or phenomena that need to be avoided: from washing the floor to the entry of wheeled vehicles. On 5 November at Ottery St Mary in Devon blazing tar barrels are paraded through the streets, carried on men's shoulders until they can stand the heat no more or until the barrels fall to pieces. As they rush into the crowd, the action generates space, instantaneously.

Field implies area, openness. But it's still very crowded – in the crowd. In order to draw attention to itself, performance may need to raise itself above head-height. To lift itself. To suspend itself. To use effects of elevation and falling and floating: fireworks and kites and skydivers. Engaging the full *volume* or arc of the space. Or it may raise the audience, in arrangements temporary or permanent. The vertical is engaged and viewpoints shift.

The reserving areas for its sole usage may involve the indication, delineation and marking out of no-go areas, from a few chalk marks on the floor, to cordons, to the inclusion of areas of a different surface, of coal, sand, water. Eddie Ladd's *Sawn-Off Scarface* (2000) that 'reduces nearly three hours of film action to twelve minutes' is performed on a rectangle of blue carpet, ten feet square, with microphone and stand the only other objects in the room. As the action proceeds, it is revealed to be soaked in water, suggesting both 'a sticky, wet nightclub' and the swimming pool in which Tony Montana meets his death. As she dances and falls, Ladd's actions create splashes and sprays that accentuate her movement. Her suit becomes soaked, her appearance dishevelled.

In an unfamiliar space, where the arrangements of presentation are yet to be demonstrated, the audience will seek clues about where to situate itself. Invariably this involves a retreat, backs to the walls, out of the light, away from suspended objects, or that place where we have made it rain. But the inclusion of raised or sloping areas may lead to confusion: are they intended for performers or audience? Any material emplacement, however rudimentary or provisional, will be taken as a potential locus for activity.

At site we need not anticipate that performance is in *plain view*. Even a wall – from brick structure to paper hanging – freestanding in an empty room will alter its performative potential: cutting out visual irrelevance and distraction, framing and grounding the work. It has two sides, potentially hidden and revealed, on and off. In *The Disasters of War* series (1986–89; Pearson, 1988, pp. 16–23) we planned a performance for two audiences, on either side of a wall. First they would view a set of actions infused with the sounds from behind the wall. They then change sides revealing how they may have mis-interpreted what was happening. The wall may facilitate the creation of two separate worlds, of public and private, of entrances and exits. As a transparent screen, it may provide glimpses of a shadowy world beyond. As a surface that may be decorated, suggesting other times and places. Against it there may be horizons of activity and of information of differing intensities and orders – projected imagery for instance – in the vertical axis. And water may run down its face.

Performers may stand in front of it, their activities now in relief: creating friezes, tableaux and two-dimensional imagery. They may scale it, gripping handholds as on a climbing wall. Or abseil down it, in a choreography of swings and leaps and inversions, as in the work of dancer Kate Lawrence whose *Descent of the Angel* was performed on the facade of the National Library in Aberystwyth in June 2009.

Build four walls, an enclosure, and space is set aside, reserved. Now there is inside and outside, with thresholds to be crossed and contracts to be made. Audience members put themselves in the hands of the performers as they enter the labyrinth, surrendering volition.

> The uniform layout of the vast factory interior seems to diffuse any sense of a foreground and background, centre stage and margin, with the effect that the black-and-white projected film of steel workers, for example, does not appear as a backdrop to Mary Shelley's recollections of the death of a child ('I was a mother, and am so no longer') any more than the emphatically Welsh female voice of Frankenstein's creature ('And what was I? Of me creation and creator I was absolutely ignorant') is a soundtrack to the rhythmic manipulations of a performer's limbs, strung within a frame on top of a platform; these exist along-side each other in an economy of equal parts. (Wilkie, 2008, pp. 94–5)

Time: as organizing principle

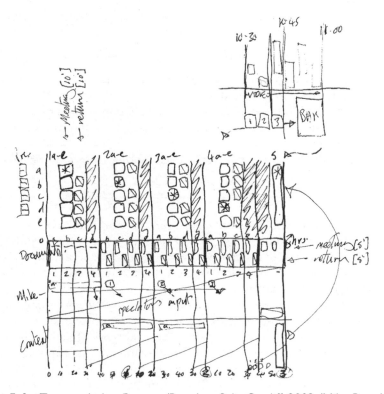

Image 5.6   Temporal plan: Pearson/Brookes, *Polis*, Cardiff, 2002 (Mike Brookes)

> The work is a broad field – operating in three dimensions and time. (McLucas, 1993, p. 7)

Performance exists in and through time. It is usually scheduled, of certain duration, with beginning and end to its parenthesis. As a *time-based* art, it demonstrates its nature by playing with time: slowing down, speeding up, attenuating and intensifying norms of social practice, in combinations of simultaneous, sequential, folded, suspended and discontinuous activity.

Performance may defy conventions of theatrical plenitude and duration. In *The Delusion of Self Immolation* (1990) – whilst strapped into a machine of his own manufacture in an empty swimming pool – Dutch artist Eric Hobijn's body was set on fire and extinguished again in a split second, though his increasingly urgent preparation lasted ninety minutes. In *One Year Performance* (1980–81) Tehching Hsieh punched a time clock at the same location on the hour every hour, twenty-four hours a day, for an entire year (see Heathfield, 2000; 2009). Every time, a movie camera shot a single frame.

The resulting film compresses each day into a second. It is six minutes and two seconds long.

In the early 1970s Richard Schechner suggested that theatrical dramaturgy employs time in three distinct ways:

> ■ In *event time* the activity takes as long as is required for completion: application without fixed duration.
> ■ In *set time* all the activity has to be completed in a given time: a fixed duration that may lead to a different sense of urgency and quality of energetic engagement.
> ■ In *symbolic time* one span represents another duration. (Schechner, 1969, pp. 87–8)

Conventionally, theatre runs in *event time*. All the business is achieved in order, narrative order, until the story is told. But it may also include phases of *symbolic time*. Three days can pass between one scene and the next. The extreme protractions of the Noh stage are only rendered comprehensible through accompanying narration.

In site-specific performance all three function as *organizing principles, structuring devices* and *operating procedures*, manifest in sequence or in parallel, from time to time over time, by different performers and types of activity – affecting the expenditure of energy, the application and quality of effort and the dynamic trajectory of the event: 'the kettle boiling in the time it takes to do the washing up. The distance one can carry a suitcase before needing to put it down to rest one's arm' (Howell and Templeton, 1976, p. 11).

Performance as the superimposition and subtle interaction of a range of time frames and scales, containing the juxtaposition of short-term events and long-term elaborations of theme and dramatic development. In *Second Skin* (1996; see Howell, 1999, p. 31) André Stitt used an angle-grinder to remove every trace of enamel from a bathtub in a closed room. Marilyn Arsem wrote on the walls of Trace: Gallery (see pp. 88–90) for twenty-four hours, in *set* time. In *Bubbling Tom* (see pp. 54–7) months of a life history passed in the *symbolic* time of walking from one location to the next.

In *Rhydcymerau* (1984) one activity set the time for another. Commencing with a tree trunk and using only Victorian joinery techniques, two performers laboured throughout to construct a child's coffin, delivering it at precisely the moment required in the attendant sequence of stories, poems and songs concerning rural decline: the sounds of work – sawing, hammering, chiselling – orchestrated against and counter-pointing the spoken text (Pearson, 1985, pp. 3–4).

Brith Gof's large-scale performances were structured as divisions of time. Against a *time-base* and within a sequence of sections of agreed, though arbitrary, duration, and with changes explicitly signalled, material could be simultaneously developed within each stratigraphic component: 'about each section, there must then be agreement concerning its nature, purpose and emotional tenor to be pursued in parallel in each element' (Pearson, quoted in Pearson and McLucas, no date, p. 13). *Gododdin* (1988) was comprised of ten sections of six minutes, *Tri Bywyd* (1995) of thirty-nine sections of two minutes each, marked by a thunderclap on the soundtrack. Of *Haearn* (1992), Cliff McLucas included: 'The Times: Four distinct time scales are stretched and compressed to the same span: (a) Mary Shelley's personal and novelistic writings from 1814 to 1822; (b) first hand accounts of key developments in Industrial Science and Medical Science during the century 1760 to 1860; (c) the "never-never" time of Greek myth; (d) the 90 minutes "real time" of the event' (ibid., p. 11). In their inclusion of the (b) texts, sections of six minutes symbolized one decade of historical time. When events unfolded against a recorded soundtrack, music and action invariably proceeded in step, in set time, necessitating the inclusion of improvised or reprised activities at the end of sections to resynchronize components.

At site, multiple temporalities may be apparent, informing and infusing performance: a Victorian chapel is inescapably a nineteenth-century edifice. It was then, it is now, and all points between. In this context, its presence may be incidentally or purposefully *anachronistic*. In relation to a certain history, performance may be *synchronic*, concerned with one moment in time, as in *Bubbling Tom* (2000), where events referred to are those of the mid-1950s. Or *diachronic*, involving multiple viewpoints in time – as in *Tri Bywyd* (1995) – where events from the mid-nineteenth century to the present day are copresent.

Performance may emulate manipulations of time familiar from video recording – fast-forward, frame advance, slow motion. Or editing – dissolve, flashback. The advent of inexpensive video and audio recorders has facilitated the virtually simultaneous recording and representation of material (without procedures of processing) in performance and the contemporaneous presence of material – as samples of different ages that confound notions of origin and authorship and serve to fold and enfold time. The absolute consistency of the *digital time-base* means that material generated in different technologies can be arranged exactly *in time* against each other. *Raindogs* (2002) (see p. 153) was an *assemblage* of multiple projections, recorded soundtrack and live narration.

In landscape settings, performance may acknowledge or be predicated upon time-scales geological, natural, seasonal, diurnal, human. Environmental *rhythms* may recommend or conspire durations – performance achieved in the hours of daylight or between the tides. It may be set against – and draw attention to – the *passage of time* in processes of marking, ageing, entropy, erosion, decay, growth. Performance proceeds as ice melts or as paint dries ...

In urban contexts, performance is inevitably located within the complex multitemporalities of the built environment, any or all of which may be summoned by, or inescapably present within, the activity. And it exists within the city's overlapping, conflicting time frames, amongst the 'conflicts, penetrations and imbrications of the cyclical and the linear'; in the gap between 'fundamental rhythms and cycles' and the 'quantified time of watches and clocks' (Lefebvre,

2004, p. 74). Here it may go with the flow, shadowing retail and transport timetables and 'the processes imposed by the socio-economic organisation of production, consumption, circulation and habitat' (ibid.). Or it may represent a point of resistance or critique, pausing, moving at a different pace.

Alan Read warns against valorizing space 'at the expense of the critical relations between temporality, built form and the performative dynamics of architecture within everyday life' (Read, 2000, p. xv). In the series of multisite works staged in Cardiff and Frankfurt, commencing with *Carrying Lyn* (2001; see Pearson and Jeff, 2001), performance existed in a number of places simultaneously, at dispersed locations in the city and for several audiences. These works employed low-grade technology – video including VHS-C, Polaroid, minidisc – equipment that still involves time-based procedures of registration, rewind, etc., and that produces artefacts that themselves can be transported – tapes, discs, photos. The city here becomes the location of performance, and dramatic material, records of what happened 'out there, just now', is brought to (and potentially returned from) a theatre space, where it is assembled, ordered and replayed in an almost instantaneous re-presentation of ephemeral occurrences within the public domain. In *Carrying Lyn* video footage returned by cycle couriers was shown within twenty minutes of its registration on the street, discrete units of dramatic material ordered against and slotted into a precise time-base, with all involved working 'against the clock'. The organizing principle here is as much of 'schedules-to-be-met' as 'places-to-be'. Time as an essential dimension of site-specificity ...

Of site-specific performances McLucas notes: 'they just stand in the same room as you, and share "plain time" with you' (McLucas, quoted in Pearson and McLucas, no date, p. 14). But performance can also, in its overwhelming affect, cut a hole in time, causing 'a losing track' as

> a time that forgets time, during which time no longer counts (and is no longer counted). ...It arrives or emerges when an activity brings plenitude, whether this activity be banal (an occupation, a piece of work), subtle (meditation, contemplation), spontaneous (a child's game, or even one for adults) or sophisticated. This activity is in harmony with itself and with the world. It has several traits of self-creation or of a gift rather than an obligation or an imposition come from without. It is in time: it is a time, but does not reflect on it. (Lefebvre, 2004, pp. 76–7)

At site, the main challenge for the performer may be of *timing*. Of successfully placing activity, as planned, in time: against all odds, in difficult circumstances, in situations where there is no pause for quiet.

Sequence: ordering material

Whilst *Gododdin* (1988–89) was envisaged as a stratigraphy of layers (see pp. 113–15), its dramaturgy was structured as a *sequence* of named, thematic

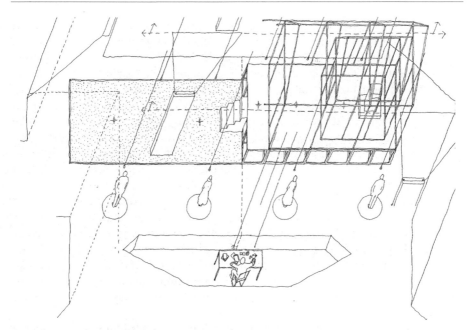

Image 5.7 Stage layout: Brith Gof, *Patagonia*, Theatr Taliesin, Swansea, 1992 (Cliff McLucas)

sections – entry, prologue, heroics, berserking, arming, journey, battle, lament, epilogue – that schematically tracked the exploits and fate of the warriors. With consensus about the character, atmosphere and emotional tenor of each section, material was generated, in relative isolation, in the various layers. Musicians and physical performers met only late in the process, confident that battle would be furious, lament poignant.

This formal but effective approach to composition was repeated in several of Brith Gof's site-specific productions. In *PAX* (1990–91) (see pp. 68–70), a meditation on the ecological plight of the planet in ten movements, angels return to Earth through a hole in the ozone. In the first staging in St David's Hall, Cardiff, titles and supplements reflected the sequence of physical action as *carrier*: (1) Descent: through the ozone; (2) Landing/Rescue: unforeseen difficulties; (3) Adjustment: the garden has changed; (4) The Message: they come with a message but who can hear it? (5) Leaving: enough is enough; (6) Observation: the effort is worth it; (7) Conflict: extreme toxic dangers; (8) Disaster: the lowest ebb – experiment leads to torment; (9) Wrath. Documentary texts were spoken by a narrator arranged against this from time to time. The sung libretto related, somewhat tangentially, the death of an elderly Welsh woman whose son was an astronaut and his encounters with angels. Whilst all components cohered around the momentum set by the live orchestral soundtrack, no one element bore full responsibility for narrative development. That seen and that heard were frequently of two different orders.

In the restaging in Aberystwyth railway station, the sections were altered to: (1) Water: 'Earth she shines brightly'; (2) Carbon: 'Tethered so closely to the Earth'; (3) Atmosphere: 'Signs of life, signs of death'; (4) Trees: 'The multitude of life flourishes as in a greenhouse'; (5) Descent: 'I've started to hear something in this unbelievable silence'; (6) Landing: 'Who are they these angels, and how shall I know them in the dark?'; (7) Signals: 'Your angels, I see them now'; (8) Conflict: 'Let their way be dark'; (9) The Message: 'Arise lest thou be consumed'; (10) Ascent: 'Will we be ready? Vengeance is theirs'. Here, the first four titles signal the presence and manipulation of scenic material. The supplements throughout are the words of the astronaut son. The sections reflect a more equal distribution of dramaturgical emphases.

Patagonia (1992) had nine sections. Sections 1–7 consisted of an *event* of one-minute duration, followed by a *state* of six to ten minutes. Section 8 comprised a radio play and the resolution of the physical activity presented in the preceding sequence of events, with an account and a replay of the shooting of Welsh pioneer Llwyd ap Iwan by Butch Cassidy and the Sundance Kid in Patagonia in 1909: 'the point at which a greater narrative meets a lesser narrative' (Cousin, 1994, p. 41). Section 9 was an epilogue: 'Lies told about Patagonia'.

The sequence of events reconstructed the trajectory of physical incidents leading to the assassination, using the conventions of the earliest silent movie acting (1903–09): non-stop movement, acting in different styles within a single frame; 'the pan was the only camera movement that was really available' (ibid., p. 40):

> First of all, virtually everyone in frame was almost always moving. There was no convention of stand and listen while one person is speaking, as you might have in theatre for instance. So actually they're really quite chaotic in a way, many of the images you see. Secondly, because there were no agreed stylistic conventions, you might see people acting in a variety of styles in any one scene, particularly when a group of people is reacting to one thing that's happening. (ibid.)

Each event began and ended with a 'freeze' or tableau as the 'camera turns over' or 'runs out'. Before commencing, the stage was 'wiped clean' by the passage of two large, suspended light-boxes at the rear, the 'freeze' appearing in silhouette. The soundtrack that accompanied the events of Sections 1–7 resembled a film score, composed as a single basic theme that gradually accumulated more orchestral voices, fully expounded and remixed in Section 8. This crisis-orientation in the events provided the dynamic impetus of the performance.

The states included textual material of different types – monologues and personal memoirs, anecdotes and lists, dialogues and biblical quotations. English and Welsh texts travelled in sequence and in parallel with little direct translation. The performers were free to use a variety of performance modes, from hymn singing to storytelling, from manual rhetoric at the microphone to mimetics, in the exposition of this material. Although the recurrent dumb shows enacted a simple narrative, the gradual accumulation of information created a vivid picture of Patagonia and its people against which events unfolded.

The aim of *Patagonia* was to make site-specific performance in an auditorium (see p. 22). To regard the stage as site with a particular set of architectural characteristics rather than a neutral space of representation. Responding to the extreme width of the stage in Theatr Taliesin in Swansea, the scenography conspired an effect akin to 'cinemascope'. Performers in period costume appeared in a formal setting – a rectangle of sand, a house of scaffolding tubing that resembled a diagram or architectural drawing. The sequence of physical *events* progressed from left to right. In the *states*, performers working in varying combinations of solo, duet, trio and quartet stepped out and away from the setting, in and out of character, even sitting on the stage apron to address the audience directly.

In her recent work *Cof y Corff* (2007) Eddie Ladd again addresses auditorium as site. The stage now resembled a film set. The audience sees her moving and being filmed as she appears and disappears in the wooden structure. In the auditorium, each group of the spectators sees the video imagery highly manipulated on small computer screens in the rows of seating. They hear the words of the narrator, a chronologically arranged sequence of texts on the body in Welsh history, on small individual radio receivers.

Such formal structuration attends to questions of scale. Around one carrier, be it physical action or sung libretto, a host of other narratives might cluster – personal and testimonial, documentary and scientific. 'It's a symphonic model; a question of trying to get the parts to work together, to resonate' (McLucas, quoted in McLucas and Pearson, 1999, p. 81).

Of *Y Pen Bas, Y Pen Dwfn* (1995), staged in a swimming pool and concerning the flooding of a Welsh valley in the building of the reservoir at Tryweryn, McLucas states: 'in order to avoid the material merely being about a historical set of events, I incorporated aspects of Daniel Defoe's Robinson Crusoe into the piece' (ibid., p. 80). The recorded bilingual soundtrack is a complex mix of sampled and specially recorded texts in English and Welsh from Defoe, the Act of Union, the prescient feature film *The Last Days of Dolwyn* (1949), contemporary news reports, hymns, the speeches of politicians, the memoirs of bombers, interviews, poetics, in a sequence of 13 scenes – such as 'Scene 3: The Queen of England, in which we hear of a futile appeal for Royal Intervention'. As Crusoe and Friday struggle to survive on a floating island, the Welsh labour underwater to build basic houses from flotsam.

Within simpler narrative, story need not unfold as *parataxis*: this *and* this *and* this. It might equally resemble *hypotaxis*: this *next to* this *behind* this *through* this. And *katachresis*: this, this, this. Such performance might exist as a string or pattern of discrete occurrences, singular events or images, as chains of events and passages, as overlapping frames in which one activity does not illustrate or allude to another. It might include *inciting incidents*, changes of consequence, crises or innovations, including *ruptures* or sudden shifts in direction, emphasis, orientation, followed by a period of disorientation, suspension, elaboration or resolution. Or *irrevocable* acts: irreversible processes of import and implication, such as flooding the room – and *decay*, as components move beyond recovery or repair. *Nodes* in which 'like' and 'unlike' phenomena are drawn together into dense images with complex and equivocal meaning. Narrative as fragmented and discontinuous, infused with the random and the discursive.

The monologue of the storyteller can exhibit a different form of 'dialogue' – a high order of intertextuality, of dialogue between texts. It can encompass the fragmentary, the digressive, the ambiguous, the appropriated, in juxtaposition and in contradiction. *From Memory* (1991) included traveller's tales, poetry, forensic data, quotations, genealogies, lies, jokes, improvised asides, physical re-enactments and autobiographical details.

However, momentum and direction are only ensured the judicious use of *dynamics*, the orchestration of elements over time. Modulations of speed, intensity, rhythm, mounting tension, pushing on and pulling back, energy expenditure, relaxation …

Stratigraphy: layering material

Image 5.8 Scaffolding structures: Brith Gof, *Tri Bywyd*, Clywedog Plantation, Lampeter, West Wales, 1995 (Mike Pearson)

Rarely does site-specific performance focus solely upon, or proceed at the pace of, that form of dramatic dialogue in which characters talk face-to-face, exchange information and their feelings about things, and constantly refer to events off-stage, elsewhere, in the real world. Too much else is vying for attention at site for it to monopolize meaning-creation, to function as the principal phenomenon to which other elements adhere or for which they provide illustration. For performance to be elaborated around verbal intercourse step by step, in step.

In a *stratigraphic* model of dramaturgy, site-specific performance is envisaged and executed as distinct strata or layers. Of the transitory component, performance, these might include *text, physical action, soundtrack* and *scenography*, the latter to include all scenic installation, lighting, amplification, prerecorded media, technological and technical aspects.

In an approach to devising embracing such a model:

> ■ Material can be conceived and manipulated in each of the individual layers.
>
> ■ Any one layer may be the starting point in the process: for instance, the soundtrack may be created first, or the site lit.
>
> ■ Any one layer may from time to time bear responsibility for carrying the prime intended meaning. Such responsibility can be reassigned and shift rapidly. No single constituent needs to bear sole responsibility for dramatic and emotional development.
>
> ■ Any one layer may provide the *carrier frequency*, the spine or consistent through-line upon which other layers are laid.

Distinct themes, moods or narratives may be carried and pursued in parallel – different, potentially *antithetical*, things being said or done in different layers, from time to time, or continuously throughout the performance, resulting in *simultaneity* and dramaturgical *complexity*.

Within individual layers there may be the sequencing of different orders of material – of stylistic discontinuity and expressive diversity. Text may be present in the form of poetics, lyrics, in-jokes, quotations, sayings; and in modes of delivery such as oratory, soliloquy, song, rhetoric, direct address, preaching, communal speaking, solo reflection, thrash-metal singing. Physical action may fluctuate between group choreography, solo improvisation and task-completion.

Performance may exist as one, two, three or four layers in a variety of *combinations* and *ratios*. It may resist or avoid the *plenitude* of dramatic exposition. Schematic, without sign of regret: as *just* text or *just* action at site.

From time to time, layers may have different relative thicknesses, threatening to overwhelm each other. They may be minimally present, or entirely absent. From time to time, individual layers may be discontinuous or suspended.

From time to time, one layer may take on or subsume the role of another – as the stamping rhythms of choreography, for instance, become soundtrack. Material in one layer will inevitably mediate that in another in the interpretation of performance, whether they have natural affinities or not: read onto, into and through each other. In listing the ten aspects of cinema vocabulary filmmaker Peter Greenaway identifies location, light, frame, audience, properties, actors, text, time, scale and illusion, attending to each in his works (Greenaway, 1997, p. 10).

Text may migrate from the mouths of the physical performers into the sung libretto or onto the walls of the scenography. At scale, it almost inevitably resides within the amplified spectrum. In *Gododdin* fragments of the poem were sung and spoken by narrators at microphones as part of the soundtrack. Conventionally this means that voices issue from the same locations, the speaker cabinet positions, potentially deadening their dynamic effect. However, through the judicious placement of amplification equipment, *sonic architectures* can be effected, within which sound can be panned between positions, allowing particular voices to be placed and shifted, and text and music to be moved over, through and around the audience.

In Brith Gof's *Patagonia* (1992) the conversational voices of on-stage performers wearing radio microphones were to be heard, much augmented, on speakers around and behind the audience, removing from performers the need to 'project' as they engaged in socially appropriate tones whilst addressing each other. Thus was the perceived relationship between action and voice, between aural and visual frames of reference, problematized.

A core narrative may be carried by the sung libretto. Crowding around this may be other narratives, documentary, literary, tangential, as sung and spoken voices unfolding in time. In *Haearn* (1992) the main narrative – selections from the diaries of Mary Shelley, and the words of Victor Frankenstein and his creation – was spoken by a female performer sitting in order on three high chairs close to the audience. Against her, a poetic working of the myth of Prometheus and Hephaestus was sung by a soprano voice. And a series of texts on industrial medical history related by male narrators. All elements were amplified and mixed against each other in performance.

Through the application of sampling technologies, the soundtrack can include documentary material from found sources mixed with live material: voices that once would have been emulated can now be present in person in their true resonance. In *EXX-1* (1990), it was R. S. Thomas who read his own poetry within the *matrix*. In *Gododdin* (1988–89) the car bonnets used as shields when struck triggered samples of shouting men, of screaming horses in the musical matrix.

Physical action, freed from its storytelling role, may be schematic and non-illustrative – from technical task, to rule-based engagements with the constructed environment, to periods of inactivity. Physical action may resemble an *interrupted practice* of different modes of expression, of varying types and intensities. Significantly, within this model the performer is no longer solely responsible for carrying dramatic meaning. In *Gododdin* performers made no attempt to tell the story of what is, after all, an elegy.

Geologically, the stratigraphy may be susceptible to processes of folding, faulting and erosion leading to discontinuities, inversions and disappearances. Layers are broken, slide diagonally and come into new configurations and juxtapositions. Story-telling transfers instantly from physical action to libretto, text is projected on to the walls.

After the analogy of the sound studio, tracks are recorded separately, then run together and *mixed* late in the process. This involves the amplification, erasure, compression, distortion, attenuation or fracture of any one track in relation to others to achieve the required overall effect. In Brith Gof's large scale performances each of the layers was written, composed, conceived and developed in relative isolation in order to reach their fullest, unmediated potential and only then combined at a late date, following the arrival and availability of all constituents on site.

Of the fixed component – site – the layers might include architecture, micro-climate, manifestations and patinas of occupancy past and present, auras and atmospheres ... All that constitutes its *depth*: archaeological, cultural, psycho-geographical. In performance some are everpresent and immediately operative. In *Gododdin*, in the unavoidable temperature of a disused factory in December, the breath of performers billows and naked bodies steam. The equipment of industrial production is inescapable, apparent in and through the sixth-century battle epic, and occasionally called into action. Such layers may be only partially controllable, the situation inherently *unstable*. In *Tri Bywyd* (1994), shortly before the performance was to commence, a cloud of mist, in itself uncanny and strangely beautiful, descended between performance and audience in the forest clearing.

NVA's *The Storr*, a night-walk on the Isle of Skye, the landscape dominated as the audience wore head-torches as they moved carefully between four settings, dramatically illuminated the poetry of Sorley MacLean and Rilke issuing from hidden speaker systems (Farquhar, 2005).

Or layers may need to be summoned up, alluded to, or invoked into operation – traces of those who have lived and died here before, along with their ghostly handiwork. In this, performance may become an active agency of archaeology: demonstrating for the popular imagination how we ourselves, and our immediate environment, are part of a historical process; how constituents of material culture exist within overlapping frames and trajectories of time; drawing attention to how we are continuously generating the archaeological record. In a renewed sensitivity to ephemerality, to an everyday rendered unfamiliar, to all we actively ignore or have forgotten, performance might avoid pointing to this or that, whilst nevertheless making them evident through its very presence. It can overlay different varieties of narrative – factual and fictive, historical and contemporary, creative and analytical, documentary and dramatic – within a given location or architecture, without laying any claim to authority or verisimilitude, whilst constantly serving to reveal the place.

And it will do this, inevitably, whether in the grain of the place or not, by its temporary occupancy.

In the street, the leakage of site into performance may be profound, its multitemporalities constantly in play; along with the random intrusions of its populace and their multifarious stories. The horizontal model:

> ■ As a means of prefabricating strands of materials, it facilitates work at sites where access is restricted, in time or by the fixity of the installation.
> ■ As a creative device, it poses a simple question: what is happening, where and when?
> ■ As an analytical device, it poses the same question.

Engagement: performers and site

Image 5.9   Underwater sequence: Brith Gof, *Y Pen Bas, Y Pen Dwfn*, Cardiff, 1995 (Cliff McLucas)

The performers had to cope with the environment they were in; this is a running preoccupation in our work. This makes things real; if someone is running about in a downpour they get cold and wet, they don't have to pretend. The physical performance in our work is real. (McLucas, quoted in McLucas and Pearson, 1999, p. 80)

Whilst much site-specific performance is ostensibly predicated upon *phenomenological* encounter and the demonstration or translation of its effect into forms of physical expression or associated account, the *engagement* of the performer at site is in essence *ergonomic* – body-to-environment, body-to-body. A simple premise here might be to regard site, including its existing and temporally installed elements, as *workplace*. It is inescapably of and in the real world but it is visited in the extra-daily guise of performance. Being in the real world, it may occasion or necessitate real world responses, but within a new frame of reference – performance – which of its nature may heighten or exaggerate immediate effects. Performers may be ill equipped or differentially prepared to deal with conditions in comparison to those who usually occupy the place – semi-naked without overalls and goggles in a factory; in street clothes underwater in a swimming pool. It is the tension between this readiness and lack of preparation at the interface of site and performance that generates substance and meaning.

Ergonomics concerns the relationship between individuals and their working or living environment, and the application of information about human physicality and behaviour to the problems of design. Our assumption is that we should be able to function effectively in everyday life. The chair allows us to sit at the table at a useful height to achieve other tasks; the cup fortunately fits the mouth without causing spillage. It is over questions of anthropometry – measurement of body size and proportions and how these may differ with age, gender and degrees of disability, and ways in which it potentially normalizes attributes – that ergonomics has been viewed with suspicion. Whose body, under what conditions?

If *ergonomics* focuses upon action and the context of its enactment, we might then regard performance as of particular interest. As place of work that attends closely to maximizing its communicative capacity, theatre has idiosyncratic practices that could appear odd in other contexts of labour. Its scenery and objects often lack verisimilitude. They are fabricated in materials and to dimensions different from their everyday equivalents in order to facilitate manipulation and reduce risk. Its actors employ vocal projection and exaggerated gesture to make themselves seen and heard in historic auditoria not entirely suited to contemporary purpose. In Japanese Noh theatre, the highly polished *hinoki* wood floor and the ethereal, gliding movement of its actors have a symbiotic relationship, floor enabling movement, style of movement possible because of floor, though it would be difficult to know which came first. In general, there is an ergonomic fit between the relatively controlled conditions of the auditorium and techniques of exposition.

In site-specific performance it may be other. Extended conditions of *surface*, *climate* and *architectural enclosure* may actually occasion dynamic engagements from the performers, beyond the routine demands of functionality. Operating conditions may oscillate between *optimal, acceptable* and *unacceptable*, enhancing opportunities and posing problems. In an inherently unstable situation, they may change rapidly, causing and requiring adjustment of response. Singly, and in combination, they may extend, limit, restrict or compromise four vectors of the performer's application: *clearance*, the headroom and legroom of the body ellipse; *reach*, the volume of the workspace envelope; *posture*, the nature and number of connections of body to workspace; and *strength*, the acceptable percentage of maximal strength in output or endurance.

The expressive capabilities and capacities of body and voice may be inhibited or altered by increases in hazard, stress, demand and overload: by the closure or limitation of sensory channels, as when performers are blindfolded. By intrusions into or invasions of personal space, as both planned and unforeseen phenomena and materials enter that envelope reserved for more or less exclusive use. By the arrangement and imposition of barriers, such as scenographic elements. Prevailing conditions may cause *duress* through increases in duration and limits to the adjustment of posture and reach. Environmental factors may include noise that causes annoyance during thinking and communication or illumination, with changes in brightness, reflection and shadow. Climate changes: in the temperature of air and surfaces, and in air velocity and relative humidity – the effects of which may, or may not, be mediated by clothing. Vibration of whole body or hand–arm: through shocks and jolts, and the toxicity of liquids, gases, vapours, dusts and solids.

The definition of an ergonomically ideal job – that it ought to consist of more than one task, to involve problem solving, to have a working cycle longer than one and a half minutes, to alternate between easy and difficult, to include individual decision-making, to provide sufficient information to control the task and to be carried out in a communal situation – indicates how problematic the conditions of performance can be. It might be a difficult, or even dangerous, place to work in, with performers attempting to apply strength against all odds, straining to maintain an effective posture, their reach restricted.

On a windy hillside or in a freezing factory, the nature of site may demand a high level of engagement and may constitute a mediating influence on its efficacy prior to any rhetorical expression: performers literally battling with the elements, trying to maintain coherence as they deal with, or try to minimize or disguise, the consequences, whilst these remain ever apparent. But the very engagement itself may form the substance of performance: ergonomics *as* performance. In the dynamic interplay of body and environment, both strategically planned and tactically improvised, performers encounter – and counter – the immediate effects of site. Audiences witness the impact of real phenomena, albeit in a work of invention. And in the installation of an active and animate environment, the scenic design may conspire sets of demanding conditions, eliciting ranges of physical and emotional response. In place of choreography in perfected conditions, performers now tackle unfamiliar circumstances.

In *Gododdin* no enemy faced the warriors. Their demise was conspired against increasingly difficult environmental conditions, as the setting gradually flooded with water, as they climbed rope nets to a deafening soundtrack in the concentrated jets of high-pressure hoses.

> They did fight against the tough and sometimes violent environmental conditions of the performance context – its loud, percussive, and pervasive sound, its slippery, hard, cold, and abrasive surfaces, its enormous, dwarfing space, the tall stacks of oil drums the performers leapt over and crashed into ... (Harvie, 2005, p. 48)

There was little in the way of acting here. As their bodies steamed, as they carried fallen comrades across the lake, collapsing, falling, rising, falling, until exhausted, it was the *symptoms* of their engagement, the outcome of their coping, that the audience witnessed: their application to the task, their constant striving. It was the methods and organization of their effort, the flexibility of response and the use of tools, both designed and provisional, that conjured dramaturgical content. *Performance* now with shades of its other meaning: of quality and degree of endeavour and achievement in competition, as performers are put to the test. Above all, the audience is watching real responses, which is not to suggest that all here is reactive. The performer may be vulnerable but has a range of rejoinders: those planned, those extemporized and those informed by previous experience.

Stuart Brisley's film *Being and Doing* (1984) is a meditation upon convergences between ritual and performance art that includes footage of calendar customs such as the Haxey Hood (see pp. 47–50) as well as examples of his own work. In *Between* (1979), staged in galleries in Amsterdam and London, two naked men struggle to keep their footing on an inclined metal ramp. Constantly they circle, trying to dislodge each other through impulsive barges and protracted pushes. Any strategy may result in success or failure for the protagonist, precipitating either performer onto the floor at the base of the slope. At times we recognize a ploy before it is even executed. At other times we foresee the folly of a tactical repost in advance. Over several hours they re-engage again and again, their bodies increasingly marked by grazes and contusions, dramatizing 'the conflict between human autonomy and the instrumental forces of bureaucratic and state power'. All here results from altered ergonomic conditions. On the flat, such hapless activity without resolution, and its attendant metaphors, would be impossible.

Such activity need not be all seriousness. Imagine the comic result of tilting a stage to an angle of forty degrees and then proceeding with the drama. Performers hacking across the space, abseiling down it, hanging on for dear life whilst trying to get on with the business.

At Haxey, the binding of men with arms prevents breakages but perhaps comprises the ability to apply strength as might be the case when head down in a rugby scrum. But their effort is mediated by topography. Body and landscape are inextricably linked. There is no separation of *self* from *scene*: an *immersion*, the convergence of individual and ground. It may be difficult to know where one begins and the other ends: ergonomics as 'an exercise in hybridisation' (Thrift, 2008, p. 84).

In site-specific performance, discussion of shifting ergonomic engagements may prove more useful than such nebulous concepts as 'motivation' and 'characterization'. But it will require paying as much attention to site as to performance.

Reception: audience and site

Image 5.10   Brith Gof, *Camlann*, Disused factory, Cardiff, 1993 (Jens Koch)

5. Audience Locations
Performers devise methods of working above their audience.
Performers devise methods of working below their audience.
Performers devise methods of working at a considerable distance from their audience.
Performers devise methods of working with the audience very close to them indeed. (Howell, 1999, p. 179)

It is 3 October 1997 and I'm performing *Dead Men's Shoes* in a former ship's chandlers, now part of the Welsh Industrial and Maritime Museum on Bute Street in Cardiff. The seventy-minute monologue is an evocation of the psychological, physical and emotional pressures of R. F. Scott's trek to the South Pole in 1912 and an attempt to recover the story of Welsh seaman Edgar Evans, the fifth man on the fateful journey. Scott's ship *Terra Nova* set out from Cardiff.

The room is long and narrow. Along one wall Mike Brookes has positioned a white screen from ceiling to floor, forty feet in length, upon which are projected expeditionary images, over six hundred in total, from seven computer-controlled slide projectors. Four large photographs abut each other. Three smaller insets straddle the joins. Against the screen at regular intervals are placed five chairs. I move gradually from one end to the other, sometimes sitting, sometimes standing, whilst telling the story. But the space available to me is very restricted. A single row of audience faces the screen not more than eight feet away. Some I approach, others I leave. Sometimes I am close, sometimes distant, but, in white dinner jacket, always immersed in the monochrome of Antarctica. For them too there is no escape from this frozen world. They sit so close that it is impossible to see the whole screen, to separate figure from ground. Although I speak to those directly in front of me, my amplified voice remains at a constant level throughout.

The institutional fixities and sureties of the auditorium are absent at site. Other displacements of, and relationships with, audience become feasible. Conventions of theatrical prudence and decorum may not apply. Previous experience may not be a useful guide as to how to go on, and preconceptions, expectations and critical assumptions may be dislocated and confounded:

> It might prevent the 'theatre' that audiences bring with them, in their heads, when they come to the theatre (i.e. theatre buildings). That 'theatre in the mind' may be made up of a physical memory of all of an individual's previous experiences in theatres. It may be a distillation or a jumble of all previous contracts between audience, individual and event, and results in a 'seemliness' that tends to define a theatrical orthodoxy. This orthodoxy pre-exists any piece of work we might want to place in the theatre. In Blaenafon rubber factory, that 'seemliness' might not exist, it might be left at home (because we're not going to the theatre and won't need it) or it might be left at the factory gate. The slate, therefore, might be cleaner and the individual might be more openhearted and ready to take things as they come. (McLucas, 1993, pp. 3–4)

Audience need not be categorized, or even consider themselves, as 'audience', as a collective with common attributes. All three sets of relationship, performer/performer, performer/spectator, spectator/spectator, become part of an active matrix of interaction and available for negotiation: momentary and durable, individual and collective. Both *proxemics*, interpersonal distances from performer to performer and performer to spectator, and *haptics*, the touch of self and others, may become part of the expressive repertoire of performers and of the dramaturgical fabric of performance. Thrown together in *sociopetal* arenas, sites where audiences are thrown into proximity, audiences may feel not only the closeness and touch of performers but also of each other:

> It may rewrite or problematise the nature of the relationships between all components of the event: (a) between audience member as individual and audience as

mass; (b) between audience member and performer; (c) between audience mass and performer; (d) between performer and performer; (e) between performer and architecture and so on. This inevitably broadens the deep, structural possibilities of theatre. (McLucas, quoted in Pearson and McLucas, no date, pp. 6–7)

Major questions for site work regarding audience include:

■ Where are they, who are they, what is the nature of the relationship and how is it enacted?
■ How are they constituted?
■ How are they addressed?

Site-specific performance may appropriate a pre-existing spatial configuration, annexing the architectural features of site to distribute its audience – staircases, balconies or the terraces of a sales ring, providing prospects unfamiliar or impossible to conspire in the auditorium. Or it may impose new arrangements with the audience in lines, alleys or blocks to conspire effects of distance, closeness, obliqueness, etc. It need not be withdrawn to a place of singular scrutiny. Whilst the auditorium often locates performance 'over there', necessitating projection and a particular economy of vocal and physical rhetoric, site-specific performance may be 'just here', 'up close'. For performers, such intimacy may require *temperance*, tones of voice, gestures and demeanours of another order. Stage practices may be insufficient to the task, or may appear ill placed and overblown in the circumstances. Always on view, without respite, they must also ensure a continuum of attention.

For audiences distributed asymmetrically, this may mean restricted or partial view-points. Anthony Howell demonstrates the repercussions of introducing a large object into an empty space (Howell and Templeton, 1976, pp. 7–10). Around the cube he places a standing figure with arms outstretched, a prone figure and a large group of performers. Depending on where the spectators are positioned, they will see a different combination of performers and may thus interpret the situation differently. 'If the performance space occupied a square mile hearing would be as affected as drastically as vision' (ibid., p. 8). As the performers begin to move, completely different narratives may be revealed in the combination of seen/unseen/half-seen/heard but not seen. They may be encouraged to witness the same action four times, each from a different perspective, or to attend several times or to create an individual narrative by moving at will 'catching as many different dramas as there are points of view' (ibid., p. 10).

Two fundamentally different sets of knowledge and expectation, degrees of preparedness and strategies of survival are brought to, and active within, the encounter of performers and spectators: these may shift. For the performer it may resemble a 'primal scene', a condition of being 'for' the other. In this new space – a place where subjectivity is embodied, face-to-face, hand-to-hand, eye-to-eye, toe-to-toe, not transcendent – there is no distance between action and its repercussion. The body becomes reinscribed as the locus of political action. It becomes a site of local protestation: 'I stand by my word!'. The encounter of performance here may be more profound and consequential than ever.

Bruno Latour reminds us that no relationship is either *isotopic* or *isobaric* (Latour, 2005, pp. 200–2). What the audience brings may come from many different places and may from time to time exert different pressures. In a situation where much might be said and done, performance may need to be accommodating and adaptable.

The audience may be other than an essentially anonymous 'general' public:

- Are they coming to meet me, or me them?
- Are they on home turf?
- Do they know more about this place than I do?

Is the audience known to me and if so what might be said and done and what is better left unsaid? In *Bubbling Tom* (2000), for an audience of family members and local inhabitants, I talked in detail about past events and characters within common currency, though the death of my father, the theme of *From Memory* (1991), an earlier monologue presented elsewhere, was not mentioned in this context.

- Am I leading them?
- Are they following me?
- How can I establish a relationship *and* some conventions of practice in the moment of articulation, some sense of 'here we are, in the here and now'?
- How do I continue to address an audience that has become a straggling line following me over the terrain?
- Or make myself apparent to them in the noise and visual confusion of the urban street?

And if they have no experience of theatre going, would I be better employing conventions with which they are familiar? Performance in the form of a lecture or slideshow or fieldtrip ...

Site-specific performance need not invoke a collective identity for its audience, though it might ascribe them a role. Or at least address them *as* jurors, mob, co-conspirators. 'Every audience member has a vast range of perceptual roles at their disposal: theatre spectator, tourist, game player, partygoer, voyeur, connoisseur, witness, scientific observer, detective' (Turner, 2000, p. 25). In

Polis (see pp. 76–9) they are cast as *participants*, 'co-creators' of the work. The demands upon them to contribute material are substantial.

In Misha Myers's perambulatory performances, they are *percipients*: 'a particular kind of participant whose active, skilful, embodied and sensorial engagement alters and determines a process and its outcomes' (Myers, 2009, p. 33).

Scenario: Exercises

In which exercises towards the creation of dramaturgy are recommended. Checklists are intended to demonstrate the intricacies of the multiple articulations of site and performance, but also to support practical applications.

As ways of devising ...

Exercise 1

Picture an occurrence, incident or personal interaction: an argument, a departure, a fall:

- Where does it happen?
- Who is involved?
- What do we know of their biographies, backgrounds and motives?
- Who else is present?

Fix a particular moment. Imagine the situation thirty seconds before and its trajectory towards the moment, then its continuation to thirty seconds beyond. Then repeat for one minute before and after, five minutes before and after, ten minutes before and after, etc. This may involve protagonists and others commencing and concluding in other places.

Exercise 2

Slice the twenty-minute sequence imagined in Exercise 1 into ten sections of two minutes duration.

Give each section a heading or title, for example 'Excitement', 'Approach', 'Kiss'.

Elaborate what else might happen in each section, that said and that done:

- Who else is present or witnesses each section?
- Who else might have an opinion?
- What other viewpoints are available?
- What other discourses might cast light on what happens in each section: news reports, weather forecast, etc.

Based on the above, devise a performance of twenty minutes:

■ Who are the performers? Audit their specific skills and abilities that might be called upon.
■ What narratives are in play?
■ What orders of expression are used? Is there stylistic consistency between sections?
■ Where is the text: is it spoken or pre-recorded? Are narrators or commentators present?
■ Does the physical action include re-enactment? Is it choreographed or task-based?
■ What is the soundtrack? Does it establish the emotional tenor? Does it include samples, especially of text? Where does it issue from?
■ What media are employed?
■ How might different orders of material be attributed to different voices or media?
■ How do they provide access to other times, places and opinions? From what angles?
■ How is the passage of time marked?
■ What is the dynamic trajectory: variations of pace and emphasis?

Exercise 3

Develop a means of notating the above as a scenario, shooting script or composition of elements against a time-base.

Exercise 4

Now imagine the performance at a site other than that of the original incident: in a lecture theatre, in a car wash, in a field, in a swimming pool.

■ Does the history or function of the site suggest further narratives that can be woven into, or referenced in, the dramaturgy?
■ Does it suggest form that might be annexed by the performance: *as* a lecture, *as* a dinner party?
■ Does it recommend new resources, practices, processes or activities that might elaborate the performance: achieved whilst swimming, whilst washing a body, lit by flaming torches?
■ How might its dimensions, the configuration of its architectural elements – walls, floors, surfaces – and existing spatial arrangements

inform the placement and dispersal of both performance and audience? Do they limit or broaden performative potential? Do they facilitate the provision of close-up, shifting focus and multifocus shots?
- What are the site's internal viewpoints and external outlooks?
- What is its relationship of site to its setting and surroundings?
- Does the site include an existing formal or social organization that might inform audience arrangement, sitting around beds in a hospital ward for instance, and modes of address that might be employed as a consequence?
- Can the audience be assigned a role: as witnesses to be questioned after the reconstruction of the incident?
- Does its nature and state of repair allow the use of techniques impossible in the auditorium, such as vehicles and their headlights?
- What scenographic elements do you introduce or install?
- Now reimagine the performance as a radio play, as an opera, as street theatre.
- What are the repercussions for its form and modes of exposition?

Exercise 5

Now adapt the performance for an audience of family relatives, of children, of the deaf, of those who cannot speak English.

- What are the repercussions?

Exercise 6

Now jettison the original incident and resultant performance and substitute another set of narratives in the dramaturgical and on-site structures whilst maintaining and carrying forward those features that appear useful or of interest.

- What other stories, existing as a sequence of ten phases, might be read into such structures, such as the Stations of the Cross?

Checklist

To recap, these are questions that might be borne in mind when creating site-specific performance.

Of that which is of site:

- Does the history, function or nature of the site suggest a particular subject matter, theme or form?
- Do the particular dimensions and architecture of the site suggest a displacement of action or dispersal of activity?
- Does the site allow the employment and formalization of unusual configurations and spectators? Where are the spectators? Where is the action in relation to them? Is the relationship fixed or changing?
- Does the site suggest types of activity that are appropriate or inappropriate here? What types of activity might be congruent, indifferent or in conflict here?
- Do the dimensions, surfaces, textures and material conditions – the shape, proportion, height, length and disposition of architectural elements of the site – suggest theatrical styles, devices and dramatic forms to be used?
- How are the architecture, history, function, location, microclimate of the site apparent as subject matter, framing, subtext?

Of that which is brought to site:

- How does your performance reveal, make manifest, celebrate, confront or criticize the site?
- Does the site necessitate the employment of particular techniques to overcome the material difficulties here?
- Does the site allow the construction of a second 'ghost' architecture within its 'host'? What is the relationship between 'host' and 'ghost'?
- Does the site allow the suspension and transgression of the prescribed practices and by-laws of the auditorium and enable the use of resources, techniques, materials and phenomena unseen or even illegal in the auditorium: the unusual, the unacceptable, the downright dangerous?
- Is it possible to create a purposeful paradox, through the employment of orders of material seemingly unusual, inappropriate or perverse at this site?
- How are the sight-lines organized? How does the audience see what it sees?
- Can we think formally in three and four dimensions at the site? Or are there backdrops and framing devices?
- How does the physical action emulate or mutate previous activities and behaviours at the site? How is the action informed by the

architectural particulars and special possibilities of site? What does the site allow you to do? Is there one basic mode, such as flying?

■ How do the multiple meanings and readings of performance and site intermingle, amending and compromising one another?

■ Does the performance allow changing points of attention, multiple focus, simultaneous or sequential action, the proximity and touch of performers?

In preparing the concepts for a site-specific performance, Mike Brookes posed a progressive series of questions regarding the placing of performance work within the public domain to undergraduate students in Aberystwyth:

■ Which are the key historical, political, social and formal frameworks within which the work is being made?

■ What are the key intentions of the work?

■ Within which context or contexts could the work most effectively and appropriately be placed?

■ What relationship is to be established or denied between the work and the realities of these contexts?

■ Do these decisions assume cooperation, agreement, specific prior knowledge or any other disposition within the audience?

■ Is the work intended to be perceived as embracing, ambivalent, confrontational or indifferent in its attitude to its audience?

■ Is the work to be structured or placed to allow delivery directly to chosen spectators?

■ What are the intended relationships between spectators, performers, subject, staging and location?

■ What are the material requirements necessary to enable/enhance these relationships?

■ What are the physical, conceptual, formal, aesthetic requirements necessary to enable the presentation of the subject and fulfil its intention?

■ Do the aspirations of the work require the location to have a particular scale, construction, temperature, historical association, light, state of repair, climate?

■ Do the aspirations of the work require a particular/controlled audience viewpoint?

■ Are these requirements inherent within the chosen location, or is the location chosen simply as a host within which these requirements may be realized?

- Is the work intended to be perceived as embracing, ambivalent, confrontational or indifferent in its ostensible attitude to its location?
- What are the intended relationships between the staging, the location, the surrounding area and the wider daily reality?
- What are the requirements necessary to enable these relationships?
- How do these decisions affect all previous decisions?
- What are the most realistic and potentially effective options for the staging of this work?

Scenario: Project: country hotel

In which a site and performance are described. The reader is invited to conceive performance for a similar site, in light of the conditions operational within such a ubiquitous location.

Image 5.11   Paul Jeff, *Life Is Perfect*, Peterstone Court Hotel, Mid-Wales, 2005 (Paul Jeff)

Site

> Legend 1: There is a man and a woman in a hotel room. The man dozes on his back in a rumpled bed. The woman, dressed in a cheap negligee, crawls very slowly up the bed on all fours, over the man. And hammers a spike through his eye.

It is 2 p.m. on Saturday 2 October 2004 and photographer Paul Jeff and dancer Sarah Dowling check into the Peterstone Court country house hotel in mid-Wales. They arrive wearing matching business suits and carrying matching luggage, packed with props and costumes – fake blood, plastic guns, knives, clubs. They are shown upstairs to a large en suite room in the Georgian building. There, over the next twenty-four hours, they prepare, enact and record fifty love scenes, each ending in a murder, a *crime passionnel*, at a rate of just over two killings per hour. Forty-eight are shared equally between them. The sequence also includes two suicide pacts.

Performance photography is for Jeff a hybrid of photography and live art within which photographs are not merely the record of a live event: the performative act and photography are combined into a single utterance, act and record collapsed into one and indistinguishable as separate parts of the work. Event and document are synchronous if not synonymous. In *Life Is Perfect* there is no live audience: the only witness is the camera itself, a Graflex 'Speed Graphic' 5 × 4 camera, the equipment favoured by Arthur Fellig. On his inner left forearm, Jeff has a circular blue permanent tattoo that reproduces the stamp on Fellig's prints: 'Credit Photo by WEEGEE the Famous'. His allegiance is clear. (For an explication of 'performed photography' and images of Jeff's projects see Jeff, 2009.)

The work began with fifty written 'legends', each detailing a short performance authored by Jeff, but referencing the films of Alfred Hitchcock and the pulp novels of Jim Thompson. Every thirty minutes one of these texts was chosen, at random, providing the stage directions for a murder. The Graflex stood on a tripod in the corner, a long lead and bulb-release attached to its shutter. Each love scene was played as realistically as possible. In any one scene the protagonist, the murderer, squeezed the bulb at what he or she regarded as the apogee of ardour, recording the 'death' on Polaroid Type 55 reversible film. In this moment, the instant of sexual passion, the instant of death and the photographic instant collapse into each other: 'into one hugely dense and significant moment', 'a moment of perfection'. Dowling subsequently kept the instant prints, Jeff the negatives.

Life Is Perfect was demanding for the performers, the inevitable consequence of completing such a rigorous, time and task-based concept. They were, after all, 'serial killers', condemned 'to replay the most significant moment of their lives over and over again as if in an infernal purgatory' (Jeff, 2009). Registering the first three images was particularly difficult: how would they sustain the requisite relentless creative application? Only gradually did they acknowledge the need to submit themselves to the programme, to surrender volition to the task. In this durational event it was the schedule to be met that eventually drove the dramaturgy. The effect of repetition was a gradual loss of self-consciousness and the forfeiting of any striving for effects. But to achieve the allegorical approximation to death, it was necessary to achieve high emotional investment in the work, requiring the realistic enactment of sex scenes and a recurrent working towards moments at which they could, at the very least, contemplate 'doing the deed'. Through this, in Jeff's words, the images became 'loaded'. 'Strange,' Dowling retorted, 'how a human being normalises even the strangest of actions.' At midnight the reception desk rang to complain about the noise they were making. From then on they only walked round the outside of the room, avoiding creaking floorboards at the centre. They began to whisper and this became a convention that continued until the end of the work.

As the sequence developed over twenty-four hours the intensity of creating consecutive love scenes resulted in heightened moments of experience transferred to the images in a way that *tableaux vivant* cannot match, an emotional intensity that closes the space between life and art, that is not attainable by other means'. 'No amount of acting could achieve the desired effect.' These are pictures of desire, excess, hallucinatory eroticism. The normal relationship between the event and the implied distance of the dispassionate photographic record is interrupted. There is here a melding of first person narrative – the subject in the photo – and third person position of the camera, of the 'I' of the protagonist and the 'he' or 'she' of the witness/photography.

What actually happened in that room? Jeff says that they would sit together on the leather sofa and read the next scenario. They then dressed, prepared the props, set up the scene and 'ran into it'. There were always, he said, three or four minutes of grappling, of unwitnessed live action moving into the point at which the protagonist felt that it was right to strike and to press the bulb. Of course we only have his word for it and the images neither confirm nor refute this. What occurred is a secret between the two performers. Apparently they no longer have much contact and there is an awkwardness between them. The photograph is an instant of testimony, when the private becomes public.

What are they like, these images? Although Jeff subsequently created a slide show, I only ever saw one print: of a man and woman entwined at the bottom of an image, and surprised that it was in focus given the somewhat erratic operation of the Graflex, with its bellows and primitive wire-frame viewfinder. I was delighted to see the halo of light created by the flash, familiar from Weegee's photographs, heightening the contrast between foreground and receding dark backgrounds and interiors. But Weegee largely photographed the aftermath of crime, though he often arrived ahead of the NYPD and was notorious for rearranging the body and objects to create the best press picture. In Paul Jeff's work we are party to the event itself, though what the exact nature of that event is is not always clear.

Their status as evidence we take on trust. They might, after all, have been shot in one hour. The murders, he says, were purposefully all different, to illustrate the multiple potentialities that could have existed in that one dark instant of passion and action in that one place. A temporal moment is unfolded to show the other potential scenarios that lie behind it and create a seriality that is neither linear nor spatial.

But on first encounter, they defy easy categorization. They are enigmatic and deeply troubling. Who are these anonymous figures? And are they loving or killing? They emerge not from a world of cheap pornography, of calculated violence casually achieved behind closed doors, but from the world of shadows caught out of the corner of the eye. On the border between real and fake, they resemble rather those images of ghosts shot in the main in country houses. Perhaps performance photography restores lost time to the medium – which is Jeff's principal concern – as 'dreamtime'. These images from 4 a.m. are the images *of* 4 a.m., of nightmare.

- Are they the work itself, a paradigmatic example of performance photography?
- Are they the planned outcome of a performance unwitnessed by a live audience, serving as evidence of past events, confirming and authenticating them, standing in for them, showing us what happened in our absence: the camera as my surrogate? Each image then represents and substitutes thirty minutes of work, arresting and compressing time, although the process is effectively aestheticized: there is no hint here of creative difficulties. Were I to know the sequence of their shooting, I could follow the event. I might search for signs of progression or of weariness in physical and emotional expenditure, of increasing decay in the setting.
- Or are they the accidental outcome of something they would have done anyway, a personal fetish perhaps?
- Are they a kind of rationale, an excuse, for an extreme encounter, framed as performance that might have had altogether other motives?
- Is this a series of discrete moments or are there narratives hidden in the sequence?
- And were you to get hold of the legends, could I restage it?

Brief

In conceiving performance for a hotel room:

- What is possible behind closed doors?
- How does it occupy the room?
- How is it positioned in the room?
- What facilities are available?

- How does it utilize furniture and fittings?
- What is the relationship or link with adjacent spaces – corridor, room next door, scene outside?
- Is the audience in the room or elsewhere?
- If elsewhere, how is the performance made available to them?
- Can dramaturgy be informed by what goes on in hotel rooms, what has famously happened there, and what takes place in moments of privacy?

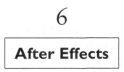

6

After Effects

Afterlife: pedagogy

In which the pedagogical potential of site-specific work is espoused.

> Attention is thus directed to practices. It is hardly astonishing to see students' interest move from *products* of research to *methods of production*. (Certeau, 1997, p. 49)

Though resistant to wider appreciation through the distribution of its documents, site-specific performance may inform transferable and broadly applicable approaches in pedagogy: it necessitates research with interdisciplinary aspects into both site and performance. 'It also permits entry into a debate around *theatreness*, raising questions of what theatre has been and might be in the future' (Wilkie, 2008, p. 102).

Aberystwyth is at the end of the railway line ... or at the beginning. It is a good place to address the questions posed by the 'Living Landscapes' conference of 18–21 June 2009:

- How are landscapes lived on, in and through?
- How are landscape and environment revealed, imagined, experienced, contested, animated and represented by, in and through performance?
- How can performance inform, extend and enhance engagement with, and the interpretation and appreciation of, landscape and environment?
- How can performance illuminate, explicate and problematize the multiplicity of attachments, meanings and emotions that resonate within and from landscapes: visual, aural and tactile?
- What strategies and forms of performance-exposition does working with landscape as medium and scene of expression inspire and necessitate?
- What is the life of landscape and how is it performed?

Within academic provision, we make a virtue and an opportunity of an assumed geographical marginality, seeking to devise distinctive pedagogical approaches, both practical and theoretical, that acknowledge and capitalize upon the specific intellectual, cultural and geographical resources of the town – its landscape, languages, architecture, history – and that value its characteristic physical, social and cultural ecology; that utilize the material assets of the environs as a creative stimulus. Students are challenged to create work in the resonant architectures of chapels, in the commercial arrangement of the cattle market, in a sand-filled horse-training arena, on the beach, in the town museum – to discern the constraints and possibilities of a given situation. To design scenographies using fences, scaffolding and lighting from the local farmers' cooperative and builders' merchants. Of their own volition, they stage performances in bedrooms, cellars, deserted public houses, in the *camera obscura* ... This active engagement with a specific locale favours the local, the particular, the 'grain' of the place. Pedagogy develops that is itself site-specific, beginning perhaps in the 'empty field' rather than on the 'empty stage'. Working primarily with applied dramaturgy – procedures through which material is organized and ordered to generate performative meaning – the intention is to identify principles, organizing principles, however schematic: approaches to conception, design, rehearsal and production in relation to a particular situation, that are then applicable in other arenas of performance, presentation and representation in and beyond Wales, within theatre and elsewhere.

Heike Roms suggests that we function within a triangular field of endeavour, constituted in the dynamic interaction of, or tension between, three notions: practice, theory and context, which constantly feed off and into each other. 'Practice' because we aim to make things – performances, knowledges – as much as we want to reflect on things, informed by extensive personal experience of professional engagement. 'Theory' because we are committed to the development of appropriate means of analysing performance from the position of participation rather than spectatorship. And 'context' because we are interested in the implications of social, cultural, political and historical context for the nature, form and function of performance, particularly as operational in this place and because we are equally concerned with the constituent elements of the performance environment – location, site, architecture, scenography – and their effect upon techniques of exposition. Within and beyond the triangle, a multitude of stances and viewpoints are available: each one of us may stand from time to time closer to one apex than the others, whilst still holding all in view. It is they that orientate our approaches. Our aim is to keep all three constantly in play. So whilst we may be considering a moment in the theory of practice (or a practice of theory), context still claims our attention. Our question is ever: what does that mean to us, here? And when, as is ever the case in Wales, we become overly concerned with the relationship between practice and context, the insistent presence of theory offers new perspectives.

Concentration upon processes of devising, presentation and documentation involves attending to space, time, pattern, detail, ordering, dynamics ... Emergent principles equip students to operate effectively across media and platforms, without being tied to particular genre or stylistic conventions. And our peripheral situation provides a stump where practices from elsewhere that will never visit this place might be interrogated, verified, criticized and confronted. The result is a set of attitudes that might be summed up thus: *Were one to attempt these kinds of things, in this or that sort of situation, then these might be the possible range of outcomes.*

We espouse a deliberate erasure of the finely etched line between the academic and the artistic, in offering undergraduate and postgraduate schemes with a substantial practical component, drawing directly upon traditions of experimental theatre-making in Wales that have proposed alternative approaches to the preoccupations, themes and placement of performance from companies such as Cardiff Laboratory Theatre and Brith Gof to a younger generation of artists concerned with place, environment and landscape, who

> share an interest in the complex relationship between ourselves, our bodies and our environment, in our physical and sensual experience and memory of place, and in the impact a particular location can have on our lives. Theirs is a theatre that acknowledges the close link between culture, subjectivity and place without reverting to nostalgia, new age mysticism or an aggressive 'native soil' ideology. (Roms, 1997, p. 80)

Practice and theory are folded together in an increasingly complex manner over the arc of provision, progressing from concept through devising to public presentation and finally documentation. And site-specificity is a pervasive and persistent consideration.

Early on, students are required to work in small groups to conceive though not to perform a performance of a given duration on a given theme for a given number of spectators and at a given location in Aberystwyth: the castle, the promenade, a swimming pool, the balconied hall of the Old College building. This is presented for assessment through live exposition though not performance, involving the use of video, slide, diagrammatic and textual material in a formal lecture situation. Although criteria include feasibility, students are invited to consider site, performance and audience and what they might achieve given the opportunity is without prescriptions of genre.

Parallel study is of contexts in which performance is negotiated and enacted; and the social, cultural and environmental implications for the nature of performance itself: what particular conditions might lead to, enable or inspire artists to create? These include landscape, village, city, border, revolution, carnival, network, feast. They are examined in a comparative and interdisciplinary manner, drawing upon history, anthropology, human geography, sociology and politics. In assessment, a written essay is matched by its performed equivalent, requiring intellectual argument to be articulated in academic presentation. This offers the student an opportunity to introduce material and media inappropriate or impossible in the written submission, from the inclusion of documentary footage to real-time demonstration and emulation: research on cycle couriers includes video shot from a camera fixed to the handlebars. That on tattooing is staged in the local parlour.

Writing for, about and as performance, encourages the integration of theoretical and creative modes. Assessment requires the location of writing within specific physical parameters. Spatial composition takes precedence over word length. In 'Page as Site' writing is confined to the foldout sheets of a small Moleskine notebook in forms of manual and mechanical inscription and collage. In 'Site as Page', writing as inscription or exposition at or on a particular site: from their own body to the interior of a wardrobe, from an embroidered bedspread to a telephone line available only in a certain kiosk, burned onto toast, as an audio tour of the university library. In both, the relationship between site and writing is topographical and dramaturgical.

Production commences with preparatory études under the direction of fellow students: five women, locked in a room for forty-eight hours, follow instructions provided by their peers. Four women in ball-gowns walk slowly down a jetty and then jump into the sea.

In a major production students then work in groups of eight for a period of four weeks to conceive, develop, rehearse, produce and present a performance of at least sixty minutes on a given topic, putting into operation, in an ordered and meaningful way, the methodological and representational principles of devising performance. At site they must organize both performance and its reception, be it in the restricted spaces of a terraced house or in a university greenhouse.

Schemes culminate with a solo performance in which the individual accepts sole responsibility for determining and achieving personal, creative outcomes: as a car journey to the local supermarket, in a cage at the zoo, in a derelict boxing club, in the privacy of a bathroom, underwater in a specially constructed tank, in a barn on the family farm, in the pulpit of Bethel chapel.

Undergraduates conclude their course with documentation. Whether this is a collection of texts or a DVD, it must fit within the flat cardboard container provided: a pizza box, frequently extended, elaborated, decorated. It must become the site of documentation of site-specific performance, addressed through principles now familiar.

Afterlife: archive

In which the documentation of site-specific performance is considered.

> Creativity is the act of reusing and recombining heterogeneous knowledge. (Certeau, 1997, p. 49)

The remnants of site-specific performance can be extensive. It generates *documents* relating to both the creation of performance and to the engagement with site *before*, *during* and *after* the event. Those *before* – scripts, plans, contracts – are proactive, utopian. They envisage. They want things to happen. Those made *during* – video and sound recordings, photographs – often assert themselves to be the true record of what really happened, or else we ascribe that capacity to them. And those *after* make claims to efficacy and ownership: reports, reviews, receipts, etc.

In addition, site-specific performance resides differentially and with differing degrees of durability in the memories of those undertaking differing types of task that contribute to its making. What might not survive, might alter profoundly or disappear totally, is site itself, rendering restaging unlikely. Site performance is also specific to period, to a moment in time.

But site-specific performance frequently lacks those totalizing and prestigious documents, equivalents of the play script, that can be published, transported, held in the palm of the hand, read, reread, subjected to literary scrutiny, to textual analysis. It is tangible, uncomplicated, unitary: all that legitimizes and validates acts of theatre. It may as a result be barely accounted for and under-represented within the purview of historiography.

How then to redress this shortfall: to recover past performance, to plan documentation? Between 1981 and 1997, the history of Brith Gof paralleled the widespread adoption of information technology, the increasing public availability of video and audio recording equipment and, in Wales, the inception of the national broadcaster S4C. Within its archive, there is a perceptible shift from hand-written notes to computer-generated designs; and from black and white photographs to videos of productions for television transmission. *Gododdin* (1988–89) was recorded for broadcast with one camera on multiple occasions in performances in Wales, Italy, Germany and Scotland. *Haearn* (1992) was recorded during six performances: by seven cameras, including two mounted on mobile booms and one 'steadycam', simultaneously.

The National Library of Wales is the custodian of a substantial deposit of material on the company's work, in a variety of media and in multiple formats: from plans, drawings, scenarios, scripts, scores, notebooks, publicity material and reviews to prints, slides, computer disks, film, audio and video tapes – including unpublished preparatory documents, discarded 'rushes' and incomplete submasters. This is now ordered production by production in 100 acid-free boxes. The Library also holds an unsorted deposit similar in amount and composition from the personal bequest of Cliff McLucas.

A collaborative project is now under way with the Library. First, to archive, catalogue and improve access to the deposit. Thereafter to enhance appreciation of the historical, cultural and aesthetic significance of the company's work. And perhaps also to recover, reassess and activate some of the artistic gains made. There are complex issues of conserving a multimedia collection and of digital transfer; of disaggregating documents made before, during and after performance; and of identifying, deciphering and translating material that was only ever intended as the workaday communication of ideas amongst collaborators.

New media may offer enhanced opportunities to synthesize the fragmentary remains of performance. On a web-based wiki environment created by Michael Shanks at Stanford University, any individual with a password, including all those who worked in any way in a Brith Gof production, were invited to add to an accumulative account of the performance. They might even alter posted opinion, in the knowledge that all versions would be archived. Few accepted the offer and the laborious effort required to upload data.

New media may also facilitate the aesthetic reconstitution of past devised performance from its archival debris: to assemble, juxtapose and interpenetrate documentary material of different orders – textual, visual and audio – in works of on-screen recovery. To apply and develop new programs, formats and platforms: to create *digital scenarios*, the equivalent of the dramatic script, through such integrations. Or through the use of computer-aided design, rendering and animation to model three-dimensional representations of a site showing the building of scenography, the disposition of moving performers and audience, light states, etc., from all angles, and located in domains such as Second Life.

Any later drawing together of material into a single document will be inevitably partial. It can make no claims to completeness. It will struggle to create an authoritative or authorized version of an occurrence where all experiences were partial, where panoptical positioning was available neither to the various orders of spectators nor to the performers. Any subsequent record, a DVD for instance, risks collapsing time and space counter to the very intentions of the work.

And yet one effective way of achieving the ambition to *evoke* the original performances for a contemporary audience has been through a series of public symposia, four thus far, each dedicated to a specific production, chosen from different periods in the company's history, under the title *Rhwng Cof ac Archif/Between Memory and Archive*. Involving the participation of former company members – directors, performers, technicians, administrators, as well as funders, critics, academic researchers and original audience members – these events include critical presentations, interviews and discussions, eye-witness accounts, practical demonstrations and the viewing of a range of surviving documentation, especially copied and prepared by the Library. Fragments of documentation are assembled, both physical remains *and* memories – a combination of images and anecdotes, of documentary accounts and personal revelations. Some colleagues arrive with all that they have kept, purposefully or accidentally. For others, viewing the archival material acts as a *mnemonic*, stirring faint recollections.

Significant questions include:

- What survives and why? And what went where? What to the archive, what to the attic, what to the rubbish dump?
- What is lost, and how might this shortfall be addressed?
- What is remembered and why? Are memories of when it went well or of all those traumas of production and mishaps during presentation?
- Is there a tension between the official version preserved in perpetuity in the Library and the remembrance of uneasy experiences, of bad times in the creative process?

The full audio and video records of these events function as multivocal oral history for further dissemination and study, and as aids to the identification of material within the archival deposit, as future discussion focuses upon the exact provenance of documents.

A key component of these symposia has been the return to site. On Aberystwyth railway station company members collectively remember the staging of *PAX* in 1991 in animated discussion and playful argument with much pointing and positioning, disclosing personal experiences of an event that resists becoming a single object. *PAX* is talked into being. Not only is the change in the performers and the passage of time poignantly revealed, as they tell heroic tales of youthful exploits and moments of failure – when it went wrong, when the plan failed, when they had to use all their skill and experience in acts of compensation – but also the nature of the site itself in the on-going transformation of material surroundings: the station concourse is now a bar, the platform an antique shop; the newspaper kiosk upon which the orchestra played is long gone. There is no pretence at restaging here, but the energetic recollection of that which was once feasible may inspire other initiatives in changed circumstances. Site-specific performance as an unlikely and fleeting moment in the history of a place, known only through the traveller's tales of those present.

Certainly, in the end, the measure of specificity may be whether the authors of its written account are willing or able to devote equal attention to perform-ance *and* to site: to extensive and detailed description of cultural and political context, architectural and topographic setting, history and ambiance.

Postscripts

In which a future is glimpsed.

1. Whatever the proscriptions of the Health and Safety Executive and contem-porary restraints upon public assembly under the watchful eye of CCTV, site-specific performance can endure as a work of imagination; as a con-ceptual exercise, a means of thinking through the implications of varying arrangements of place, performance and audience; and as a touchstone in recognizing that the practices of the auditorium are themselves site-specific, not a universally applicable means to go on in all circumstances.
2. On 5 November 2009 the newly formed National Theatre Wales announced that its first programme of productions is to include site-specific works.

Bibliography

Adams, H. (2004) 'This house today is a theatre ...', in Rees, M. and Tyson, J. (eds) *The House Project* (Cardiff: Chapter (Cardiff) Ltd).

AHT (Antarctic Heritage Trust New Zealand)

—— (2003) *Conservation Report: Shackleton's Hut* (Christchurch, NZ: Antarctic Heritage Trust)

—— (2004a) *Conservation Plan: Discovery Hut, Hut Point* (Christchurch, NZ: Antarctic Heritage Trust)

—— (2004b) *Conservation Plan: Scott's Hut, Cape Evans* (Christchurch, NZ: Antarctic Heritage Trust)

—— (2009) http://www.hertitage-antactic.org/AHT, date accessed 9 May 2009.

Andreotti, L. and Costa, X. (eds) (1996) *Theory of the dérive and other Situationist writings on the city* (Barcelona: Museu d'Art Contemporani de Barcelona/ACTAR).

Augé, M. (1995) *Non-places: introduction to an anthropology of supermodernity* (London: Verso).

Augé, M. (2000) 'Non-places', in Read, A. (ed.) *Architecturally Speaking: Practices of Art, Architecture and the Everyday* (London and New York: Routledge), 7–11.

Auster, P. (2005) *Ground Zero: A Sonic Memorial Soundwalk* (New York: Soundwalk), CD.

Balfour, M. C (1891) 'Legends of the Cars'. *Folk-Lore,* II, 145–70; 257–83; 401–18.

Barrell, J. (1980) *The dark side of the landscape: The rural poor in English painting 1730–1840* (Cambridge: Cambridge University Press).

Baudelaire, C. (1972) *Selected Writings on Art and Literature* (London, Penguin).

Baumann, Z. (2000) *Liquid Modernity* (Cambridge: Polity).

BBC Wales (2009) Coal House. Cardiff, http://www.bbc.co.uk/wales/coalhouse2/index.shtml, date accessed 8 May 2009.

Benjamin, W. (1992) *Illuminations* (London: Fontana Press).

Benjamin, W. (1999) *The Arcades Project* (Cambridge MA: Harvard Belknap).

Berger, J. (1983) 'Boris', *Granta,* 9, 21–51.

Biggs, I. (2008) 'Transect – margins and registers re-figured: notes from the Avonmouth–Severn Beach "Littoral"', AHRC 'Living in a Material World: Performativies of Emptiness' network, unpublished report.

Blaenavon (2009) Blaenavon Industrial Landscape World Heritage Site, http://www.world-heritage-blaenavon.org.uk, date accessed 8 May 2009.

Bourriaud, N. (1998) *Relational Aesthetics* (Paris: Les presse du réel).

Bourriaud, N. (2004) 'Berlin Letter about Relational Aesthetics', in Doherty, C. (ed.) *Contemporary Art: From Studio to Situation* (London: Black Dog Publishing).

Brueggemann, W. (1989) 'The land', in Lilburne, G. (ed.) *A Sense of Place: Christian Theology of the Land* (Nashville: Abingdon Press).

Brown, C.C. (2000) *Under Erebus.* Creative New Zealand, Christchurch, New Zealand, audio CD.

Brown, N. (2005) Walking as knowing as making, http://www.walkinginplace.org, date accessed 7 May 2009.

Buchli, V. and Lucas, G. (eds) (2001) *Archaeologies of the Contemporary Past* (London: Routledge).

Buckland, D., MacGilp, A. and Parkinson, S. (eds) (2006) *Burning Ice: Art and Climate Change* (London: Cape Farewell).

Calle, S., Macel, C., Bois, Y-V. and Rolin, O. (2003) *Sophie Calle: M'as tu vue? – Did yoy see me?* (London: Prestel).

Campbell, F. and Ulin, J. (2004) *BorderLine Archaeology* (Goteborg University, Sweden), joint PhD thesis.

Carieri, F. (2002) *Walkscapes: Walking as an aesthetic practice* (Barcelona: Gustavo Gili).

Casey, E. (1998) *The Fate of Place: A Philosophical History* (Berkeley: University of California Press).

Casey, E. (2001) 'Body, Self, and Landscape: A Geophilosophical Inquiry into the Place-World', in Adams, P. C., Hoelscher, S. and Till, K.E. (eds) *Textures of Place: Exploring Humanist Geographies* (Minneapolis: University of Minnesota Press), 403–25.

Certeau, M. de. (1988) *The Practice of Everyday Life* (Berkeley: University of California Press).

Certeau, M. de (1997) *Culture in the Plural* (Minneapolis: University of Minnesota Press).

Clough, P.T. (2007) *The Affective Turn: Theorizing the Social* (Durham: Duke University Press).

Cooper, J.J. (1993) 'A Fool's Game'; The Ancient Tradition of Haxey Hood (Wroot: Lord and Boggins of the Haxey Hood).

Cosgrove, D. (1984) *Social Formation and Symbolic Landscape* (Beckenham: Croom Helm).

Cosgrove, D. (2004) 'Landscape and Landschaft', *German Historical Institute Bulletin*, 35, 57–71.

Coult, T. and Kershaw, B. (eds) (1983) *Engineers of the Imagination* (London, Methuen).

Cousin, G. (1994) 'An Interview with Mike Pearson of Brith Gof', *Contemporary Theatre Review*, 2, 2, 37–47.

Crickhowell, N. (1997) *Opera House Lottery: Zaha Hadid and the Cardiff Bay Project* (Cardiff: University of Wales Press).

Cumberland, G. (1996 [1796]) *An Attempt to Describe Hafod* (Aberystwyth, Hafod Trust).

Cusack, P. (2009) http://www/lcc.arts.ac.uk/17617.htm, date accessed 4 May 2009.

Deakin, R. (1999) *Waterlog: A Swimmer's Journey Through Britain* (London: Chatto & Windus).

Deleuze, G. and Guattari, F. (1988) *A Thousand Plateaus* (London: The Athlone Press).

Deller, J. (2009). Http://www.jeremydeller.org. 4 May 2009.

Doherty, C. (ed.) (2004) *Contemporary Art: From Studio to Situation* (London: Black Dog Publishing).

Earthfall (2009) http://www.earthfall.org.uk, date accessed 1 May 2009.

Eastley, M. (2007) *Arctic* (London: Cape Farewell), CD.

Emerson, R.W. and Thoreau, H.D. (n.d.) *Nature Walking* (Boston: Beacon Press).

Etchells, T. (1999) *Certain Fragments* (London: Routledge).

Farquhar, A. (ed.) (2005) *The Storr: Unfolding Landscape* (Glasgow: Scottish Arts Council).

Farquhar, A. (2007) *Half Life* (Glasgow: nva)

Feenstra, W. (2007) *The Best Place* (Rotterdam: Veenman publishers/Gijs Stork).

Foucault, M. (1986) 'Of Other Places', *Diacritics*, 16, 22–7.

Garoian, C.R. (1999) *Performing Pedagogy: Toward an Art of Politics* (Albany, NY: State University of New York Press).

Geertz, C. (1973) *The Interpretation of Cultures* (New York: Basic Books).

Grant, S. (2006) 'How to Stand in Australia?', in McAuley, G. (ed.) *Unstable Ground: Performance and the Politics of Place* (Brussels: P.I.E. Peter Lang), 247–70.

Greenaway, P. (1991) *The Physical Self* (Rotterdam: Boymans van Beuningen).

Greenaway, P. (1997) *Flying over water* (London: Merrell Holberton).

Greenaway, P. (2009) http://www.petergreenaway.info, dated accessed 4 May 2009.

Harvie, J. (2005) *Staging the UK* (Manchester: Manchester University Press).

Hauptmann, D. (ed.) (2006) *The Body in Architecture* (Rotterdam: 010 Publishers).

Heathfield, A. (2000) 'End Time Now', in Heathfield, A. (ed.) *Small Acts: Performance, the Millennium and the Marking of Time* (London: Black Dog Publishing), 104–11.

Heathfield, A. (2009) *Out of Now: The Lifeworks of Tehching Hsieh* (Cambridge, MA: MIT Press).

Heddon, D. (2002) 'Performing the archive: following in the footsteps', *Performance Research*, 7, 4, 68–77.

Heddon, D. (2008) *Autobiography and Performance* (Basingstoke: Palgrave Macmillan).

Heddon, D. and Turner, C. (2009) 'The Art of Walking: An Embodied Practice' (*Living Landscapes*: Aberystwyth), conference paper.

Heim, W. (2006) 'Navigating Voices', in Giannachi, G. and Stewart, N. (eds) *Performing Nature: Explorations in Ecology and the Arts* (Bern: Peter Lang), 199–216.

Hill, L. and Paris, H. (2006) *Performance and Place* (Basingstoke: Palgrave Macmillan).

Hodge, S., Smith, P., Turner, C., and Weaver, T. (2003) *An Exeter Mis-Guide* (Exeter: Wrights & Sites).

Hofer, P. (1967) *The Disasters of War by Francisco Goya y Lucientes* (New York: Dover).

Howell, A. (1999) *The Analysis of Performance Art* (Amsterdam: Harwood Academic).

Howell, A. and Templeton, F. (1976) *Elements of Performance Art* (London: The Ting – Theatre of Mistakes).

Hughes, H. (1998) *An Uprooted Community: A History of Epynt* (Llandysul: Gomer).

Hunter, R. (2007) *Civil Twilight & Other Social Works* (Cardiff, Trace: Samizdat Press).

Huws, S. (2009) http://www.sionedhuws.com, date accessed 4 May 2009.

Ingold, T. (2000) *The Perception of the Environment: Essays on Livelihood, Dwelling and Skill* (London, Routledge).

Ingold, T. (2007) *Lines: A Brief History*, London and New York, Routledge.

IOU (2009) http://www.ioutheatre.org, date accessed 8 May 2009.

Irwin, K. (2007) *The Ambit of Performativity: How Site Makes Meaning in Site-Specific Performance* (University of Art and Design: Helsinki), PhD thesis.

Jeff, P. (2009) http://www.morebeautifulthangod.com, date accessed 4 May 2009.

Kastner, J. and Wallis, B. (1998) *Land and Environmental Art* (London: Phaidon).

Kaye, N. (1996a) *Art Into Theatre: Performance Interviews and Documents* (London: Routledge).

Kaye, N. (1996b) 'Site/Intermedia', *Performance Research*, 63–9.

Kaye, N. (2000) *Site-Specific Art: Performance, Place and Documentation* (London: Routledge).

Kurtz, C.F. and Snowden, D.J. (2003) 'The new dynamics of strategy: Sense-making in a complex and complicated world', *IBM Systems Journal*, 40, 3, 462–83.

Kwon, M. (2004) *One Place After Another* (Cambridge, MA: MIT Press).

Ladd, E. (2009) http://www.eddieladd.com, date accessed 8 May 2009.

Latour, B. (2005) *Reassembling the Social: An Introduction to Actor-Network-Theory* (Oxford: Oxford University Press).

Lefebvre, H. (2004) *Rhythmanalysis: Space, Time and Everyday Life* (London: Continuum).

Lewis Jones, B. (1985) 'Cynefin – The word and the concept', *Nature in Wales*, 121–2.

Libeskind, D. (2001) *The Space of Encounter* (London: Thames & Hudson).

Lippard, L. (1997) *The Lure of the Local* (New York: The New Press).

Lorimer, H. (2006) 'Herding memories of humans and animals', *Environment and Planning D: Society and Space*, 24, 497–518.

Lorimer, H. (2009) http://www.ges.gla.ac.uk:433/staff/hlorimer, date accessed 4 May 2009.

Malpede, J. (2009) The Robert F. Kennedy Performance Project, http:www.rfkineky. org, date accessed 4 May 2009.

Massey, D. (1994) *Space, Place and Gender* (Cambridge: Polity).

Massey, D. (1999) 'Spaces of politics', in Massey, D., Allen, J and Sarre, P. (eds) *Human Geography Today* (Oxford: Polity), 279–94.

Massey, D. (2005) *For Space* (London: Sage).

Mayhew, H. (1985 [1861]) *London Labour and the London Poor* (Harmondsworth: Penguin).

McAuley, G. (ed.) (2006) *Unstable Ground: Performance and the Politics of Place* (Brussels: P.I.E. Peter Lang).

McAuley, G. (2000) 'BodyWeather in the Central Desert of Australia: towards an ecology of performance', in de Quincey, T. (2009) Bodyweather, http://www.bodyweather. net, date accessed 4 May 2009.

McAuley, G. (2007) 'Local Acts: Site-Specific Performance Practice, Introduction', *About Performance*, 7, 7–11.

Mcfarlane, R. (2007) *The Wild Places* (London: Granta).

McLucas, C. (1989) *Leeuwarden: The Workbook* (Brith Gof Archive, NLW).

McLucas, C. (1993) 'The Host and the Ghost' (Brith Gof Archive, NLW), lecture notes.

McLucas, C. (1998) 'The Host, the Ghost and the Witness. Some approaches to site in the theatre works of Brith Gof 1989–1999. The Roehampton Remix' (Brith Gof Archive, NLW), lecture notes.

McLucas, C. (2001) 'The Pointing Finger and the Moo "Wales". Some Approaches to Cutural Specificity in the Works of Brith Gof' (Brith Gof Archive, NLW), multi-media presentation.

McLucas, C. (no date) 'Brith Gof: Large Scale Site Specific Theatre Works. Some Notes Prepared for an Illustrated Lecture' (Brith Gof Archive, NLW), lecture notes.

McLucas, C. and Pearson, M. (1995) 'Performance/Place/Public' (Brith Gof Archive, NLW), company document.

McLucas, C. and Pearson, M. (1996) 'Cliff McLucas and Mike Pearson (Brith Gof)', in Kaye, N. (ed.) *Art into Theatre* (Amsterdam: Harwood Academic).

McLucas, C. and Pearson, M. (1999) 'Clifford McLucas and Mike Pearson', in Gianacchi, G. and Luckhurst, M. (eds) *On Directing: Interviews with Directors* (London: Faber and Faber), 78–89.

Miller, G. (2009) Linked, http://www.linkedm11.info, date accessed 4 May 2009.

Morgan, R. (1995) *Y Llyfyr Glas; Brith Gof 1988–95* (Cardiff: Brith Gof).

Myers, M. (2006) 'Journeys To, From and Around: Founding Home in Transition', in Coulter-Smith, G. and Owen, M. (eds) *Art in the Age of Terrorism* (London: Paul Holberton Press), 213–27.

Myers, M. (2009) *Homing Place: Performing Emplacement* (University of Plymouth), PhD thesis.

Nancy, J-L. (2005) *The Ground of the Image* (New York: Fordham University Press).

National Trust for Scotland (2009) 'Culloden', http://nts.org.uk/Culloden, date accessed 8 May 2009.

Natural England (2009) 'Sites of Special Scientific Interest', http://sssi.naturalengland. org.uk/Special/sssi/index/cfm, date accessed 8 May 2009.

Newall, V. (1980) 'Throwing the hood at Haxey: a Lincolnshire Twelfth-Night custom', *Folk Life*, 18, 7–23.

Nora, P. (1996) *Realms of Memory: Rethinking the French Past, Vol. I* (New York: Columbia University Press).

Olivier, L. (2001) 'The archaeology of the contemporary past', in Buchli, V. and Lucas, G. (eds) *Archaeologies of the Contemporary Past* (London and New York: Routledge), 175–88.

Owen, T. (1987) *Welsh Folk Customs* (Llandysul: Gomer).

Parratt, C.M. (2000) 'Of place and men and women: gender and topophilia in the "Haxey Hood"', *Journal of Sport History*, 27, 2, 222–49.

Pavis, P. (1998) *Dictionary of the Theatre: Terms, Concepts, and Analysis* (Toronto: University of Toronto Press).

Pearson, M. (1980) *Glimpses of the Map: Cardiff Laboratory Theatre 1974–1980* (Cardiff: Cardiff Laboratory Theatre).

Pearson, M. (1985) *Brith Gof: A Welsh Theatre Company 1. 1981–5* (Aberystwyth: Brith Gof).

Pearson, M. (1988) *Brith Gof: A Welsh Theatre Company* (Aberystwyth: Brith Gof).

Pearson, M. (1991) 'Performance' (Brith Gof archive, NLW), company document.

Pearson, M. (1996) 'The Dream in the Desert', *Performance Research*, 1, 1, 5–15.

Pearson, M. (1997) 'Special Worlds, Secret Maps: A Poetics of Performance', in Taylor, A-M. (ed.) *Staging Wales: Welsh Theatre 1979–1997* (Cardiff: University of Wales Press), 85–99.

Pearson, M. (2000) 'Bubbling Tom', in Heathfield, A. (ed.) *Small Acts: Performance, the Millennium and the Marking of Time* (London: Black Dog Publishing), 172–85.

Pearson, M. (2001) 'You can't tell by looking', *Performance Research*, 6, 2, 31–8.

Pearson, M. (2004) '"No joke in petticoats": British polar expeditions and their theatrical presentations', *The Drama Review*, Spring 2004, T181, 44–59.

Pearson, M. (2005a) 'P-P-P-Pick Up a Penguin: Men and Animals in Antarctic Exploration', in Gianacchi, G. and Stewart, N. (eds) *Performing Nature: Explorations in Ecology and the Arts* (Bern: Peter Lang), 119–32.

Pearson, M. (2005b) 'Way Out West!', *Studies in Theatre and Performance*, 25, 3, 253–62.

Pearson, M. (2006a) *In Comes I: Performance, Memory and Landscape* (Exeter: University of Exeter Press).

Pearson, M. (2006b) 'Marshfield Mummers: The Old Time Paper Boys', in Kelleher, J. and Ridout, N. (eds) *Contemporary Theatres in Europe* (London and New York: Routledge), 136–48.

Pearson, M. (2007a) 'It Came Apart in My Hands: Reflections On Polis by Pearson/ Brookes', *About Performance*, 7, 13–23.

Pearson, M. (2007b) *Carrlands*, http://www.carrlands.org.uk, date accessed 8 May 2009.

Pearson, M. (2007c) 'Site-specific Performance' (University of Art and Design, Helsinki), lecture notes, August 2007.

Pearson, M. (2009) '"Professor Gregory's Villa" and Piles of Pony Poop: Early Expeditionary Remains in Antarctica', in Holtorf, C. and Piccini, A. (eds) *Contemporary Archaeologies: Excavating Now* (Frankfurt am Main: Peter Lang), 83–94.

Pearson, M. and Jeff, P. (2001) 'Pearson/Brookes: Carrying Lyn', *Performance Research*, 6, 3, 23.

Pearson, M. and McLucas, C. (no date) 'The Host and the Ghost: Brith Gof's large scale site specific works' (Brith Gof archive, NLW), company document.

Pearson, M. and Shanks, M. (1997) 'Performing a Visit', *Performance Research,* 2, 2, 41–53.

Pearson, M. and Shanks, M. (2001) *Theatre/Archaeology* (London: Routledge).

Persighetti, S. (2000) 'Wrights & Sites & Other Regions', *Studies in Theatre and Performance,* Supplement 5, 7–22.

Piccini, A. (2009) 'Guttersnipe: A Micro Road Movie', in Holtorf, C. and Piccini, A. (eds) *Contemporary Archaeologies: Excavating Now* (Frankfurt am Main: Peter Lang), 183–99.

Pimlott, M. (2006) 'Being in Places', in Hauptmann, D. (ed.) *The Body in Architecture.* (Rotterdam: 010 Publishers), 266–73.

Platform (2009) http://platformlondon.org, date accessed 8 May 2009.

de Quincey, T. (2009) Bodyweather, http://www.bodyweather.net, date accessed 4 May 2009.

Read, A. (ed.) (2000) *Architecturally Speaking: Practices of Art, Architecture and the Everyday* (London and New York: Routledge).

Read, S. (2006) 'The Urban Image: Becoming Visible, in Hauptmann, D. (ed.) *The Body in Architecture* (Rotterdam: 010 Publishers), 48–63.

Rees, M. (2009) http://www.r-i-p-e.co.uk, date accessed 1 May 2009.

Rees, M. and Tyson, J. (2004) *The House Project* (Cardiff: Chapter (Cardiff) Ltd.).

Rees, S. (2003) 'Threshold', *Platfform*, 1, 24–7.

Rendell, J. (1998) 'Displaying sexuality: gendered identities and the early nineteenth-century street', in Fyfe, N. R. (ed.) *Images of the Street* (London and New York: Routledge), 75–91.

Rendell, J. (2009) http://www.bartlett.ucl.ac.uk/research/architecture/profiles/Rendell/ htm, date accessed 4 May 2009.

Rendell, J. (2010 forthcoming) *Site Writing: Art, Architecture and Criticism* (London: I. B. Tauris).

Ripper (2009) Jack the Ripper Tour, http://www.jack-the-ripper-tour.com, date accessed 4 May 2009.

Robinson, T. (2007) *Connemara: Listening to the Wind* (London: Penguin).

Rogoff, I. (2000) *Terra Infirma* (London: Routledge).

Roms, H. (1997) 'Making Landscapes', *Planet*, 126, 79–92.

Roms, H. (2001) 'The Battle of Orgreave', *Planet*, 148, 124–6.

Roms, H. (2004) 'Performing *Polis*: theatre, nationness and civic identity in post-devolution Wales', *Studies in Theatre and Performance*, 24, 3, 177–92.

Roms, H. (2008) 'Staging an Urban Nation', in Holdsworth, N. and Luckhurst, M. (eds) *Contemporary British and Irish Drama* (Oxford: Blackwell), 107–24.

Rose, M. (2006) 'Gathering "dreams of presence": a project for the cultural landscape', *Environment and Planning D: Society and Space*, 24, 537–54.

Sante, L. (1992) *Evidence* (New York: Farrar, Strauss and Giroux).

Savage, J. (2004) *Mapping 001* (Cardiff: Jenny Savage).

Savage, J. (2009) The Arcades Project, http://www.arcadesproject.org, date accessed 1 May 2009.

Savill, C.C. (1990) 'Dismantling the Wall', *Planet*, 79, 20–8.

Savill, C.C. (1997) 'Brith Gof', in Taylor, A-M. (ed.) *Staging Wales: Welsh Theatre 1979–1997* (Cardiff: University of Wales Press), 100–10.

Scarry, E. (1999) 'Participal acts: work and the body in Thomas Hardy', in Payne, A. (ed.) *Lie of the Land: Earth Body Material* (Southampton: John Hansard Gallery).

Schechner, R. (1969) *Public Domain* (New York: Discus/Avon).

Schuring, J. (2008) *Graven waar je staat* (Amsterdam: Theater Instituut Nederland).

Sebald, W.G. (1999) *The Rings of Saturn* (London: Harvill).

Shanks, M. (2004) 'Three rooms: archaeology and performance', *Journal of Social Archaeology*, 4, 2, 147–80.

Sheller, M. and Urry, J. (2006) 'The new mobilities paradigm', *Environment and Planning D: Society and Space*, 38, 207–26.

Solnit, R. (2000) *Wanderlust: A History of Walking* (London: Verso).

Stan's Café (2009) http://www.stanscafe.co.uk, date accessed 8 May 2009.

Stewart, K. (1996) *A Space on the Side of the Road: Cultural Poetics in an "Other" America* (Princeton: Princeton University Press).

Svinhufvud-Lockett, L. E. (2008) 'Kotkaniemi: family, kinship and personal narrative', University of Wales, PhD thesis.

Thrift, N. (2008) *Non-Representational Theory* (Routledge: Abingdon).

Topping, M. (2004) 'The House Project', *Plattform*, 2, 34–7.

Trace: (2009) http://www.tracegallery.org, date accessed 4 May 2009.

Tschumi, B. (1994) *The Manhatten Transcripts* (London: Academy Editions).

Tschumi, B. (1995) *Event-Cities (Praxis)* (Cambridge, MA: MIT Press).

Tuan, Y.-F. (1974) *Topophilia* (Englewood Cliffs, NJ: Prentice-Hall).

Tufnell, M. and Crickmay, C. (2004) *A Widening Field: Journeys in Body and Imagination* (Alton, Hants: Dance Books).

Turner, C. (2000) 'Framing the Site', *Studies in Theatre and Performance*, Supplement 5, 23–40.

Turner, C. (2004) 'Palimpsest or Potential Space? Finding a Vocabulary for Site-Specific Performance', *New Theatre Quarterly*, 20, 4, 373–90.

Turner, J. (1996) *The Abstract Wild* (Cambridge: Harvard University Press).

Volcano Theatre (2009) http://www.volcanotheatre.co.uk, date accessed 4 May 2009.

Warr, T. (2001) Circuitry. *Performance Research*, 6, 3, 8–12.

Whitehead, S. (2006) *Walking to Work* (Abercych, Pembrokeshire: Shoeless).

Wiles, D. (2003) *A Short History of Western Performance Space* (Cambridge: Cambridge University Press).

Wilkie, F. (2001) 'Archaeologies of memory: Mike Pearson's *Bubbling Tom*', (FIRT: Amsterdam), conference paper.

Wilkie, F. (2002a) 'Mapping the Terrain: a Survey of Site-specific Performance in Britain', *New Theatre Quarterly*, 18, 2, 140–60.

Wilkie, F. (2002b) 'Archaeologies of memory: Mike Pearson's *Bubbling Tom*', unpublished paper.

Wilkie, F. (2008) 'The Production of "Site": Site-Specific Theatre', in Holdsworth, N. and Luckhurst, M. (eds) *Contemporary British and Irish Drama* (Oxford: Blackwell).

Williams, D. (1998) 'Frontwords', *Performance Research*, 3, 2, v–viii.

Williams, J. (ed.) (2005) *Sideways Glances* (Cardigan: Parthian).

Williams, R. (1973) *The Country and the City* (Oxford: Oxford University Press).

Wright, P. (1995) *The Village that Died for England* (London: Jonathan Cape).

Wrights and Sites (2006) *A Mis-Guide to Anywhere* (Exeter: Wrights & Sites).

Wunderlich, F.M. (2008) 'Walking and Rhythmicity: Sensing Urban Space', *Journal of Urban Design*, 13, 1, 125–39.

Wylie, J. (2002) 'Becoming-icy: Scott and Amundsen's South Polar voyages, 1910–1913', *Cultural Geographies*, 9, 249–66.

Wylie, J. (2005) 'A single day's walking: narrating self and landscape on the South West Coast Path', *Transactions of the Institute of British Geographers*, NS 30, 234–47.

Wylie, J. (2006) 'Depths and Folds: On Landscape and the Gazing Subject', *Environment and Planning D: Society and Space*, 24, 2, 519–35.

Wylie, J. (2007) *Landscape* (Abingdon: Routledge).

Young, J.E. (2000) *At Memory's Edge* (New Haven: Yale University Press).

Index